THE TUSKEGEE AIRMEN CHRONOLOGY

A Detailed Timeline of the Red Tails and Other Black Pilots of World War II

DANIEL L. HAULMAN

With a Foreword by Charles E. McGee, Colonel (Ret.)
302ND FIGHTER SQUADRON, 332ND FIGHTER GROUP

NEWSOUTH BOOKS

Montgomery

NewSouth Books
105 S. Court Street
Montgomery, AL 36104

Publisher's Cataloging-in-Publication Data

Haulman, Daniel L.
The Tuskegee airmen chronology : a detailed timeline of the Red Tails and
other black pilots of World War II / Daniel Haulman ;
with a foreword by Charles E. McGee.
p. cm.

ISBN 978-1-58838-341-9 (paperback)
ISBN 978-1-60306-341-8 (ebook)

1. United States. Army Air Forces. Fighter Group, 332nd—History. 2. United
States. Army Air Forces. Fighter Squadron, 99th—History. 3. United States. Army
Air Forces. Composite Group, 477th—History. 4. United States. Army Air Forces—
African American troops. 5. African American pilots—History—20th century.
6. World War, 1939–1945—Participation, African American. 7. World War, 1939–
1945—Aerial operations, American. 8. World War, 1939–1945—Campaigns—
Western Front. I. Haulman, Daniel L. (Daniel Lee), 1949– II. Title.

2017939732

Design by Randall Williams
Printed in the United States of America

To my wife, Ellen,
and my son, Evan

Contents

Foreword

Charles E. McGee, Colonel (Ret.)
302ND FIGHTER SQUADRON, 332ND FIGHTER GROUP

When World War II began, the United States military had no African American flying units. Early in 1940 the Army Air Forces Southeast Training Center stated that young men accepted to become pilots, bombardiers, and navigators would receive "the best training in the world," but as yet there were no black pilots.

Early Army policy presumed that black Americans could and would not 'measure up' in any technical field. It was into this aviation training environment that the now called "Tuskegee Airmen" entered and received their army silver wings and officer commissions. Tuskegee Institute provided preflight and primary training through its Civilian Pilot Training Program and newly established Moton Field. Seven or so miles North, Tuskegee Army Air Field was built for Basic and Advanced training and tactical aircraft checkout.

The early training produced the pilots and necessary support for four single engine fighter squadrons becoming the 332nd Fighter Group, and subsequently the training for four medium bomber squadrons making up the 477th Bomber Group. Research has provided a picture of the creditable combat performance of the fighter squadrons, and the fight of the bomb group personnel to eliminate segregation at their combat training sites.

Human judgment seems often to misstate or omit events that have taken place. This chronicle seeks to provide the accurate and complete record and to eliminate such omissions or misconceptions. This chronology of the Tuskegee Airmen Experience is good reading to refresh the memory for those involved, provide the full history for those interested, and support the researcher reviewing the history of African Americans in the US Army Air Corps, Army Air Forces and the United States Air Force during and just after World War II.

Charles E. McGee is one of the most famous of the Tuskegee Airmen, partly because he flew fighter aircraft in three wars and accumulated a total of 409 combat missions, more than any other Tuskegee Airman. He graduated from advanced pilot training at Tuskegee Army Air Field on June 30, 1943, and became a member of the 302nd Fighter Squadron of the 332nd Fighter Group. He flew P-51 Mustang fighters in combat from Ramitelli Air Field in Italy. On one mission to escort B-17 bombers against an enemy target in Czechoslovakia, he shot down an enemy aircraft, earning an aerial victory. Following World War II, he elected to stay in the Air Force, and in Korea he flew 100 combat missions in the F-51 as a member of the 67th Fighter Bomber Squadron of the 18th Fighter Group. During his Korean combat experience he earned a Distinguished Flying Cross. He attended the Air Command and Staff College at Maxwell Air Force Base in 1953. Between 1959 and 1961, McGee commanded the 7230th Support Squadron at Gioia del Colle Air Base in Italy. During the war in Vietnam, Colonel McGee served as commander of the 16th Tactical Reconnaissance Squadron and flew 173 combat missions in the RF-4. He earned another Distinguished Flying Cross in Vietnam. In 1972, Colonel McGee commanded Richards-Gebaur Air Force Base in Missouri. In retirement, Colonel McGee has served as former president of the Tuskegee Airmen Incorporated. He also earned that organization's first Noel Parrish Award, its most distinguished honor. — D. H.

Introduction

For decades after World War II, the first black pilots in American military history were relatively unknown. Americans became increasingly aware of the contributions of African Americans to their cultural heritage during and after the Civil Rights Movement in the 1950s and 1960s. By the end of the twentieth century, the "Tuskegee Airmen" had become famous in newspaper and magazine articles, books, films, television programs, and museum exhibits. Unfortunately, their story was told not only by historians using primary source documents, but also by others less familiar with history than with legend. A number of false claims circulated, many of them based on an ignorance of the chronological sequence of events that formed the skeleton of the true story. This book is an effort to provide a framework for Tuskegee Airmen history while at the same time revealing their historically significant accomplishments.

Having worked at the Air Force Historical Research Agency for more than thirty-two years, I have developed an appreciation for the invaluable collection of documents on Army Air Forces organizations in World War II that is maintained there. Many of the documents describe the most famous Tuskegee Airmen organizations such as the 99th, 100th, 301st, and 302nd Fighter Squadrons that were assigned to the 332nd Fighter Group during World War II, which escorted American B-17 and B-24 bombers over Nazi targets in central Europe, its pilots flying red-tailed P-51 Mustangs. But the story is much more complex than that. For example, before flying P-51s to escort heavy bombers, the squadrons flew P-40, P-39, and P-47 fighters to support the advance of ground forces in Italy. Before that, the Tuskegee Airmen in the United States flew other kinds of aircraft in training, including aircraft specifically designed for primary, basic, and advanced flying training. The Tuskegee Airmen story also involves bomber crews who trained with the 477th Bombardment Group and the 616th, 617th, 618th, and 619th Bombardment Squadrons to fly B-25s for the war against Japan, although they never got the chance to go into combat overseas.

What many Americans do not realize, without an acquaintance with the chronology, is that many of these phases of the Tuskegee Airmen story were occurring simultaneously. What they imagine is that there was a time when the Tuskegee Airmen trained for flying at bases within the United States, and then a later time they all deployed overseas to fight in aerial combat, and then even later they all returned to prepare for combat with the Japanese, after the war in Europe had been won. In truth, even while fighter pilots were flying combat missions overseas in 1944 and 1945, new Tuskegee airmen cadets were training to fly at the flying training bases around Tuskegee, and bomber squadrons were training for combat operations, moving from base to base in Michigan, Kentucky, and Indiana. At the same time that black officers were incarcerated for resisting segregation at Freeman Field, for example, other black officers were earning Distinguished Flying Crosses and aerial victory credits by shooting down enemy airplanes in combat over Europe, while still other black cadets were learning to fly military airplanes. Even after the World War II was over, new black military pilots were training at Tuskegee Institute's Moton Field and the Army Air Forces' Tuskegee Army Air Field back in Alabama. Readers may be surprised that the chronology seems to jump between the war in Europe and training within the United States, but those events proceeded simultaneously.

Still, it might be useful, as an introduction to the chronology, to tell the story more thematically, all the time realizing that these parts of the history were not always sequential.

PRIMARY AND BASIC FLYING TRAINING

After primary training in PT-17 and PT-19 airplanes at Tuskegee Institute's Moton Field, the first African-American pilots in the Army Air Forces transferred to Tuskegee Army Air Field, a military airfield belonging to the Army Air Forces, for the basic, advanced, and transition phases of flying training. Tuskegee Army Air Field, as new as Moton Field, covered a much larger area, and included four paved runways and three large double hangars.

It lay a few miles to the northwest of Moton Field. Basic flying training consisted of both ground school and flying training in military aircraft. Ground school courses included meteorology, radio communication, radio code, airplanes, engines, and navigation. The flying training took place in BT-13 airplanes, which, unlike the biplanes of Moton Field, had only one set of wings. The first advanced class began at Tuskegee Army Air Field on November 8, 1941.

Advanced and Transition Training

After pilots completed basic training at Tuskegee Army Air Field, using BT-13 monoplanes, they were ready for the next stage of their flying training, which was advanced training. The first advanced training class at Tuskegee began in January 1942. For the flying training, the pilots flew AT-6 aircraft, which did not appear very different from the BT-13s, but which were more advanced and maneuverable, like the fighters most of the graduates would eventually fly. Ground courses consisted of armament, gunnery, tactics and techniques of air fighting, advanced navigation, maintenance, and engineering. For the gunnery and combat tactics, the pilots in the advanced training stage used ranges at Eglin Field, Florida. The advanced training was followed at Tuskegee Army Air Field, unlike most other basic and advanced flying training bases, by transition training. Single engine pilots learned how to fly P-40 aircraft, which were of the same type as fighters flown in combat theaters. The 99th Fighter Squadron flew P-40s when it first entered combat in North Africa and later in Italy. Twin-engine pilots learned instead how to fly AT-10s, which prepared them to fly medium bombers such as the B-25, which also had two engines. Some of the A-10 pilot graduates from Tuskegee Army Air Field moved on to Mather Field, California, where they learned how to fly the B-25 aircraft types used by the 477th Bombardment Group. By March 1945, Tuskegee Army Air Field had a training version of the B-25 of its own, to replace the AT-10.

Training Beyond Tuskegee

Primary, basic, advanced, and transition training for pilots at Tuskegee Army Air Field was just the beginning for the black pilots who trained there.

Although the 99th Fighter Squadron deployed directly from Tuskegee for overseas duty in North Africa in April 1943, the three other fighter squadrons at Tuskegee, along with the 332d Fighter Group to which they belonged, moved to Selfridge Field in Michigan for further training. The group and its 100th, 301st, and 302nd Fighter Squadrons remained at Selfridge from the end of March 1943 to early April 1943, when they moved to Oscoda, also in Michigan. In early July, the group and its squadrons moved back to Selfridge where they remained until the end of the year. During its time at Selfridge and Oscoda in Michigan, the 332d Fighter Group honed its skills with fighters designed in part to strike ground targets on tactical missions, including P-39s that it would use after deployment overseas.

After the 332d Fighter Group and its three squadrons deployed from Selfridge at the end of 1943, the first and only African-American bombardment group was activated at Selfridge, in January 1944. The training of a bombardment group took longer than a fighter group, partly because the bombers required training not only for pilots but also for crewmen such as navigators, bombardiers, radio operators, and gunners. While the bomber pilots trained in B-25s at Selfridge, the bombardiers and navigators trained at other bases. The 477th Bombardment Group moved in May 1944 to Godman Field, Kentucky, not merely because it was in the South, which was more familiar with racial segregation, but also because the climate was better there for flying, particularly in the winter.

The 477th Bombardment Group moved again in early March 1945, as the weather warmed up, from Godman Field to Freeman Field, Indiana, a larger base that seemed to be an improvement over Godman. However, it was a blessing and a curse. The larger field allowed the commander to designate two different buildings as officers' clubs, claiming one would be for training officers, and one for trainees. The real purpose was racial segregation, which violated the current Army Air Forces regulations. Many of the African-American officers at Freeman Field refused to be limited to the club reserved for them, and mutinied. They were arrested, and the group was transferred back to Godman Field, Kentucky, in late April 1945. To resolve the racial problems, the Army Air Forces replaced the 477th Bombardment Group's white commander with Colonel Benjamin O. Davis

Jr., who had commanded the 332d Fighter Group in successful combat in Europe. In fact, all of the white officers in the group were transferred. The 99th Fighter Squadron was also reassigned from the 332d Fighter Group to the 477th Bombardment Group, and the group was redesignated as the 477th Composite Group, because it then had both bombers and fighters. The 332d Fighter Group in the meantime was inactivated, leaving the 477th as the only black group in the Army Air Forces.

With black leadership, the 477th Composite Group continued to prepare for combat overseas, but the chance never came. Faced with atomic attacks and a Soviet declaration of war, the Japanese surrendered before the black pilots of the 477th could use their bombers and fighters against them.

Behind the Tuskegee Airmen pilots were many others who could also call themselves Tuskegee Airmen but who never got to fly an airplane. Many were other officers, such as the navigators and bombardiers who flew as air crew members on the B-25s. Many of them trained at bases beyond those where the pilots trained. For example, Tuskegee Airmen navigators trained at the Army Air Forces Navigation School at Hondo Army Air Field in Texas. Behind every Tuskegee Airman officer was a team of enlisted men who supported them and without which they would not have succeeded. They included maintenance personnel, ordnance personnel, quartermasters, guards, engineers, supply personnel, and other specialists. Among the bases where enlisted personnel in the Tuskegee Airmen organizations trained were Chanute Field, Illinois (where the 99th Fighter Squadron was first activated); Keesler Field, Mississippi; Midland Army Air Field in Texas; Fort Monmouth, New Jersey; the Curtis-Wright Factory Training School in Buffalo, New York; and cities and towns that included Atlanta, Georgia; Lincoln, Nebraska; Indianapolis, Indiana; Tomah, Wisconsin. In fact, personnel who served as Tuskegee Airmen trained and served at bases all over the United States and in a host of units beyond the squadrons of the 332d Fighter Group and the 477th Bombardment Group.

The Tuskegee Airmen in Combat

Commanding more interest than any other aspect of the Tuskegee Airmen experience is their combat record. While flying missions from North Africa,

Sicily, and the mainland of Italy, the Tuskegee-trained pilots demonstrated not only that they could fly fighters in combat, but also that they could fly any kind of fighter aircraft on any kind of fighter mission, and do it as well as their non-black compatriots and enemies.

The 99th Fighter Squadron was not only the first American black flying unit but also the first such unit in combat. It deployed from Tuskegee to North Africa during April 1943. Flying P-40s fighters, the squadron at first flew patrol missions to protect Allied shipping in the Mediterranean Sea. While attached to various white fighter groups, although not assigned directly to them, the 99th joined white P-40 squadrons in attacking enemy targets on the Mediterranean Islands of Pantelleria and Sicily. After moving to Sicily and then to the mainland of Italy, the 99th scored impressive numbers of aerial victories while protecting American ground forces at Anzio from enemy aircraft attacks. During its combat operations in Italy, before it joined the 332d Fighter Group, the 99th Fighter Squadron earned two Distinguished Unit Citations.

In early 1944, the 332d Fighter Group and its 100th, 301st, and 302nd Fighter Squadrons also deployed to Italy. Although the group at first flew P-39s in combat instead of P-40s, it performed attacks on ground targets and flew patrol missions for the Twelfth Air Force, like the 99th, and occasionally escorted medium bombers raiding battlefield targets near the front.

By the summer of 1944, the mission of the Tuskegee Airmen changed dramatically, as the 332d Fighter Group began escorting heavy bombers such as B-17s and B-24s on long-range raids deep into enemy territory for the Fifteenth Air Force. Flying P-47s and later P-51 high-speed long-range fighters with tails painted red for group identification, the Tuskegee Airmen shot down increasing numbers of enemy fighters that threatened the bombers they were guarding. Enemy aircraft shot down bombers the 332nd Fighter Group was assigned to protect on only seven of the 179 bomber-escort missions the group flew between early June 1944 and late April 1945. The total number of escorted bombers shot down was significantly less than the average number of bombers lost by the six other fighter escort groups of the Fifteenth Air Force. On the longest fighter-escort mission from Italy, on March 24, 1945, to Berlin, three Tuskegee Airmen each shot down a

German jet aircraft that could fly significantly faster than their own red-tailed P-51 Mustangs. When the 332d Fighter Group returned from Italy, it had proven that black fighter pilots could fly advanced aircraft in combat as well as their white compatriots or their enemies.

AFTER WORLD WAR II

In March 1946, after the war ended, the 477th Composite Group moved from Godman Field to Lockbourne Army Air Base in Ohio. On July 1, 1947, the 332nd Fighter Group replaced the 477th at Lockbourne. That same year, the Army Air Forces was replaced by the United States Air Force, independent from the Army. The 332nd Fighter Group became the only active black group in the new service.

In 1949, members of the 332d Fighter Group won the conventional aircraft category at an Air Force-wide gunnery meet in Las Vegas, proving again the flying and fighting ability of black pilots. On July 1, however, the group was inactivated and its black personnel were all reassigned to other formerly all-white organizations as the Air Force implemented racial integration in accordance with President Truman's Executive Order 9981.

The Tuskegee Airmen opened the door of opportunity for black people in aviation wider than it had ever been opened before. They proved that black men could not only fly military aircraft, but also the most advanced fighters, in successful combat with the enemy. The Tuskegee Airmen also demonstrated that they could fly multi-engine bombers, leading crews that included bombardiers, navigators, and radio operators. The success of the Tuskegee Airmen in combat, and in successful resistance at home to seg-regationist policies, contributed immeasurably to the ultimate integration of the Air Force.

But what became of the original Tuskegee Airmen? After World War II many of them left the Army Air Forces and became successful businessmen in the civilian world. Many also stayed in the new United States Air Force, and continued to demonstrate that African-Americans could fulfill missions assigned to them, regardless of whether the mission had ever been assigned to them before. Benjamin O. Davis, Jr., who had commanded both the 332nd Fighter Group and the 477th Composite Wing, remained in the service, and rose to become the first African-American general in the United States Air Force. He eventually commanded the Thirteenth Air Force. Daniel "Chappie" James, another Tuskegee Airman, also rose to become a general, and was named the first four-star African-American general in the Air Force, after flying fighter missions during both the Korean and Vietnam wars. He eventually became commander of the North American Air Defense Command. Other Tuskegee Airmen remained in the Air Force and continued to serve with distinction, among them Colonel Clarence "Lucky" Lester and Colonel Charles McGee. Like many of his fellow Tuskegee Airmen, Colonel McGee flew in three wars (World War II, Korea, and Vietnam). He accumulated a total of 409 combat missions.

There were many other Tuskegee Airmen who continued to serve their country in the Air Force, and they inspired other African-Americans to become pilots in the military. Jesse L. Brown became the first black pilot in the U.S. Navy in 1949, and later Frank E. Peterson became the first black Marine Corps pilot to command a squadron in the Navy Department. He later rose to the rank of lieutenant general. Years later, Guion "Guy" Bluford became the first African-American in space, taking part in the Space Shuttle program of the National Aeronautics and Space Administration. Lloyd "Fig" Newton became the first black Thunderbird pilot, and he later rose to become commander of the Air Education and Training Command, one of the most important major commands in the Air Force.

There are numerous other examples that could be named. Suffice it to say that African-Americans since World War II have continued to excel in the fields of aviation and space, not only as members of the Air Force, but as members of other military services. They and countless others can thank the Tuskegee Airmen for helping to open the door of opportunity for them and for inspiring them to excel in a world still full of obstacles to overcome.

THE
TUSKEGEE AIRMEN
CHRONOLOGY

Chronology of the
TUSKEGEE AIRMEN

KEY TO ABBREVIATIONS

BS	Bombardment Squadron
BG	Bombardment Group
BW	Bombardment Wing
FS	Fighter Squadron
FG	Fighter Group
FW	Fighter Wing
PS	Pursuit Squadron
TAAF	Tuskegee Army Air Field

EVENTS BEFORE THE TUSKEGEE AIRMEN

1903–1909

17 December 1903: Orville and Wilbur Wright completed the first powered and controlled heavier-than-air aircraft flights, at Kill Devil Hill, near Kitty Hawk, North Carolina.

1 August 1907: The U.S. Army's Signal Corps established a new Aeronautical Division to take charge of military ballooning and air machines. The Army did not yet have any pilots or airplanes.

19 May 1908: Lt. Thomas E. Selfridge became the first Army officer to solo in an airplane, but the Army did not yet have its first airplane. He also became the first U.S. military member to die in an airplane crash in September of the same year.

2 August 1909: The Army accepted its first airplane, from the Wright Brothers, after it met or surpassed all specifications.

26 October 1909: At College Park, Maryland, after instruction from Wilbur Wright, Lt. Frederick E. Humphreys and Lt. Frank P. Lahm became the first Army officers to solo in a Wright airplane. All of the first U.S. Army pilots were white.

1917–1918

April 1917: The United States entered World War I. The Air Service deployed personnel to France and flew many aircraft. Many of the American volunteers who had served in the Lafayette Escadrille of the French Air Service before American entry into the war later became members of the 103rd Aero Squadron. The U.S. Air Service did not admit any black pilots.

5 May 1917: Corporal Eugene Bullard, a black American who volunteered to serve with the French Air Service, received his military pilot's license, becoming the first black American to be a military pilot, although he was not in American military service. (Larry W. Greenly, *Eugene Bullard: World's First Black Fighter Pilot* [Montgomery, AL: New South Books, 2013], 69.)

November 1917: Eugene Bullard, while in the service of France, claimed to have shot down two enemy airplanes, but neither was confirmed officially by the French. (Larry W. Greenly, *Eugene Bullard: World's First Black Fighter Pilot* [Montgomery, AL: New South Books, 2013], 95–99; National Air and Space Museum blog.)

November 1918: Armistice ends World War I and U.S. Army Air Service involvement.

1921–1926

15 June 1921: Bessie Coleman became the first civilian licensed African American pilot in the world, receiving her license in France from the Federation Aeronautique Internationale. She soon returned to the United States, where she performed in air shows. (Von Hardesty, *Black Wings* [New York: Harper Collins, 2008], 9.)

30 October 1925: The War College of the U.S. Army in Washington, D.C. published a report claiming that black military members were inferior to whites, and lacked the capacity to serve in certain capacities. It was entitled "The Use of Negro Manpower in War," and was used to by the War Department to continue to keep the military segregated and to exclude blacks military pilot training. (Alan Gropman, *The Air Force Integrates, 1945–1964* [Washington: Office of Air Force History, 1985], 2.)

2 July 1926: President Coolidge signed Congress' Air Corps Act, which redesignated the Army's Air Service as the Air Corps. There were still no black pilots allowed in any of the U.S. military services, although there were black civilian pilots.

1931–1938

May 1931: John C. Robinson was the first black student to graduate at the Curtiss-Wright Aeronautical School, where he trained to become a civilian pilot.

9 October 1932: James Banning and Thomas Allen became the first black pilots to complete a transcontinental flight, after 22 days and many stops along the way. (Von Hardesty, *Black Wings* [Washington: Smithsonian, 2008], 51.)

28 July 1933: Charles Alfred Anderson and Albert E. Forsythe completed the first roundtrip transcontinental flight. The next year they flew from the United States to the Caribbean, further demonstrating the potential of blacks in aviation. (Von Hardesty, *Black Wings* [Washington: Smithsonian, 2008], 52.)

1933: John C. Robinson and Cornelius Coffey, who had organized the Challenger Air Pilots' Association as the first all-black flying club, in Chicago, supervised the construction of the club's first airstrip at Robbins, Illinois. (Von Hardesty, *Black Wings* [Washington: Smithsonian, 2008], 35.)

May 1935: John C. Robinson, an African American civilian pilot, journeyed to Ethiopia to serve Emperor Haile Selassie, who soon appointed Robinson head of the tiny Imperial Ethiopian Air Force and granted him the rank of Colonel. Hubert Julian, another African American civilian pilot, had also gone in 1930 to serve the emperor of Ethiopia, but with less distinction. (Phillip Thomas Tucker, *John C. Robinson, Father of the Tuskegee Airmen* [Washington: Potomac Books, 2012], 71, 99–100, 117.)

1937: Willa Brown became the first African American woman to earn her pilot's license in the United States. She joined the Challenger Air Pilot's Association in the Chicago area, and later married Cornelius Coffey.

27 December 1938: President Franklin D. Roosevelt called for a government-sponsored civilian pilot training program which was tried at thirteen colleges in early 1939. None of those colleges was black. (Robert J. Jakeman, *The Divided Skies*, 90–91)

1939

12 January: President Roosevelt asked Congress to pass legislation to expand the Air Corps tremendously, and for a permanent civilian pilot training program that went well beyond the experimental program. (Robert J. Jakeman, *The Divided Skies* [Tuscaloosa: University of Alabama Press, 1992], 89)

January: Census reports revealed that there were then only 25 licensed Negro pilots in the United States. None were in the U.S. military. (George L. Washington history)

1939: Chauncey Spencer and Dale White completed a demonstration flight from Chicago to Washington, D.C., stopping at several cities on the way. The flight generated publicity for the cause of increased opportunities for blacks in aviation. (J. Todd Moye, *Freedom Flyers* [Oxford, UK: Oxford University Press, 2010], 24.)

5 February: Triangle Airport opened in Tuskegee, on land owned by John Connor. Stanley O. Kennedy Sr., whose father leased the field, served as the airfield manager. Kennedy and two other white men, Forrest Shelton and Joe Wright Wilkerson, built the field originally for their personal use. This is the same field that Tuskegee Institute later acquired for its part in the Civilian Pilot Training Program, and it was popularly called Kennedy Field, although to Tuskegee Institute, it was airport number 1. Eventually Tuskegee Institute acquired a second airfield, which was called Moton Field. (Robert J. "Jeff" Jakeman, *The Divided Skies* [Tuscaloosa: University of Alabama Press, 1992], 127; *The Heritage of Macon County* [Clanton, AL: Heritage Publishing, 2003], 3.)

3 April: President Franklin D. Roosevelt signed a Public Law 18, which was sometimes called the Army Expansion Act of 1939, that appropriated funds to the War Department. While many interpreted a provision in the law as mandating the War Department to begin training black pilots in the Army Air Corps, others thought it was too vague for that, since it only authorized the Secretary of War, at his discretion, to choose a school or schools where black civilian pilots might be training, and lend it equipment for further training. The War Department did not immediately begin training black pilots, but it did begin considering that if it ever had to do so, that such training would be on a segregated basis. (Ulysses Lee, *The Employment of Negro Troops* [Washington: Office of the Chief of Military History, 1966], 56–60; Lt. Col. Michael Lee Lanning, *The African-American Soldier* [New York: Citadel Press, 2004] p. 189)

April: Charles Alfred Anderson, a black pioneer aviator, visited Tuskegee Institute while transporting a passenger from Philadelphia there. (George L. Washington history)

May: Chauncey Spencer and Dale White, two black pilots who belonged to the National Airmen's Association of America (NAAA), conducted a cross-country flight that originated in Chicago and stopped at ten cities, including Washington, D.C. The purpose of the flight was to generate interest in black aviation and to increase opportunities for black pilots. In Washington, Spencer and White met with NAAA lobbyist Edgar Brown, who introduced them to various members of Congress, including Congressman Everett Dirksen of Illinois, who in April had proposed an amendment to pending legislation so that blacks would not be excluded from the planned civilian pilot training program. They also met Senator James Slattery of Illinois, black Congressman William Mitchell, and Senator Harry S. Truman of Missouri. The flight encouraged Congress to include the Dirksen amendment in the legislation. (Robert J. Jakeman, *The Divided Skies* [Tuscaloosa: University of Alabama Press, 1992], 108–110; Chauncey E. Spencer, *Who is Chauncey Spencer* [Detroit, MI: Broadside Press, 1975; Lawrence P. Scott and William M. Womack Sr., *Double V: The Civil Rights Struggle of the Tuskegee Airmen* [East Lansing: Michigan State University Press, 1994), 91–93)

27 June: Congress passed the the Civilian Pilot Training Act. It included a provision inserted by Representative Everett Dirksen of Illinois that no one would be excluded from the program because of race. Six black colleges eventually took part in the program, including Hampton Institute, Howard University, North Carolina A&T, Delaware State College for Colored Students, Tuskegee Institute, and West Virginia State College. (Robert J. Jakeman, *The Divided Skies* [Tuscaloosa: University of Alabama Press, 1992], 108–110; J. Todd Moye, *Freedom Flyers* [Oxford University Press, 2010], 24)

15 October: The Civil Aeronautics Authority certified Tuskegee Institute and the Alabama Air Service, a private firm at the municipal airport in Montgomery, Alabama, as a civilian pilot training school. The cadets would receive ground training at Tuskegee and flight training at the Montgomery airport, some forty miles away. ("Civilian Training School, Tuskegee Institute," call number 289.28–17 at Air Force Historical Research Agency; George L. Washington history)

November: 14 men and 2 women qualified physically to enter civilian pilot training at Tuskegee Institute. (Randy Johnson, *From Cubs to Hawks*)

1940

January: Students in the civilian pilot training program at Tuskegee Institute began flying, using the airport at Montgomery, Alabama. (Randy Johnson, *From Cubs to Hawks*)

Late February: The Civil Aeronautics Authority approved Tuskegee's Kennedy Field (originally called Triangle Field) for Civilian Pilot Training, after improvements to the field, eliminating Tuskegee Institute's need to use the Montgomery Airport. Kennedy Field was also called airport number 1. (Robert J. Jakeman, *The Divided Skies*)

25 March: George A. Wiggs arrived in Tuskegee to administer the standard written examination required of all Civilian Pilot Training students. Every student who took the examination passed, surpassing the passing rate of other schools in the South. (Robert J. Jakeman, *The Divided Skies.*)

20 May: Tuskegee Institute applied to teach secondary civilian pilot training after securing approval to use the Alabama Polytechnic Institute (API) airfield at Auburn. (Randy Johnson, *From Cubs to Hawks*)

29 July: Charles Alfred Anderson arrived at Tuskegee Institute to assume duties as its first flight instructor. He came from the civilian pilot training program at Howard University. He flew a Waco airplane. (George L. Washington history)

30 July: Pilots from Tuskegee began Civilian Pilot Training (CPT) secondary flight training at Alabama Polytechnic Institute at Auburn. (George L. Washington history)

End of July: Tuskegee Institute began secondary civilian pilot training, with new instructors who had been trained at Chicago, and using the Alabama Polytechnic Institute (API) airfield at Auburn. (Randy Johnson, *From Cubs to Hawks*)

16 September: President Franklin D. Roosevelt signed the Burke-Wadsworth Act, also called the Selective Training and Service Act, which Congress had already passed. The law forbid racial restrictions on voluntary enlistments in the branches of the Armed Forces, including, presumably, the Army Air Corps. (Jakeman, *The Divided* Skies, 183). On the same day, the War Department announced that the Civil Aeronautics Authority, in cooperation with the U.S. Army, would start the development of "colored personnel" for the aviation service. (Public Law 783, 16 September 1940; War Department Press Release, 16 September 1940; 99th Fighter Squadron summary history in the lineage and honors folder of the 99th Flying Training Squadron at the Air Force Historical Research Agency (AFHRA), Maxwell AFB, AL)

8 October: President Franklin D. Roosevelt approved a new War Department policy of allowing blacks to serve in all branches of the service (including the Air Corps), but on a segregated basis. His action was announced the next day, 9 October. (Robert J. Jakeman, *The Divided Skies* [Tuscaloosa: University of Alabama Press, 1992], 187). At about the same time, the War Department promoted Benjamin O. Davis Sr. to be the first black general in the U.S. Army and Judge William H. Hastie, the first black federal judge, as a civilian advisor to Secretary of War Henry L. Stimson. All three actions were designed to encourage black voters to support Roosevelt instead of Republican candidate Wendell Wilkie in the November 1940 Presidential election. (J. Todd Moye, *Freedom Flyers* (New York: Oxford University Press, 2010), 28, 72)

16 October: The War Department issued a letter sent to its commanding generals implementing the policy President Roosevelt approved on 8 October and announced on 9 October, noting that blacks would be serving in all branches of the Army (including the Air Corps). (Robert J. Jakeman, *The Divided Skies* [Tuscaloosa: University of Alabama Press, 1992], 189)

24 October: The War Department directed the Air Corps to submit a plan for the establishment and training of a black pursuit squadron. (Robert J. Jakeman, *The Divided Skies* [Tuscaloosa: University of Alabama Press, 1992], 197.)

20 November: Yancey Williams, a Howard University student who completed civilian pilot training, applied to enter the Army Air Corps as an aviation cadet. Three days later he received a response that the War Department was holding his application because "appropriate Air Corps units are not available at this time, in which colored applicants can be given flying cadet training." (Robert J. Jakeman, *The Divided Skies* [Tuscaloosa: University of Alabama Press, 1992], 204–205)

6 December: General Walter R. Weaver of the Southeast Air Corps Training Center at Maxwell Field, Alabama, submitted to General Henry H. Arnold, commander of the Army Air Corps, a plan prepared by Major L. S. Smith for a black pursuit squadron to be based and trained at Tuskegee, Alabama.

(Robert J. Jakeman, *The Divided Skies* [Tuscaloosa: University of Alabama Press, 1992], 206]

10 December: The Air Staff of the U.S. Army adopted the 6 December 1940 plan of Major L. S. Smith for a black pursuit squadron whose pilots would be trained at Tuskegee, and and added that technical training for support personnel of the black pursuit squadron should be accomplished at Chanute Field, Illinois. (Robert J. Jakeman, *The Divided Skies* [Tuscaloosa: University of Alabama Press, 1992], 211)

18 December: the Air Corps sent plans for a black pursuit squadron at Tuskegee to the adjutant general of the War Department. (Robert J. Jakeman, *The Divided Skies* [Tuscaloosa: University of Alabama Press, 1992], 212)

20 December: The War Department issued Army Regulation 210–10 that required post commanders to insure that all officers at an installation be allowed full membership in the officers' club, mess, or other social organization.

Late December: The War Department deliberated over the Air Corps plans for a black flying unit to be trained at Tuskegee. Among those reviewing the plan were Assistant Secretary of War Robert Patterson and Judge William Hastie, an African American who was then serving as a civilian advisor to the War Department. Hastie objected to segregated training for black military pilots, arguing that the training should be integrated instead, and that black pilots should be trained at existing flying schools where white military pilots were already training. (Robert J. Jakeman, *The Divided Skies* [Tuscaloosa: University of Alabama Press, 1992], 212–214)

1941

15 January: A. Philip Randolph, president of the Brotherhood of Sleeping Car Porters, an influential black railroad union, called for 10,000 blacks to march on Washington, D.C. to demand an end to segregation in the armed forces and an end to racial discrimination in hiring for defense industries under contract with the federal government. (*Reporting Civil Rights* [New York: The Library of America, 2003], 897)

16 January: The War Department announced publicly that a "Negro pursuit squadron" would be established within the Army Air Corps, the support personnel to be trained initially at Chanute Field, Illinois, and the pilots to be trained at Tuskegee, Alabama. (Robert J. Jakeman, *The Divided Skies* [Tuscaloosa: University of Alabama Press, 1992], 221, 228, 240)

17 January: Yancey Williams, a civilian pilot who was a senior at Howard University, filed suit in Washington, D.C., to compel the War Department to consider his application for enlistment as a flying cadet in the Army Air Corps. He had applied in November 1940, but had been told his application was being held because no suitable units for "colored applicants" were available yet to train him. (*The Crisis*, vol. 48, no. 3 [March 1941], 87–88) The National Association for the Advancement of Colored People (NAACP) legal department prepared to support the Yancey Williams lawsuit. (J. Todd Moye, *Freedom Flyers* [Oxford University Press, 2010], 37–38)

January: The Civil Aeronautics Authority approved Tuskegee Institute's Kennedy Field, which had been improved, for secondary civilian pilot training. The training had taken place at the Alabama Polytechnic Institute (API) airfield in Auburn. (Randy Johnson, *From Cubs to Hawks*)

February: The Civil Aeronautics Authority certified Tuskegee Institute for both elementary and secondary civilian pilot training. The training would take place at an improved Kennedy Field. (Randy Johnson, *From Cubs to Hawks*)

11 March: Henry Ford visited Tuskegee Institute's Airport Number One (Kennedy Field) to observe civilian pilot training there. (George L. Washington history)

19 March: The 99th Pursuit Squadron was constituted. (Maurer, *Combat Squadrons of the Air Force, World War II* [Washington: United States Government Printing Office, 1969], 329)]. At the same time, a new "Air Base Detachment" was constituted, which later became the 318th Air Base Squadron and finally the 318th Base Headquarters and Air Base Squadron (Colored) at Tuskegee. The organizations had no personnel assigned until they were activated. (organization record cards)

THE TUSKEGEE AIRMEN EXPERIENCE BEGINS

22 March: The 99th Pursuit Squadron was activated at Chanute Field, Illinois, under the command of Captain Harold R. Maddux, a white officer, but composed of African-American enlisted men. (Maurer, *Combat Squadrons of the Air Force, World War II* [Washington: United States Government Printing Office, 1969], 329; lineage and honors history of the 99th Fighter Squadron)

Eleanor Roosevelt flew as a passenger of "Chief" Charles Alfred Anderson, who led the flight instructors at Tuskegee Institute, in March 1941, before the military flight training began. The 99th Pursuit Squadron had already been activated, but it did not yet have any pilots.

29 March: Eleanor Roosevelt, wife of President Franklin D. Roosevelt, visited Kennedy Field in the Tuskegee area and was taken up in an aircraft piloted by Chief C. Alfred Anderson, Tuskegee Institute's chief instructor pilot. Mrs. Roosevelt was a Rosenwald Fund trustee who helped secure funding for the construction of Moton Field at Tuskegee. (Robert J. Jakeman, *The Divided Skies* [Tuscaloosa: University of Alabama Press, 1992], 245–246) A popular story claims that Mrs. Roosevelt was discouraged by her Secret Service escorts from going on the flight, but a historian who has researched the lives of the First Ladies noted that not long after Roosevelt first took office, Eleanor Roosevelt "adamantly refused Secret Service protection," and Secret Service agents might have not been with her that day. (Lewis Gould, *American First Ladies: Their Lives and Their Legacy* [Routledge, 2014], 294)

Early April: With approval of officials from Maxwell Air Force Base, Tuskegee Institute selected land 3 miles north of the campus to develop into a primary flight training base under contract with the Army Air Corps. The site would be called Moton Field. (Robert J. Jakeman, *The Divided Skies* [Tuscaloosa:

University of Alabama Press, 1992], 249)

1 May: An "Air Base Detachment" was activated at Chanute Field, Illinois, to support the 99th Pursuit Squadron. It was later redesignated as the 318th Air Base Squadron and still later the 318th Base Headquarters and Air Base Squadron (Colored) at Tuskegee. (unit's organization record card)

1 May: A War Department contract with Tuskegee Institute for a primary flight training school was drafted. (George L. Washington history)

1 June: Construction of Moton Field, for primary flight training of Army Air Corps black cadets, commenced. Alexander and Repass Company of Des Moines, Iowa, handled the project. Alexander was black, and Repass was white.

7 June: The War Department approved a contract that established a primary flying school at Tuskegee Institute. (Tuskegee Army Flying School history yearbook, AFHRA call number 289.28–100; George L. Washington history)

Mid-June: Captain Noel F. Parrish, a white officer, who had taught pilots at the Chicago School of Aeronautics in the Civilian Pilot Training program, reported to Tuskegee Institute to supervise the primary flight training that would take place at Moton Field. (George L. Washington history)

10 June: The Air Corps activated a series of aviation squadrons around the country, composed of black personnel. Despite the name of the squadrons, they had no pilots or aircraft, but were designed to construct or maintain airfields. (Organization record cards at the Air Force Historical Research Agency). The 99th Pursuit Squadron remained the only black flying unit in the country, but it did not yet have pilots.

18 June: A. Philip Randolph, president of the Brotherhood of Sleeping Car Porters, and Walter White, executive secretary of the National Association for the Advancement of Colored People, met with President Franklin D. Roosevelt at the White House in Washington, D.C. They discussed what the federal government could do to increase opportunities for black people in the armed services and defense industries, since the nation was becoming the "arsenal of democracy." Randolph had threatened to lead at least 10,000 blacks in a March on Washington, which he had announced on 15 January and scheduled for the summer. (*Reporting Civil Rights* [New York: The Library of America, 2003], 897)

19–20 June: Frederick Patterson, president of Tuskegee Institute, and George L. Washington, Director of Aeronautics at the institute, inspected the training of ground crew personnel of the 99th Pursuit Squadron at Chanute

Field, Illinois, because the squadron was destined to move to Tuskegee.

20 June: The War Department established the Army Air Forces under General Henry "Hap" Arnold, which included resources of the Air Corps.

25 June: President Franklin D. Roosevelt issued Executive Order 8802, which prohibited racial discrimination in hiring by federal departments and by defense industries with contracts with the federal government. *(Reporting Civil Rights* [New York: The Library of America, 2003], 897)

28 June: A. Philip Randolph announced indefinite postponement of his planned March on Washington, which was scheduled for 1 July 1941. He did this probably because President Roosevelt had issued Executive Order 8802 three days earlier. While Roosevelt acted to increase opportunities for blacks in the armed forces and in defense industries, he still had not ended segregation in the military. *(Reporting Civil Rights* [New York: The Library of America, 2003], 897)

12 July: Construction began on Tuskegee Army Air Field, a military airfield a few miles northwest of Moton Field, which would provide basic and advanced military flight training for the pilots who had already received primary flight training at Moton Field. The base would cover 1,650 acres. It was located 7 miles northwest of Tuskegee. It would eventually become the only base offering basic, advanced, and transition flying training to black personnel. (Lou Thole, *Forgotten Fields of America,* volume III [Missoula: Pictorial Histories Publishing Co., Inc., 2003], 1–5)

19 July: The first class of aviation cadets (42-C) entered Preflight Training at Tuskegee Institute. It included Captain Benjamin Oliver Davis Jr., who was also appointed that day as Commandant of Cadets. The other twelve cadets, besides Davis, were: John C. Anderson Jr., Charles D. Brown, Theodore E. Brown, Marion A. Carter, Lemuel R. Custis, Charles H. DeBow Jr., Frederick H. Moore, Ulysses S. Pannell, George S. Roberts, Mac Ross, William H. Slade, and Roderick C. Williams, for a total of thirteen (only five of these cadets completed the flying training at Tuskegee, in March 1942). On the same date, 19 July 1941, Captain Noel F. Parrish, a white officer, assumed command of the 66th Army Air Forces Flying Training Detachment at Moton Field. 2d Lieutenant Harold C. Magoon, another white officer, arrived the next month to assist him as assistant supervisor. Both Davis and Magoon would serve as check pilots, helping determine who would continue the training and who would be eliminated, or "washed out." (66th Army Air Forces Flying Training Detachment, Moton filed, Tuskegee Institute, Alabama, Feb 1941–7 Dec 1941, vol. 1; J. Todd Moye, *Freedom Flyers* [Oxford University Press, 2010], 58; Lynn H. Homan and Thomas Reilly, *Black Knights: The Story of the Tuskegee Airmen* [Gretna: Pelican Publishing Company, 2006], 38, 52–53; Robert J. Jakeman, *The Divided Skies* [Tuscaloosa and London: University of Alabama Press, 1992], 256, 258). Only five of the thirteen completed advanced flight training in March 1942.

22 July: The first enlisted Army Air Forces (Air Corps) personnel reported to Moton Field of Tuskegee Institute. The field was three miles northeast of the town of Tuskegee. (66th Army Air Forces Flying Training Detachment, Moton Field, Tuskegee Institute, Alabama, Feb 1941–7 Dec 1941, vol. 1, 5, 11)

23 July: The War Department constituted an Air Corps Advanced Flying School at Tuskegee, Alabama, to be under the immediate supervision of the Commanding General, Southeast Air Corps Training Center (at Maxwell Air Force Base) but under the control of the Chief of the Air Corps. (Organization record card at Air Force Historical Research Agency). It was to be activated at a new airfield several miles to the northwest of the town of Tuskegee and a few miles northwest of Moton Field. It was 13 miles away from the main campus of Tuskegee Institute. Unlike Moton Field, the new facility was not owned by Tuskegee Institute but by the Air Corps (later, Army Air Forces). (George L. Washington history)

1 August: The first of several white enlisted men, specialists in various support functions, arrived at Tuskegee Army Air Field. (Randy Johnson, *From Cubs to Hawks*) Most personnel arriving at the field traveled by train to a small station at Chehaw, 3 miles east of the base. (Thole)

6 August: The Air Corps Advanced Flying School at Tuskegee was activated at Tuskegee Army Air Field. (organization record card) The first commander at Tuskegee Army Air Field was Major James A. Ellison, a white officer. (Randy Johnson, *From Cubs to Hawks*) The first Commandant of Cadets was 2d Lt. Robert L. Lowenberg, and 1st Lt. Hayden C. Johnson was his administrative assistant. Detachment clerks included Private First Class Richard M. Lee and Private Ralph E. Jones. 1st Lt. Fred Minnis served as Special Service Officer. (History of The Corps of Aviation Cadets, Tuskegee Army Air Field, Alabama, AFHRA call number K289.28–1, 1 Aug 1941–1 Mar 1944)

11 August: 2d Lieutenant Harold C. Magoon reported for duty at Moton Field, to serve as Assistant Supervisor under Captain Noel F. Parrish, who was serving as commander of the 66th Army Air Forces Flying Training Detachment there. (66th Army Air Forces Flying Training Detachment, Moton Field, Tuskegee Institute, Alabama, Feb 1941–7 Dec 1941, p. 10)

21 August: The first class of aviation cadets entered the first phase of military flight training (Primary) administered by Tuskegee Institute, under contract with the War Department, at Kennedy Field near Tuskegee, because Moton Field was not yet completed. The class included the same 13 cadets who had begun preflight training at Tuskegee on 19 July. (Jakeman, *The Divided Skies*, p. 267) Capt. Noel Parrish commanded the primary flight training, first at Kennedy, and later at Moton Field. (Tuskegee Airmen National Historic Site) The first instructor pilots for primary flight training for the Army were Charles Alfred Anderson and Frank Shelton, the first black and the second white, who transferred from the civilian pilot training school. George W. Allen, also black, succeeded Anderson as chief of the civilian pilot training school. Other instructor pilots who remained at the civilian pilot training school at first were Lewis A. Jackson, Joseph T. Camilleri, Dominick J. Guido, and Frank Rosenberg. Allen and Jackson were black, but Camilleri, Guido, and Rosenberg were white. (Robert J. Jakeman, *The Divided Skies* [Tuscaloosa: University of Alabama Press, 1992], 264)

25 August: Primary flight training of the first class of black pilots to enter the Army Air Corps moved from Kennedy Field to Moton Field, but the field still needed more construction and still suffered from drainage problems. Civilian pilot training continued at Kennedy Field, for a time, but the military primary flight training was thereafter at Moton Field, home of the 66th Army Air Corps Primary Flying School. (Jakeman, *The Divided Skies*, p. 266; George L. Washington history). The first supervisor of the primary flying school at Moton Field, Capt. Noel Parrish, was assisted by Capt. Harold C. Magoon, assistant supervisor, and Capt. John G. Penn, the first Commandant of Cadets there.

Late August: The second class of black aviation cadets arrived at Tuskegee for pre-flight training, as members of class 42-D. They included Charles W. Dryden, Clarence C. Jamison, Sidney P. Brooks, William C. Boyd, Benjamin A. Brown Jr., Earl L. Bundara; Hercules L. Joyner; Emile J. Lewis; Harold E. McClure; Charles H. Moore; and James R. Smith. There were eleven of them, but only the first three graduated from advanced flight training (on 29 April 1942). (Lynn M. Homan and Thomas Reilly, *Black Knights: The Story of the Tuskegee Airman* [Gretna: Pelican Publishing Company, 2006], 58; Charles W. Dryden, *A-Train: Memoirs of a Tuskegee Airman* [Tuscaloosa: University of Alabama Press, 1997], 21, 30, 36.

1 September: The runway at Moton Field became fully operational for primary flight training, under contract with the U.S. Army, at Moton Field. (Randy Johnson, *From Cubs to Hawks*). Flight training before that had taken place at Kennedy Field, about 7 miles away. It was four miles south of Tuskegee, while Moton Field was three miles northeast of the town. The airplanes for the primary training moved at the same time from Kennedy Field to Moton Field, as did administration for the school. Mrs. Evelyn Curtright served as typist for the school administration. (66th Army Air Forces Flying Training Detachment, Moton Field, Tuskegee Institute, Alabama, Feb 1941–7 Dec 1941, vol. 1, 5, 8, 19, 21)

19 September: The first black enlisted support personnel arrived at Tuskegee Army Air Field. There were eighteen of them. Since the base did not yet have housing available, the newcomers were quartered at Tuskegee Institute. (Randy Johnson, *From Cubs to Hawks*) Tents were eventually erected at Tuskegee Army Air Field. The tent area came to be called Camp Hazard, named after base executive officer Capt. John T. Hazard. (Thole)

October: Lt. Col. Donald G. McPherson, a white officer, became Director of Basic Flying Training at Tuskegee Army Air Field.

27 October: 2nd Lt. Robert B. Lowenberg was appointed the first Commandant of Cadets at Tuskegee Army Air Field. The first cadets, however, would not arrive until 8 November. The Commandant of Cadets at Moton Field was Capt. John G. Penn. (History of Tuskegee Army Air Field, 23 Jul 1941–6 Dec 1944, vol. 1 and 2, AFHRA call number 289.28–1; plaque at Tuskegee Airmen National Historic Site referring to Capt. John G. Penn)

5 November: The 99th Pursuit Squadron moved from Chanute Field, Illinois, to Maxwell Field, Alabama. (Maurer, *Combat Squadrons of the Air Force, World War II*)

8 November: Four BT-13 basic flying training aircraft arrived at Tuskegee Army Air Field. On the same day, six of the thirteen cadets in the first black military pilot class, who had graduated from primary flight training at Tuskegee Institute's Moton Field, moved to the Army Air Forces' Tuskegee Army Air Field to begin the basic flying training phase. Five of them would eventually complete advanced flight training there. (Histories of Tuskegee Army Air Field at the Air Force Historical Research Agency; Randy Johnson, *From Cubs to Hawks*)

10 November: The 99th Pursuit Squadron moved from Maxwell Field to Tuskegee Army Air Field (Tuskegee Army Air Base), Alabama. (99th Fighter Squadron history, Mar 1941-Oct 1943) On the same day, 2d Lieutenant Clyde H. Bynum, a white officer, became the squadron's new commander. (Maurer, *Combat Squadrons of the Air Force, World War II*). On the same day, the Air Base Detachment that would later serve with the 99th Pursuit Squadron as the 318th Air Base Squadron and later as the 318th Base

Headquarters and Air Base Squadron (Colored) at Tuskegee moved from Chanute Field, Illinois, to Maxwell Field, Alabama, where the 99th Pursuit Squadron had been. On the same day, ground school began in an unfinished barracks at Tuskegee Army Air Field for the pilots in the first class. (Randy Johnson, *From Cubs to Hawks*) Lt. Joseph W. Grunow served as Director of the new Cadet Ground School. (History of the Corps of Aviation Cadets, Tuskegee Army Air Field, AL, AFHRA call number 289.28–1)

4 December: Major Noel F. Parrish transferred from the Primary Flying School at Tuskegee Institute to the Air Corps Advanced Flying School at Tuskegee Army Air Field and was appointed as Director of Training. (Tuskegee Army Flying School yearbook, AFHRA call number 289.28–100). At the same time, 1st Lieutenant William T. Smith assumed command of the primary flying training program at Moton Field, and command of the 66th Field Training Detachment. Both officers were white. (66th Army Air Forces Flying Training Detachment, Moton Field, Tuskegee Institute, Alabama, Feb 1941–7 Dec 1941, vol. 1, 9 and appendix V; Tuskegee Airmen National Historic Site) The original civilian flight instructors at Moton Field, for the primary phase of flight training, were Charles Alfred Anderson, who served as "Chief Pilot," Milton P. Crenshaw, Charles R. Foxx, and Forrest Shelton. Of these four civilian flight instructors, only Shelton was white. Warren G. Darty, another white man, served as ground school instructor at Moton Field in 1941. (66th Army Air Forces Flying Training Detachment, Moton Field, Tuskegee Institute, Alabama, Feb 1941–7 Dec 1941, vol. 1, 13)

6 December: Captain Alonzo S. Ward became the third commander of the 99th Fighter Squadron. Like the first two commanders of the unit, he was white. (99 Fighter Squadron history, Mar 1941–17 Oct 1943)

7 December: The Japanese attacked Pearl Harbor in Hawaii, bringing the United States into World War II. The need for combat pilots skyrocketed.

12 December: Colonel Frederick Von H. Kimble assumed command of Tuskegee Army Air Field, succeeding Major James A. Ellison. Like Ellison, he was a white officer. (*Hawk's Cry*, vol. II, no. 11, dated 14 May 1943)

20 December: Major C. Albright arrived at Tuskegee Army Air Field as a flying instructor. Like Kimble, he was a white officer. (*Hawk's Cry*, vol. II, no. 32, dated 8 Oct 1943, commemorating his long service at the base)

22 December 1942–13 January 1943: Pilots of the 99th Fighter Squadron trained at Dale Mabry Field near Tallahassee, Florida, in preparation for combat overseas. They had already deployed for gunnery training at Eglin Field, Florida.

27 December: The 100th Pursuit Squadron was constituted. (Maurer, *Combat Squadrons of the Air Force, World War II*)

1942

5 January: The Air Base Detachment that had served with the 99th Pursuit Squadron at Chanute Field, Illinois and then moved to Maxwell Field, Alabama on 10 November 1941 (when the 99th Pursuit Squadron moved to Tuskegee) moved from Maxwell to Tuskegee Army Air Field, Alabama. It would later be redesignated as the 318th Air Base Squadron and still later as the 318th Base Headquarters and Air Base Squadron (Colored). (organization record card)

11 January: Five of the aviation cadets of Class 42-C entered advanced flying training at Tuskegee Army Air Field, using AT-6 advanced training aircraft. (Randy Johnson, *From Cubs to Hawks;* History of The Corps of Aviation Cadets, Tuskegee Army Air Field, Alabama, AFHRA call number K289.28–1, 1 Aug 1941–1 Mar 1944)

14 February: 2nd Lt. Wallace P. Reed was commissioned as the first African American weather officer. (Gerald White, 99 ABW/HO)

19 February: The 100th Pursuit Squadron was activated at Tuskegee Army Air Field, Alabama. It was the second African-American Army Air Forces flying unit ever to be activated. (Maurer, *Combat Squadrons of the Air Force, World War II*)

23 February: The first class of advanced flying training cadets from Tuskegee Army Air Field arrived at Eglin Field, Florida, for gunnery and combat tactics fighter training. (Randy Johnson, *From Cubs to Hawks*)

7 March: The first class of African-American pilots at Tuskegee Army Air Field, 42-C, completed advanced pilot training. There were only five who completed the training: Capt. Benjamin O. Davis, Jr and 2d Lieutenants Mac Ross; Lemuel R. Custis; Charles H. DeBow Jr.; and George S. Roberts. Davis was assigned to the base, and the other four became the first African-American flying officers in the 99th Pursuit Squadron. Captain Davis was the first black American to hold a regular commission in the nation's air arm, having transferred on graduation from the infantry to the Air Corps. (Jakeman, *The Divided Skies;* 99th Fighter Squadron history, Mar 1941–17 Oct 1943)

9 March: Approximately 800 men arrived at Chehaw, Alabama, near Tuskegee Army Air Field, after a train ride from Camp Upton, New York, and

Fort Dix, New Jersey. They became the nucleus of the Recruit Detachment at the field, and many of them later joined the 366th Materiel Squadron after it was activated there on March 13, 1942. (366th Service Squadron history, call number SQ-SV-366-HI)

13 March: The "Air Base Detachment" at Tuskegee was redesignated as the 318th Air Base Squadron. (organization record card of the 318th Base Headquarters and Air Base Squadron (Colored). On the same date, the 96th Maintenance Group was constituted. (96th Service Group history, Mar 1942-Aug 1944)

21 March: The 96th Maintenance Group (Reduced) (Colored) was activated at Tuskegee Army Air Field, Alabama. At the same time, the 366th and 367th Materiel Squadrons were activated under the 96th Maintenance Group. (Organization record cards at Air Force Historical Research Agency). The same day, the Tuskegee Army Flying School Weather Detachment was activated, and the Tuskegee weather station became active. (67 AAFBU history, 21 Mar 1942–30 Sep 1944; Gerald A. White Jr.)

25 March: The 689th Signal Aircraft Warning Company was activated at Tuskegee Army Air Field, Alabama. (organizational record card of 689 Sig AW Co)

26 March: Lt. Wallace P. Reed became commander of the Tuskegee Weather Detachment at Tuskegee Army Air Field, becoming the station weather officer. (67 AAFBU history, 21 Mar 1942–30 Sep 1944)

29 March: Five members of the Army Nurse Corps were assigned to Tuskegee Army Air Field. Among them was 1st Lt. Della H. Raney, who became the chief nurse at the base. (Tuskegee Army Air Field history, call number 289.28–1 at the Air Force Historical Research Agency)

31 March: 2nd Lieutenant Harold C. Magoon, second highest ranking white officer at Moton Field, and Assistant Supervisor there under 1st Lieutenant William T. Smith, was promoted to 1st Lieutenant. (66th Army Air Forces Flying Training Detachment, Moton Field, Tuskegee Institute, Alabama, Feb 1941–7 Dec 1941, vol. 1, appendix VI)

1 April: In a controversy over custody of a black military member from Tuskegee Army Air Field who had been arrested by Tuskegee white city police for disturbing the peace in the town of Tuskegee, one of the base black military police (MP) members drew his gun and insisted that town police allow him and his associates to take the prisoner back to the base. Representatives from the Macon County sheriff's office and the Alabama Highway Patrol arrived to reinforce the city police, and disarmed the MP and his fellow guards.

Local law enforcement officials beat one of the MPs badly enough to need medical treatment at the nearby Veterans Administration hospital. Although no shots were fired, a race riot almost resulted, as armed white civilians from Tuskegee and Macon County gathered to confront black military personnel from Tuskegee Army Air Field. Word spread to the base, where black airmen armed themselves to go into town to rescue their compatriots. The Tuskegee Army Air Field post commander, Colonel Frederick von Kimble, who lived in Tuskegee, rushed to the scene and ordered all base personnel back to Tuskegee Army Air Field. Colonel Noel Parrish convinced Tuskegee Army Air Field personnel who had armed themselves and boarded a truck, to turn around and return to the base. Col. von Kimble, ordered that henceforth military policeman from Tuskegee Army Air Field would not be allowed to carry their arms outside the base. The incident resulted in 1st Lt. Bernice E. Compton, who had experience with the Alabama state police, to serve as acting Provost Marshal at Tuskegee Army Air Field. Exaggerated stories in the press also convinced the base commander to hire a public relations officer. (Tuskegee Army Air Field history, 7 Dec 1941–31 Dec 1942, AFHRA call no. 289.28–2; J. Todd Moye, *Freedom Flyers* [Oxford University Press, 2010], 87; Benjamin O. Davis Jr., *Benjamin O. Davis, Jr., American* [Washington: Smithsonian Institution Press, 1991], 77)

14 April: A Factory Training School associated with the Curtiss Wright Service School, Williamsville Branch, was activated in Buffalo, New York. It would later train African-American P-40 airplane mechanics. (organization record card)

17 April: The Air Corps Advanced Flying School at Tuskegee Army Air Field was redesignated as Tuskegee Advanced Flying School. (organization record card at AFHRA)

24 April: Bus service between Tuskegee and Tuskegee Army Air Field began, with both black and white riders. The white passengers were mostly employees of contractors and engineering personnel. (Tuskegee Army Air Field history, 7 Dec 1941–31 Dec 1942, AFHRA call number 289.28–2)

29 April: The second class of African-American pilots graduated from flying training at Tuskegee Army Air Field. It was class SE-42-D, and there were three graduates. (99th Fighter Squadron history, Mar 1941-Oct 1943; Roster of graduates by class)

April: P-40 Warhawk airplanes arrived at Tuskegee Army Air Field during the month, for transition flying training for the pilots who had graduated from the advanced flying training. (Thole, *Forgotten Fields in America*, vol. 3)

15 May: The 99th Pursuit Squadron was redesignated as the 99th Fighter Squadron and the 100th Pursuit Squadron was redesignated as the 100th Fighter Squadron. (Maurer, *Combat Squadrons of the Air Force, World War II*)

20 May: The third class of African-American pilots graduated from flying training at Tuskegee Army Air Field. It was class SE-42-E, and there were four graduates. (99th Fighter Squadron history, Mar 1941-Oct 1943)

1 June: 1st Lt. George S. Roberts assumed command of the 99th Fighter Squadron. He was the first African American to command the squadron. The previous three commanders had been white. (99th Fighter Squadron history, Mar 1941–17 Oct 1943)

1942: Robert A. Dawson from San Antonio, Texas, lost his life during advanced flying training at Tuskegee Army Air Field.

13 June: The 318th Air Base Squadron at Tuskegee was redesignated as the 318th Base Headquarters and Air Base Squadron (Colored). It served with the 99th Fighter Squadron at Tuskegee. (organization record card of the 318th Base Headquarters and Air Base Squadron)

15 June: Capt. James Hunter became commander of the 100th Fighter Squadron. Hunter was white. (100th Fighter Squadron lineage and honors history)

3 July: The fourth class of African-American pilots graduated from advanced flying training at Tuskegee Army Air Field. It was class SE-42-F, and there were 14 graduates, the largest class to that time. (99th Fighter Squadron history, Mar 1941-Oct 1943)

4 July: The 332d Fighter Group was constituted. (Maurer, *Air Force Combat Units of World War II*) The 301st and 302d Fighter Squadrons were also constituted that day, for eventual assignment to the group. (Maurer, *Air Force Combat Units of World War II*)

25 July: The 96th Maintenance Group was redesignated as the 96th Service Group (Colored) at Tuskegee Army Air Field. (Organization record card)

25 July: The 96th Maintenance Group was redesignated as the 96th Service Group. At the same time, the 366th and 367th Materiel Squadrons were redesignated as the 366th and 367th Service Squadrons at Tuskegee. (Organization Record cards at AFHRA)

5 August: The fifth class of African-American pilots graduated from flying training at Tuskegee Army Air Field. (99th Fighter Squadron history, Mar 1941-Oct 1943) It was class SE-42-G, and their were eight graduates. Enough African-American pilots had completed training to bring the 99th

Fighter Squadron to its full strength of 33 pilots.

19 August: The 99th Fighter Squadron was attached to the III Fighter Command. (Maurer, *Combat Squadrons of the Air Force, World War II*)

Late August: Several white pilots from the 20th and 58th Fighter Groups, both stationed in Florida, were assigned temporarily as instructors to the 99th Fighter Squadron. (99th Fighter Squadron history, Mar 1941-Oct 1943)

22 August: Lt. Col. Benjamin O. Davis Jr. became commander of the 99th Fighter Squadron, replacing Lieutenant George S. Roberts in that position. Colonel Davis was the second black commander of the unit. (99th Fighter Squadron lineage and honors history; 99th Fighter Squadron history, Mar 1941–17 Oct 1943)

27 August: The War Department organized the Advisory Committee on Negro Troop Policies, with Assistant Secretary of War John J. McCloy as chairman. (Ulysses Lee, *The Employment of Negro Troops* [Washington: Office of the Chief of Military History, United States Army, 1966], 157)

August: Only 2.8 percent of Army Air Forces personnel were black by this month, although the percentage of blacks in the general population of the United States was around 10 percent. By this month, the Army Air Forces had only 78 black commissioned officers. (Wesley Frank Craven and James Lea Cate, editors, *The Army Air Forces in World War II*, volume VI, *Men and Planes* [Washington: Office of Air Force History, 1983], 523)

1 September: Captain John G. Cooke Jr. succeeded Lt. Robert B. Lowenberg as Commandant of Cadets at Tuskegee Army Air Field. (History of Tuskegee Army Air Field, 23 Jul 1941–6 Dec 1944, vol. 1 and 2, AFHRA call number 289.28–1)

6 September: The sixth class of African-American pilots graduated from flying training at Tuskegee Army Air Field. (99th Fighter Squadron history, Mar 1941-Oct 1943) It was class SE-42-I, and there were nine graduates.

12 September: Lt. Faythe A. McGinnis crashed on a routine flight and became the first casualty of the 99th Fighter Squadron. (99th Fighter Squadron history, Mar 1941–17 Oct 1943)

15 September: The 1000th Signal Company, the 1051st Quartermaster Service Group Aviation Company, the 1765th Ordnance Supply and Maintenance Company, Aviation, and the 1901st and 1902d Quartermaster Truck Company (Aviation) were all activated at Tuskegee Army Air Field. (Organization record cards of each organization)

19 September: At a bus station in Montgomery, Alabama, 2nd Lt. Norma

Class 42-H , which graduated from advanced flight training at Tuskegee Army Air Field in September 1942. There were a total of 44 classes.

Greene, an African American U.S. Army nurse, was forced to vacate an express bus on which she expected to return to Tuskegee Army Air Field after a Saturday shopping trip to the city. Bus station personnel called the Montgomery police, who arrested her and detained her for several hours. At the time of her arrest, she was wearing civilian clothes, and the policemen did not at first realize she was a member of the military. When they discovered that, they released her to authorities at Tuskegee Army Air Field and dropped the charges. Another source, which misspelled her name as Nora Green, claimed she had been beaten, a claim Montgomery police officials denied. When Lt. Greene returned to Tuskegee Army Air Field, she went to the base hospital, probably not because of any injuries she suffered, but because she worked there. (Zellie Orr; "Army Nurse Jailed After Montgomery Bus Dispute," *Pittsburgh Courier*, 26 September 1942; another source that misspelled Greene's name as Nora Green, and claimed the beating, is Walter White's autobiography, *A Man Called White* [New York: The Viking Press, 1948], 222)

September: After further gunnery training at Eglin and Dale Mabry Fields in Florida, the 99th Fighter Squadron returned to Tuskegee and was declared ready for combat. However, its planned deployment to defend Liberia was indefinitely delayed because of the diminished enemy threat to that country. During the same month, a post chapel was completed. (*Hawk's Cry*, vol. II, no. 29, dated 17 Sep 1943, which referred to the first anniversary of the chapel). By the end of September 1942, there were at least 33 trained black military pilots, enough for the squadron to be operational. (Lawrence P. Schott and William M. Womack Sr., *Double V: The Civil Rights Struggle of the Tuskegee Airmen* [East Lansing: Michigan State University Press, 1994], 159)

7 October: Secretary of War Henry L. Stimson visited the 99th Fighter Squadron at Tuskegee Army Air Field. (99th Fighter Squadron history, Mar 1941-Oct 1943)

9 October: The seventh class of African-American pilots graduated from flying training at Tuskegee Army Air Field. (99th Fighter Squadron history, Mar 1941-Oct 1943) It was class SE-42-I, and there were eight graduates.

13 October: The 332d Fighter Group was activated at Tuskegee Army Air Field, Alabama, and the pre-existing 100th Fighter Squadron was assigned to it. The 301st and 302d Fighter Squadrons were also activated for the first time at Tuskegee, and assigned to the 332d Fighter Group. This group was the first African-American group in the Army Air Forces. (Maurer, *Air Force Combat Units of World War II*; Maurer, *Combat Squadrons of the Air Force, World War II*). Eventually, all four of the African-American squadrons in the Army Air Forces were assigned to the 332d Fighter Group. On the same date, 13 October 1942, the 332d Fighter Control Squadron (Colored) was activated at Tuskegee Army Air Field. (organization record card)

19 October: Lt. Col. Sam W. Westbrook Jr., was appointed commander of the 332d Fighter Group. He physically took command of the group on 3 December. (Maurer, *Air Force Combat Units of World War II*) By this date, the group had only 7 enlisted men and 2 officers, the latter being white. (332nd Fighter Group history, Oct 1942–1947))

10 November: The eighth class of African-American pilots graduated from flying training at Tuskegee Army Air Field. (99th Fighter Squadron history, Mar 1941-Oct 1943) It was class SE-42-J, and there were four graduates.

12 November: 1st Lt. Charles W. Walker became the first black officer assigned to the 332d Fighter Group. He was a chaplain. (332d Fighter Group History, Oct 1942–1947)

17 November: Lt. Col. Benjamin O. Davis Jr. addressed the assembled 99th Fighter Squadron for the first time, at Tuskegee Army Air Field. (99 Fighter Squadron history, Mar 1941–17 Oct 1943)

23 November: The 99th Fighter Squadron paraded for the first time, at Tuskegee Army Air Field. (99th Fighter Squadron history, Mar 1941–17 Oct 1943)

26 November: 1st Lieutenant Harold C. Magoon, second highest ranking white officer at Moton Field, was promoted to captain. The field's military commander, also white, William T. Smith, had already been appointed the rank of captain. (66th Army Air Forces Flying Training Detachment, Moton Field, Tuskegee Institute, Alabama, Feb 1941–7 Dec 1941, vol. 1, appendix VI)

December: Lt. Col. Noel F. Parrish, who had served as Director of Training at the Tuskegee Army Air Field since early December 1941, became commanding officer of the base, replacing Col. Frederick von Kimble. Parrish allowed more desegregation of the facilities on the field than his predecessors. (Tuskegee Army Flying School Yearbook, AFHRA call number 289.28–100, and Jakeman)

3 December: Although he was appointed first commander of the 332nd Fighter Group on 19 October, Major Sam W. Westbrook arrived at Tuskegee to take command of the organization. He was white and from Alabama, a graduate of Alabama Polytechnical College (later, Auburn University) and he was an experienced pilot. Although he was commander of the group, he was attached to it rather than assigned to it. (332nd Fighter Group history, Oct 1942–1947)

13 December: The ninth class of African-American pilots graduated from flying training at Tuskegee Army Air Field. It was class SE-42-K, and there were eight graduates. (Homan and Reilly, *Black Knights;* roster of graduates from TAAF)

22 December 1942–13 January 1943: The 99th Fighter Squadron deployed at Dale Mabry Field in Tallahassee, Florida, for maneuvers. (99th Fighter Squadron history, Mar 1941-Oct 1943)

End of 1942: All major construction at Tuskegee Army Air Field was complete. The base had 3414 men, 67 of whom were white. 121 of the men were flying cadets. The base was congested, with one fighter group, four fighter squadrons, a service group, and three phases of flying training. To control severe soil erosion, tens of thousands of trees were planted around the field. (History of Tuskegee Army Air Field, Mar-Jun 1944, AFHRA call number 289.28-4, vol. 1; Thole, *Forgotten Fields in America*, vol. 3) By the end of 1942, 63 cadets had graduated from flying training, and 30 had been eliminated. (History of The Corps of Aviation Cadets, Tuskegee Army Air Field, Alabama, AFHRA call number K289.28–1, 1 Aug 1941–1 Mar 1944)

1943

14 January: The tenth class of African-American pilots graduated from advanced pilot training at Tuskegee Army Air Field. It was class SE-43-A, and there were six graduates. (Roster of graduates, TAAF)

15 January: The emblem of the 332d Fighter Group as approved. On a blue shield with a gold band across the middle, a black panther breathing fire. (Maurer, *Air Force Combat Units of World War II*). On that same date, 1st Lt. Frederick E. Miles assumed command of the 301st Fighter Squadron. (Lineage and Honors histories of the 100th Fighter and 301st Fighter Squadrons)

25 January: The first class of African-American military personnel in any of the Army Air Forces technical schools began a twelve-week aerial photography course at the Army Air Forces Technical School at Lowry Field, Colorado. Forty-six students completed the course on April 16. (*The Lowry Field Rev-Meter* base newspaper, January 22, 1943, 3, and April 15, 1943, 2, both articles supplied by Craig Huntly)

26 January: The 366th and 367th Service Squadrons and the 43d Medical Support Platoon, Aviation were all assigned to the 96th Service Group at Tuskegee. (Organization record card of the 96 Air Service Group). On the same date, 1st Lt. Mac Ross assumed command

Colonel Noel F. Parrish, who commanded the flying school at Tuskegee Army Air Field during most of World War II, was remembered by most of the Tuskegee Airmen pilots as a fair man who was genuinely interested in their success.

of the 100th Fighter Squadron, and Capt. Charles H. Debow became commander of the 301st Fighter Squadron. Both had been in the first black pilot graduating class at Tuskegee Army Air Field, and both became the first black commanders of their respective squadrons. The previous two commanders of the 100th Fighter Squadron, before Lt. Mac Ross, had been white, and the previous commander of the 301st Fighter Squadron, before Capt. Charles H. DeBow, had been white. (Lineage and Honors histories of the 100th and 301st Fighter Squadrons)

30 January: Lt. Richard A. Davis crashed, becoming the second casualty of the 99th Fighter Squadron. (99th Fighter Squadron, Mar 1941–17 Oct 1943)

8 February: Capt. James P. Ramsey was appointed first medical officer of the 332nd Fighter Group. (332nd Fighter Group history, Oct 1942–1947)

8 February: Tuskegee Advanced Flying School at Tuskegee Army Air Field was assigned to the Flying Training Command, but remained under the jurisdiction of the Southeast Air Corps Training Center. (Organization record card at Air Force Historical Research Agency)

9 February: Six 99th Fighter Squadron pilots engaged in a mock dogfight over Tuskegee Army Air Field with six pilots visiting from Craig Field, Alabama, for practice. During the mission, 1st Lt. Sherman W. White had an engine malfunction and was forced to crash-land, but he survived. (99 Fighter Squadron history, Mar 1941–17 Oct 1943)

15 February: Major Gabe C. Hawkins Jr., a white pilot, became Director of Basic Flying Training at Tuskegee Army Air Field. (History of Tuskegee Army Air Field, Mar-Jun 1944, AFHRA call number 289.28-4, vol. 1)

16 February: Class SE-43-B graduated from advanced pilot training at Tuskegee Army Air Field. There were seven graduates. It was the eleventh class of pilots to graduate. (Roster of TAAF graduates)

March: Lt. Col. Donald G. McPherson, a white officer who had served as Director of Basic Flying Training at Tuskegee Army Air Field, moved up to become Director of Flying Training there. (Histories of Tuskegee Army Air Field at the Air Force Historical Research Agency)

March: Col. Roscoe G. Conklin of the Third Fighter Command led the final three and a half weeks of training of the 99th Fighter Squadron at Tuskegee Army Air Field.

3 March: The War Department directed that there be "equal opportunity to enjoy recreational facilities at each post." The directive was largely ignored. (Noel Parrish thesis for Air Command and Staff College, "Segregation of

Negroes in the Army Air Forces," 1947, AFHRA call number 239.04347)

11 March: 2nd Lt. William T. Mattison assumed command of the 302nd Fighter Squadron. He is the first known black commander of the squadron. (302nd Fighter Squadron lineage and honors history)

15 March: The 332nd Fighter Control Squadron (Colored) was disbanded at Tuskegee Army Air Field. (organization record card). On the same day, the 403rd Fighter Squadron was activated at Selfridge Field, Michigan, as an operational training unit under I Fighter Command, to prepare the way for the movement of the 332d Fighter Group from Tuskegee Army Air Field to Selfridge. The 403rd Fighter Squadron was a white unit designed to help train the squadrons of the 332nd Fighter Group at Selfridge. (Maurer, *Combat Squadrons*, 493–494; 332nd Fighter Group history, Oct 1942–1947)

24 March: Lt. Earl E. King became the third casualty of the 99th Fighter Squadron. (99th Fighter Squadron history, Mar 1941–17 Oct 1943)

25 March: Class SE-43-C graduated from advanced pilot training at Tuskegee Army Air Field. This was the twelfth class to graduate, and there were 13 graduates that day. (Roster of TAAF graduates)

26 March: The ground echelon of the 332d Fighter Group and its 100th, 301st, and 302d Fighter Squadrons departed Tuskegee Army Air Field, heading for Selfridge Field, Michigan. The men boarded a train at a nearby station for the move. The move eased overcrowding at Tuskegee Army Air Field. (332d Fighter Group History, Oct 1942–1947)

28 March: The air echelon of the 332nd Fighter Group flew from Tuskegee Army Air Field, Alabama, to Selfridge Field, Michigan. (332nd Fighter Group history, Oct 1942–1947)

29 March: The ground echelon of the 332d Fighter Group completed its move from Tuskegee Army Air Field in Alabama to Selfridge Field in Michigan. (Maurer, *Air Force Combat Units of World War II*)

2 April: The 99th Fighter Squadron departed Tuskegee Army Air Field, Alabama, for movement overseas for combat operations. (Maurer, *Combat Squadrons of the Air Force, World War II*). Helping the men load on trucks for the journey to the train station were Col. Frederick V. H. Kimble and Colonel Noel F. Parrish, former and current commanders of Tuskegee Army Flying School, who wanted to express their support for the first black flying unit to deploy. (99th Fighter Squadron history, Mar 1941-Oct 1943)

2 April: The 366th Materiel Squadron, later 366th Service Squadron, began moving from Tuskegee Army Air Field to Selfridge Field, Michigan. (366th Service Squadron history, call number SQ-SV-366-HI). It had serviced the airplanes of the 99th Fighter Squadron, which was moving overseas, and the 332nd Fighter Group and its other three fighter squadrons, which had already moved to Selfridge.

4 April: The 99th Fighter Squadron arrived at Camp Shanks, New York, in preparation for deployment overseas for combat. The squadron remained there for eleven days. (99th Fighter Squadron history, Mar 1941–17 Oct 1943) On the same day, the 96th Service Group completed its move to Selfridge Field, Michigan, in order to serve with the 332d Fighter Group. (Lineage and honors history of the 96th Logistics Group)

5 April: 1st Lt. George L. Knox succeeded 1st Lt. Mac Ross as commander of the 100th Fighter Squadron. (Lineage and honors history of the 100th Fighter Squadron)

12 April: Part of the 332d Fighter Group moved from Selfridge Field to Oscoda, Michigan, but the headquarters remained at Selfridge until 21 May. (Maurer, *Air Force Combat Units of World War II*; 332nd Fighter Group history, Oct 1942–1947)

16 April: The 99th Fighter Squadron sailed aboard the steamship *Mariposa* from New York harbor, bound eastward across the Atlantic Ocean for Africa. It arrived later at Casablanca, French Morocco. On the voyage, black officers of the 99th Fighter Squadron commanded lower-ranking personnel on the ship. (99th Fighter Squadron history, Mar 1941-Oct 1943)

16 April: The first class of African-American military personnel in any of the Army Air Forces technical schools completed a twelve-week aerial photography course at the Army Air Forces Technical School at Lowry Field, Colorado. Forty-six students completed the course. (*The Lowry Field Rev-Meter* base newspaper, January 22, 1943, 3, and April 15, 1943, 2, both articles supplied by Craig Huntly)

24 April: The 99th Fighter Squadron arrived at Casablanca, French Morocco, its first overseas base, and began serving the Twelfth Air Force. (Maurer, *Combat Squadrons of the Air Force, World War II*)

25 April: The 320th College Training Detachment (Aircrew) was activated at Tuskegee Institute, Alabama. It provided college-level training to blacks with high school educations to prepare them for pre-flight training at Tuskegee Army Air Field. Captain Theodore H. Randall was appointed commander of the detachment the same date. (320th College Training Detachment history, Tuskegee Institute, Alabama, March 1943-Mar 1944, Air Force Historical Research Agency call number 234.821, Mar 1943-Mar 1944) and the detachment's organization record card at the Air Force Historical Research Agency)

29 April: The 99th Fighter Squadron moved to Oued N'ja, French Morocco. There it engaged in maneuvers and prepared for combat. (Maurer, *Combat Squadrons of the Air Force, World War II*)

29 April: Class SE-43-D graduated from advanced pilot training at Tuskegee Army Air Field. There were 19 in the class.

1 May 1944: The 2143d Army Air Forces Base Unit was organized at Tuskegee Army Air Field. Colonel Noel B. Parrish, who already commanded the flying school there, and the base, became the commander.

4 May: The 403rd Fighter Squadron moved from Selfridge Field, Michigan, to Oscoda Army Air Field, Michigan.

5 May: Lieutenants James T. Wiley and Graham Smith were the first two P-40 pilots of the 99th Fighter Squadron to land in North Africa, at Oued N'ja in French Morocco. (99th Fighter Squadron history, Mar 1941-Oct 1943)

5 May: Well after midnight, Private First Class Willie McRae of the 44th Aviation Squadron at Selfridge Field, an African American driver, was called to base headquarters to provide transportation for Col. William T. Colman, the white base commander. When McRae arrived at 1:10 in the morning, Colman shot McRae, wounding him. Lt. Col. Sam W. Westbrook, commander of the 332nd Fighter Group, relieved Colman of command, had him confined, and prepared a court martial. Colman was convicted in September, not for assault with intent to do bodily harm, but for careless discharge of a pistol. (History of Selfridge Field, Michigan, 1943, AFHRA call number 288.52–3, vol. I, 140–141; Lawrence P. Scott and William M. Womack Sr., *Double V: The Civil Rights Struggle of the Tuskegee Airmen* [East Lansing, MI: Michigan State University Press, 1994], 192–193)

7 May: 2nd Lt. Jerome T. Edwards of the 100th Fighter Squadron crashed in his aircraft, becoming the first 332nd Fighter Group pilot to lose his life. (332nd Fighter Group history, Oct 1942–1947)

9 May: Personnel of the 99th Fighter Squadron took part in a victory parade in Fez, North Africa to celebrate the liberation of Tunisia. Captain Hayden C. Johnson led the squadron contingent in the ceremony. (99th Fighter Squadron history, Mar-Oct 1943)

9 May: Back in Michigan, 2nd Lt. Wilmeth Sidat-Singh of the 332nd Fighter Group was killed when he crashed with his airplane into Lake Huron. His body was recovered 49 days later. (332nd Fighter Group history, Oct 1942–1947)

13 May: The 477th Bombardment Group (Medium) was constituted, along with the 616th, 617th, 618th, and 619th Bombardment Squadrons. (Maurer, *Air Force Combat Units of World War II;* Maurer, *Combat Squadrons of the Air Force, World War II*). Meanwhile, enemy forces in Tunisia surrendered, leaving all North Africa in Allied control.

May: An Air Intelligence School was established at Selfridge Field, where 332nd Fighter Group black intelligence personnel began their training. (332nd Fighter Group history, Oct 1942–1947)

16 May: Col. Robert R. Selway Jr. became commander of the 332d Fighter Group back in the United States. (Maurer, *Air Force Combat Units of World War II*). Like his predecessor, Lt. Col. Sam Westbrook, Selway was a white officer. Selway was a graduate of the United States Military Academy at West Point. He was a native of California. (332nd Fighter Group history, Oct 1942–1947)

19 May: Lieutenant General Carl Spaatz, commander of the Twelfth Air Force, inspected the flying field of the 99th Fighter Squadron at Oued N'ja. (99th Fighter Squadron history, Mar-Oct 1943)

21 May: The headquarters of the 332nd Fighter Group moved from Selfridge Field to Oscoda Field, Michigan, joining other elements of the group that had deployed there on 12 April. (332nd Fighter Group history, Oct 1942–1947)

May: Experienced white combat pilots from other P-40 squadrons in North Africa began visiting the 99th Fighter Squadron as instructors in tactical maneuvers. Among them were Col. Philip Cochran, Maj Ralph E. Keyes, Lt. Robert F. Thackler, and Lt. Robert J. Conner. (99th Fighter Squadron history, Mar 1941-Oct 1943)

22 May: The first group of aviation students to complete a new 6-week intensive study at the College Training Detachment at Tuskegee Institute transferred to Tuskegee Army Air Field for the preflight stage of aviation cadet training. Formerly, the college training took 5 months. (*Hawk's Cry*, vol. II, no. 13, dated 28 May 1943)

28 May: The 99th Fighter Squadron was assigned to the XII Air Support (later, XII Tactical Air) Command. (Maurer, *Combat Squadrons of the Air Force, World War II*)

28 May: Class SE-43-E graduated from advanced pilot training at Tuskegee Army Air Field. There were 21 graduates.

29 May: The 99th Fighter Squadron was attached to the 33d Fighter Group, which was under the command of Col. William M. Momyer. (Maurer, *Combat Squadrons of the Air Force, World War II*). On the same date, back in the United States, 1st Lt. Robert B. Tresville assumed command of the 302nd Fighter Squadron, succeeding 2nd Lt. William T. Mattison. (302nd Fighter Squadron lineage and honors history)

30 May: The air echelon of the 99th Fighter Squadron flew its P-40s from Qued N'ja, French Morocco, to Fardjouna, Tunisia, near Cape Bon, east of Tunis. One section of the ground echelon left Qued N'ja the same day, but most of the ground echelon departed three days later. The ground echelons of the squadron did not arrive at Fardjouna until June 7. (99th Fighter Squadron history, May-Oct 1943)

31 May: The 332nd Fighter Group in Michigan by this date had 1,004 enlisted men and 110 officers. (332nd Fighter Group history, Oct 1942–1947)

Late spring: Frank Carr, the white mayor of Tuskegee, offered the use of the city swimming pool to military personnel residing in Tuskegee. Presumably, all of these personnel were white, since the black personnel were residing at Moton Field, Tuskegee Army Air Field, or on the campus of Tuskegee Institute. It is possible that Carr wanted to enhance the appeal of living in Tuskegee for white military personnel stationed at Tuskegee Army Air Field, since many of them had chosen to live in Auburn instead. (History of Tuskegee Army Air Field, Mar 1944-Jun 1944, call number 289.28-4, vol. 1, at the Air Force Historical Research Agency)

1 June: The 477th Bombardment Group (Medium) was activated at Mac-Dill Field, Florida, as a white organization, with the 616th 617th, 618th, and 619th Bombardment Squadrons. Lt. Col. Andrew O. Lerche served as the commander, but the group was not yet a black organization. In August 1943, the group and its squadrons were inactivated. (Maurer, *Combat Squadrons of the Air Force, World War II;* Maurer, *Air Force Combat Units of World War II*). In 1944, the group and its four squadrons were activated again, but that second time as black organizations. (477th Bombardment Group lineage and honors history)

2 June: The 99th Fighter Squadron flew its first combat mission, flying P-40 aircraft on patrol over the Mediterranean Sea while attached to the 33d Fighter Group. The 99th did not encounter enemy aircraft that day. (99th Fighter Squadron history, Mar-Oct 1943) Squadron P-40s flew from Fardjouna, Tunisia, although the ground echelon of the squadron did not arrive at the new base until June 7.

2–9 June: The 99th Fighter Squadron flew an average of two missions daily for the 33d Fighter Group during the campaign against Pantelleria Island, which ended on 11 June. Some of the missions targeted enemy gun sites on the island, and some escorted A-20 and B-25 aircraft on raids against enemy targets there. (99th Fighter Squadron history, Mar-Oct 1943) White fighter squadrons also targeted the island.

7 June: The ground echelon of the 99th Fighter Squadron completed its move from Qued N'ja, French Morocco, to Fardjouna, Tunisia. The first elements had departed the old base on May 30. (99th Fighter Squadron history, May-Oct 1943; Maurer, *Combat Squadrons of the Air Force, World War II*)

9 June: The 99th Fighter Squadron encountered enemy aircraft for the first time during a mission on which it escorted 12 A-20s over Pantelleria Island. P-40s of the squadron intercepted four Me-109 German fighters and the enemy fled. P-40s of another squadron escorted the A-20s home. (99th Fighter Squadron history, Mar-Oct 1943)

10 June: The 96th Service Group moved from Selfridge Field to Oscoda Field, Michigan, to which the 332d Fighter Group had moved in April. (96th Service Group organization record card)

11 June: The surrender of enemy forces on Pantelleria paved the way for the Allied invasion of Sicily. (99th Fighter Squadron history, Mar 1941–17 Oct 1943)

15 June: The 99th Fighter Squadron flew four missions in one day, to cover Allied shipping in the Mediterranean Sea. (99th Fighter Squadron history, Mar-Oct 1943)

16 June: Back with the 332nd Fighter Group in Michigan, 2nd Lt. Nathaniel N. Hill of the 100th Fighter Squadron and 2nd Lt. Luther H. Blakeney, a weather officer, were killed in a plane crash in thick fog. (332nd Fighter Group history, Oct 1942–1947)

18 June: The 99th Fighter Squadron encountered enemy aircraft for the second time, and 1st Lieutenant Lee Rayford's P-40 was hit several times. (99th Fighter Squadron history, Mar 1941-Oct 1943)

20–21 June: A major race riot broke out in Detroit, Michigan, leaving 34 people dead, including 25 whites and 9 blacks, and 670 people injured. (Arthur Herman, *Freedom's Forge* [New York: Random House, 2012], 261–262). Selfridge Field deployed 2,000 men (white) to help restore order. (History of Selfridge Field, Michigan, 1943, AFHRA call number 288.52–3). The riots concerned members of the 332nd Fighter Group, most of which were stationed at Oscoda, Michigan, at the time. The group's white commander, Colonel Robert Selway, ordered black airman to stay on base. (Lawrence P. Schott and William M. Womack Sr., *Double V: The Civil Rights Struggle of the Tuskegee Airmen* [East Lansing: Michigan State University Press, 1994],

194–195)

26 June: Eight black intelligence officers assigned to the 332nd Fighter Group were reassigned from Selfridge Field, Michigan to the Army Air Forces Intelligence School at Harrisburg, Pennsylvania, where they trained with white personnel. The officers were Second Lieutenants John R. Beverly Jr., Paul V. Freeman, Morris M. Hatchett, Theodore G. Lumpkin, Robert G. Pitts, Samuel C. Scott, Robert S. Scurlock, and Ray B. Ware. (332nd Fighter Group history, Oct 1942–1947)

29 June: 1st Lt. Elwood T. Driver succeeded 1st Lt. George L. Knox as commander of the 100th Fighter Squadron. (Lineage and honors history of the 100th Fighter Squadron)

c. 29 June: The 99th Fighter Squadron was attached to the 324th Fighter Group, under the command of Col. William K. McNown, and began flying escort missions between Tunisia and Sicily. (Maurer, *Combat Squadrons of the Air Force, World War II*)

30 June: Class SE-43-F graduated from advanced pilot training at Tuskegee Army Air Field. There were 24 graduates, more than any other class to that time.

June: During this month, King George VI of the British Empire visited Grombalia Airfield in north Africa and reviewed approximately 50 enlisted men of the 99th Fighter Squadron. (99th Fighter Squadron history, Mar 1941–17 Oct 1943) The 789th Technical School Squadron at Lincoln, Nebraska, graduated its first class of African-American fighter mechanics. (newspaper article and program from Craig Huntly)

July: The 332nd Fighter Group continued preparing for combat in Michigan. Airplane mechanics arrived from training at Buffalo, New York, and Chanute Field, Illinois. Armorers came from Buckley Field, Colorado; radar mechanics from Tomah, Wisconsin; and radio personnel from Fort Monmouth, New Jersey and Camp Crowder, Missouri. (332nd Fighter Group history, Oct 1942–1947)

2 July: While escorting B-25 medium bombers on a raid on Castelvetrano in southwestern Sicily, Italy, 1st Lt. Charles B. Hall of the 99th Fighter Squadron earned the first Tuskegee Airmen aerial victory credit by shooting down an FW-190 enemy aircraft. Lt. W. I. Lawson also claimed probable destruction of another FW-190 and damaged an Me-109. On the same day, 1st Lt. Sherman H. White and 2d Lt. James L. McCullin were the first Tuskegee Airmen lost in combat. Although both went missing, one is believed to have landed on enemy-held Sicily. That afternoon, General Dwight D. Eisenhower also visited the 99th Fighter Squadron. (99th Fighter Squadron history, Mar-Oct 1943; XII ASC General Order 32 dated 7 Sep 1943; article by Joseph Caver, Jerome Ennels, and Wesley Newton)

3 July: The 99th Fighter Squadron joined three other fighter squadrons of the 324th Fighter Group, to which it was attached, in escorting medium bombers to Sicily. During that mission, enemy fighters shot down at least one of the bombers. (324th Fighter Group Operational and Intelligence Summary, Operations for July 3, 1943)

3 July: Back at Tuskegee Army Air Field, Alabama, a new NCO Club opened. (*Hawk's Cry*, vol. II, no. 18, dated 2 Jul 1943)

June-July: The 99th Fighter Squadron earned the first of its three World War II Distinguished Unit Citations for missions over Sicily. The unit provided air support for Allied landing operations and for Allied offensives on the island. The 324th Fighter Group, to which the 99th Fighter Squadron was attached, also earned the award. (Maurer, *Combat Squadrons of the Air Force, World War II*)

6 July: Air Vice Marshal Sir Arthur Conningham of the Royal Air Force, who commanded the North African Tactical Air Force, visited the 99th Fighter Squadron at Fardjouna. (99th Fighter Squadron history, Mar 1941–17 Oct 1943) On the same date, back in the United States, 1st Lt. Edward C. Gleed assumed command of the 302nd Fighter Squadron, succeeding 1st Lt. Robert B. Tresville. (302nd Fighter Squadron lineage and honors history). At the same time, Capt. Robert B. Tresville succeeded 1st Lt. Elwood T. Driver as commander of the 100th Fighter Squadron. (100th Fighter Squadron lineage and honors history)

8 July: The 99th Fighter Squadron escorted medium bombers to Milo, Sicily. Two of the pilots claimed to have damaged enemy airplanes on the mission. (99th Fighter Squadron history, Mar 1941–17 Oct 1943)

9–10 July: The 332d Fighter Group moved from Oscoda, Michigan, back to Selfridge Field, Michigan, but the 96th Service Group, which maintained the airplanes, remained at Oscoda. (Maurer, *Air Force Combat Units of World War II;* 96th Service Group organization record card) At the same time, the white 403rd Fighter Squadron moved from Oscoda to Selfridge. (Maurer, *Air Force Combat Units of World War II*)

10 July: During the invasion of Sicily, the 99th Fighter Squadron covered the landing of Allied troops at Licata. (99th Fighter Squadron history, Mar-Oct 1943)

11 July: The 99th Fighter Squadron drove off 12 German FW-190 fighters attempting to attack Allied naval vessels in the Mediterranean Sea. 1st Lt. George R. Bolling was hit by antiaircraft artillery coming from some of the vessels and bailed out. Five days later, Bolling returned to the squadron after being rescued by an Allied destroyer. (99th Fighter Squadron history, Mar 1941–17 Oct 1943)

19 July: The 99th Fighter Squadron was attached again to the 33d Fighter Group, under Col. William W. Momyer, to help provide cover for Allied shipping in the Mediterranean Sea and air support for the Seventh Army. On the same day, 29 C-47 transport planes helped carry personnel and equipment of the air echelon of the 99th Fighter Squadron from Tunisia to Licata, Sicily. Most of the ground echelon moved by ship later. (Maurer, *Combat Squadrons of the Air Force, World War II*)

21 July: The 99th Fighter Squadron flew its first missions from Sicily, from the new base at Licata. It flew 13 missions that day. (99th Fighter Squadron history, Mar 1941–17 Oct 1943)

23 July: The first three replacement pilots arrived for the 99th Fighter Squadron overseas. They included Lieutenants Howard L. Baugh, Edward L. Toppins, and Morgan (first name not given). (99th Fighter Squadron history, Mar 1941–17 Oct 1943)

23 July: Tuskegee Advanced Flying School, at Tuskegee Army Air Field, Alabama, was redesignated as AAF Pilot School (Basic-Advanced). (organization record card)

23 July: Col. William L. Boyd, a white officer, assumed command of Selfridge Field, Michigan, where the predominantly black 332nd Fighter Group was stationed (the commander of the group and his staff were also white). The former base commander, Col. William T. Colman, another white officer, was awaiting court martial trial for shooting and wounding a black driver. (History of Selfridge Field, Michigan, 1943, AFHRA call number 288.52–3, 166–167)

26 July: The 99th Fighter Squadron flew 12 missions in one day. (99th Fighter Squadron history, Mar 1941–17 Oct 1943)

27 July: Major General Edwin J. House, commander of the XII Air Support Command of the Twelfth Air Force, visited the 99th Fighter Squadron. (99th Fighter Squadron history, Mar 1941–17 Oct 1943)

28 July: The 99th Fighter Squadron moved from Tunisia in North Africa to Sicily. (Maurer, *Combat Squadrons of the Air Force, World War II*). On the same day, Lieutenant Colonel Benjamin O. Davis Jr. and 1st Lieutenant Herbert Carter, engineering officer of the 99th Fighter Squadron, flew to Tunis to meet with Secretary of War Henry L. Stimson. (99th Fighter Squadron history, Mar 1941–17 Oct 1943)

28 July: Raymond Cassagnol of Haiti became the first foreign cadet to graduate from pilot training at Tuskegee Army Air Field. (Zellie Rainey Orr, historian, Atlanta Chapter, Tuskegee Airmen, Incorporated; Lynn M. Homan and Thomas Reilly, *Black Knights: The Story of the Tuskegee Airmen* (Gretna: Pelican Publishing Company, 2006), 278.

28 July: Class SE-43-G graduated from advanced pilot training at Tuskegee Army Air Field. There were 28 in the class, more than any class to that time.

29 July: The ground echelon of the 99th Fighter Squadron completed its move to the base at Licata, Sicily, where the air echelon was already operating. The ground echelon had moved by sea from Bizerte in north Africa to Palermo and thence by truck convoy to Licata. (B. O. Davis Jr. autobiography)

2 August: Liaison pilot training began at Griel Field, an auxiliary airfield six miles from Tuskegee Army Air Field. 21 students arrived that day. (Thole)

5 August: Tuskegee Advanced Flying School, at Tuskegee Army Air Field, was redesignated as Army Air Forces Pilot School (Basic-Advanced), Tuskegee Army Air Field, Alabama. (organization record card at the Air Force Historical Research Agency)

7 August: Tuskegee Army Air Field celebrated its second anniversary, a day after the actual anniversary. Lt. Col. Noel Parrish gave a speech and base band performed in Hangar no. 3, and the P-40 and advanced trainer aircraft were placed on display near the "broad sun-bathed runways." (*Hawk's Cry*, vol. II, no. 24, dated 13–14 Aug 1943)

11 August: Lieutenant Paul G. Mitchell was killed when his airplane crashed in mid-air with another airplane in his formation. He was the third 99th Fighter Squadron pilot lost in combat. (99th Fighter Squadron history, Mar 1941–17 Oct 1943)

15 August: Brigadier General John K. Cannon, commander of Northwest African Training Command, visited the 99th Fighter Squadron. (99th Fighter Squadron history, Mar 1941–17 Oct 1943)

17 August: The Sicilian campaign ended. (99th Fighter Squadron history, Mar 1941–17 Oct 1943)

23 August: The second class of liaison pilots began training at Tuskegee Army Air Field's Griel Field. (Samuel Broadnax, *Blue Skies, Black Wings*, 118)

24 August: The 99th Fighter Squadron received six replacement pilots from the United States. (99th Fighter Squadron history, Mar 1941–17 Oct 1943)

25 August: The 477th Bombardment Group (Medium) and the 616th, 617th, 618th, and 619th Bombardment Squadrons were inactivated, but the group was activated again as a black unit in January 1944. (Maurer, *Air Force Combat Units of World War II*; Maurer, *Combat Squadrons of the Air Force, World War II*)

30 August: Class SE-43-H graduated from advanced pilot training at Tuskegee Army Air Field. There were 22 in the class.

September: The War Department announced that the training of Negroes as bomber pilots would begin at Tuskegee Army Air Field within 30 days. During the month, A-10 twin-engine training aircraft arrived at the field, and were assigned to the 1155th Flying Training Squadron. The prospective bomber pilots were selected from cadets in basic flying training. The plan was for them to receive 70 hours of advanced flying training with the A-10s, then move to another base for training in actual bombers. Late in the month, the first liaison pilots graduated at Tuskegee, after they had trained with L-4 airplanes to become field artillery officers. They would move on from Tuskegee to Fort Sill, Oklahoma, for further tactical training. During the same month, certain enlisted personnel at Tuskegee Army Air Field were appointed as warrant officers. (*Hawk's Cry*, vol. II: no. 29, dated 17 Sep 1943; no. 30, dated 24 Sep 1943; no. 31, dated 1 Oct 1943)

September: A board of re-evaluation of pilots was activated at the 332nd Fighter Group base in Michigan. The board was composed of four white pilots from the 403rd Fighter Squadron, stationed at the same base (Selfridge Field). (332nd Fighter Group history, Oct 1942–1947). During the same month, the 332nd Fighter Group began receiving P-39 aircraft to replace its P-40s.

September: The 332nd Fighter Group, which had been flying P-40 aircraft, began flying P-39 aircraft. (332nd Fighter Group history, Oct 1942–1947)

2 September: Major George S. Roberts replaced Lieutenant Colonel Benjamin O. Davis as commander of the 99th Fighter Squadron as Davis began a return trip to the United States, where he would assume command of the 332d Fighter Group. Major Roberts had been the first black commander of the unit before Colonel Davis. Captain Lemuel R. Curtis succeeded Roberts as the squadron operations officer. (99th Fighter Squadron lineage and honors history; 99th Fighter Squadron history, Mar 1941–17 Oct 1943)

4 September: The 99th Fighter Squadron moved to Termini, Sicily. (Maurer, *Combat Squadrons of the Air Force, World War II*)

6–15 September: Col. William T. Colman, a white officer who had commanded Selfridge Field from 23 April 1942 to 5 May 1943, was tried in a court martial. The most serious of several charges against him was assault with intent to do bodily harm against Private First Class Willie McRae, an African American driver whom Colman had shot and wounded when McRae arrived to provide him transportation at 1:10 in the morning of 5 May. Colman was convicted on a lesser charge of carelessly discharging a pistol. (History of Selfridge Field, Michigan, 1943, AFHRA call number 288.52–3, 153–155)

11 September: Advance elements of the 99th Fighter Squadron landed on a beach at Battapaglia in Italy, under enemy fire. For several days, enemy forces strafed the advance echelon by day and bombed it by night, after it retreated to a site near Paestum, Italy, where the 33rd Fighter Group was based. The main body of the 99th Fighter Squadron remained in Sicily. (99th Fighter Squadron history, Mar 1941–17 Oct 1943)

13 September: the first class of liaison pilots graduated at Tuskegee Army Air Field. They would eventually be assigned to U.S. Army ground organizations, but fly liaison airplanes in their support.

13–14 September: The white 33rd Fighter Group, to which the 99th Fighter Squadron was attached, moved from Sicily to Paestum on the mainland of Italy, along with its three assigned fighter squadrons, the 58th, 59th, and 60th. The 99th Fighter Squadron, however, remained behind in Sicily, and stayed there until October 17, the day after it was detached from the 33rd and attached to the 79th Fighter Group. It was during this period, between mid-September and mid-October 1943, that a memorandum from 33rd Fighter Group went up the Army Air Forces chain of command questioning the 99th Fighter Squadron's combat efficiency. (Maurer, *Combat Squadrons of the Air Force, World War II*, and Charles Francis, *Tuskegee Airmen: The Men Who Changed a Nation* [Wellesley, MA: Branden Books, 2008].

16 September: Major General Edwin J. House, commander of the XII Air Support Command, sent a memorandum to Major General John K. Cannon, Deputy Commander of the Northwest African Tactical Air Force, regarding the "Combat Efficiency of the 99th Fighter Squadron". The letter criticized the black squadron as performing poorly in combat, based partly on information supplied by Colonel William Momyer, commander of the 33rd Fighter Group, to which the 99th Fighter Squadron was attached. The report recommended that the squadron trade in its P-40s for P-39s and be assigned to coastal patrols. It also recommended that a black fighter group not be deployed overseas for combat. (Ulysses Lee, *The Employment of Negro Troops* [Washington: Office of the Chief of Military History, United

States Army, 1966], 157; AFHRA call number 141.281–22; IRIS number 0011444)

16 September: The September 20, 1943 issue of *Time* magazine appeared on newsstands containing an article, "Experiment Proved?" that raised the question about whether or not the 99th Fighter Squadron would be taken out of combat because of an alleged poor combat performance. (Lawrence P. Schott and William M. Womack Sr., *Double V: The Civil Rights Struggle of the Tuskegee Airmen* [East Lansing: Michigan State University Press, 1994], 187)

17 September: The 99th Fighter Squadron moved to Barcellona, Sicily. (Maurer, *Combat Squadrons of the Air Force, World War II*). On the same day, 1st Lt. Sidney P. Brooks crashed, and died the next day, for the fourth pilot lost in combat. (99th Fighter Squadron history, Mar 1941–17 Oct 1943)

18 September: Responding to the memorandum from Major General House of the XII Air Support Command, Major General J. K. Cannon, Deputy Commander of the Northwest African Tactical Air Force, prepared a memorandum for the commanding general of the Northwest African Air Force critical of the 99th Fighter Squadron.

19 September: Lieutenant General Carl Spaatz, commander of the Northwest African Air Forces, and commander of the Twelfth Air Force, prepared a memo as he forwarded the memoranda from Generals House and Cannon on the combat performance of the 99th Fighter Squadron. Spaatz expressed his "full confidence in the fairness of the analysis made by both General Cannon and General House," he also noted that he had personally inspected the 99th Fighter Squadron several times, and found that "there has been no question of their ground discipline and their general conduct. It has been excellent." He noted that "In processing them for combat action they were given the benefit of our training system of the supervision of instructors with much combat experience. They were processed into combat action very carefully." Spaatz forwarded the memoranda and his own note to the Commanding General, Army Air Forces, who was General Henry "Hap" Arnold, in Washington, D.C.

September: During this month, German forces bombarded and strafed the base of the 99th Fighter Squadron for five consecutive days and nights, but there were no squadron casualties. (99th Fighter Squadron history, Mar 1941–17 Oct 1943)

September: Twin-engine pilot training began at Tuskegee Army Air Field, using A-10 aircraft. It was Class 43-J-TE (twin engine). When the twin engine pilots graduated, the pilots began transition flying in B-25 medium bombers, first at Mather Field, California, and later with the 477th Bombardment Group.

20 September. *Time* magazine published an article called "Experiment Proved?" regarding the combat performance of the 99th Fighter Squadron, the only black Army Air Forces squadron in combat, which included comments of its commander, Colonel Benjamin O. Davis Jr. Although the article mentioned that the squadron "seems to have done fairly well," it also noted that the Army Air Forces was considering reducing its combat role to coastal patrol duty. (Ulysses Lee, *The Employment of Negro Troops* [Washington: Office of The Chief of Military History, United States Army, 1966], 452; *Time*, XLII [Sep 20, 1943], 66–68)

23 September. Ten P-40s of the 99th Fighter Squadron landed on the Italian mainland for the first time, but returned to the main base at Barcellona, Sicily after one day of operations, which included four patrol missions. (99th Fighter Squadron history, Mar 1941–17 Oct 1943)

23 September. Back at Tuskegee Army Air Field, Lt. Col. Noel F. Parish received news that he was being promoted to colonel. (*Hawk's Cry*, vol. II, no. 30, dated 24 Sep 1943)

28 September. 2nd Lt. Johnson C. Wells of the 332nd Fighter Group at Selfridge Field, Michigan, was killed during a training flight. He crashed about 7 miles north of Selfridge. (332nd Fighter Group history, Oct 1942–1947)

30 September. The first class of liaison pilots (CL-43–1) graduated at Tuskegee Army Air Field. Some of the liaison pilots went on to serve with the 92nd and 93rd Infantry Divisions, which were Army ground organizations. The 92nd Division served in Italy, but the 93rd Division served in the South Pacific. (David G. Styles, *The Tuskegee Airmen and Beyond: The Road to Equality* [Deerfield, IL: Dalton Watson Fine Books, 2013], 259; correspondence with Karyn J. Taylor, whose father was one of the black liaison pilots during World War II)

October. The 332nd Fighter Group began its first full month flying P-39 aircraft instead of P-40s. (332nd Fighter Group history, Oct 1942–1947)

1 October. Class SE-43-I graduated from advanced pilot training at Tuskegee Army Air Field. There were 23 in the class.

3 October. The 403rd Fighter Squadron moved back from Selfridge Field, Michigan, to Oscoda Army Air Field, Michigan. (Maurer, *Combat Squadrons*)

8 October. Colonel Benjamin O. Davis Jr., who had served as commander of the 99th Fighter Squadron in combat in North Africa and Italy, became the first black commander of the 332d Fighter Group, replacing Col. Robert R. Selway Jr. (Maurer, *Air Force Combat Units of World War II*). Both Selway and Davis were graduates of the U.S. Military Academy at West Point. (332d Fighter Group History, Oct 1942–1947)

11 October: A formal reception was held at Selfridge Field, Michigan, to honor the new first black commander of the 332nd Fighter Group, Lt. Col. Benjamin O. Davis Jr. In attendance were his father, Brig. Gen. Benjamin O. Davis Sr., who was the first black general in the U.S. Army; Col. Robert R. Selway, Jr, the outgoing commander of the group; Col. William L. Boyd, the Selfridge Field post commander, and Major Harriet M. West, one of two black majors in the Women's Army Corps (WAC). (332nd Fighter Group history, Oct 1942–1947)

13 October: The Report on the Combat Efficiency of the 99th Fighter Squadron, prepared by Major General Edwin J. House of the XII Air Support Command, based in part on information from Colonel William Momyer, commander of the 33d Fighter Group, and endorsed by Major General John K. Cannon, Deputy Commander of the Mediterranean Allied Tactical Air Force and Lieutenant General Carl Spaatz, commander of the Twelfth Air Force, was presented to the War Department's Advisory Committee on Negro Troop Policies. (Ulysses Lee, *The Employment of Negro Troops* [Washington: Office of the Chief of Military History, United States Army, 1966], 458) The report recommended a reduced combat role for the 99th Fighter Squadron, based on a perception of poor performance.

14 October: 2nd Lt. William H. Walker and 2nd Lt. Leroi S. Williams of the 100th Fighter Squadron of the 332nd Fighter Group were killed in an air collision at Selfridge Field, Michigan. (332nd Fighter Group history, Oct 1942–1947)

16 October: Colonel Benjamin O. Davis Jr. met with members of the War Department's Advisory Committee on Negro Troop Policies (the McCloy Committee) and answered questions about the combat performance of the 99th Fighter Squadron he had led. Colonel Davis defended the unit's record, and recommended that it be allowed to remain in combat. On that same day, the War Department detached the 99th Fighter Squadron from Colonel William Momyer's 33d Fighter Group and attached it instead to the 79th Fighter Group, under the command of Col. Earl E. Bates Jr. As the 99th Fighter Squadron served with the 79th Fighter Group, perceptions of its combat performance improved. (Ulysses Lee, *The Employment of Negro Troops* [Washington: Office of the Chief of Military History, United States

Army, 1966], 459; Maurer, *Combat Squadrons of the Air Force, World War II* and the lineage and honors history of the group)

17 October: The advance echelon of the 99th Fighter Squadron arrived at landing field 3 at Foggia, Italy, having departed Paestum and the 33rd Fighter Group the previous day. (99th Fighter Squadron history, March 1941-October 1943; Maurer, *Combat Squadrons of the Air Force, World War II*) From that base it provided close air support for Allied ground troops and attacked surface targets such as ammunition dumps and enemy shipping.

17 October: Brig. Gen. Frank O. D. Hunter, commander of the First Air Force, visited Selfridge Field and addressed the officers of the 332nd Fighter Group, stressing the need for discipline. (B. O. Davis Jr. autobiography)

18 October: The advance air echelon of the 99th Fighter Squadron arrived at Foggia #3 airfield, joining the advance echelon that had arrived the previous day. (99th Fighter Squadron history, March 1941-October 1943) The entire squadron had moved to Italy by the end of the day, 20 October.

22 October: The first Negroes arrived at Hondo Field, Texas, to begin training as navigators. The training was scheduled for 18 weeks. Afterwards they would be assigned to bomber crews. (*Hawk's Cry*, vol. II, no. 40, dated 17 Dec 1943)

22 October: The second class of liaison pilots (CL-43–2) graduated at Tuskegee Army Air Field. Some of the liaison pilots went on to serve with the 92nd and 93rd Infantry Divisions, which were Army ground organizations. The 92nd Division served in Italy, but the 93rd Division served in the South Pacific. (David G. Styles, *The Tuskegee Airmen and Beyond: The Road to Equality* [Deerfield, IL: Dalton Watson Fine Books, 2013], 259; correspondence with Karyn J. Taylor, whose father was one of the black liaison pilots during World War II)

30 October: Thirty men who had failed to complete pilot training at Tuskegee Army Air Field were sent to Hondo Army Air Field, Texas, for navigator training.

October: During this month, the number of P-40s assigned to the 99th Fighter Squadron averaged 28. By the end of the month, 1st Lt. Thomas Malone and PFC James W. Jones each had been awarded the Purple Heart. (99th Fighter Squadron history, March 1941-October 1943)

November: Psychological testing, which had long been used to classify and accept white airmen as potential pilots, bombardiers, or navigators, was begun at Tuskegee Army Air Field. (History of Tuskegee Army Air Field, Jan-Feb 1945, AFHRA call number 289.28–8, vol. 1)

November: By this month, 145,327 blacks were serving in the Army Air Forces, out of a total of 2,383,370 Army Air Forces personnel. That was 6.1 percent of the total (blacks constituted about 10 percent of the USA population at the time). Of the blacks in the Army Air Forces at the time, 1,280 were officers. Not all of them were Tuskegee Airmen, although most of them were. (Wesley Frank Craven and James Lea Cate, editors, *The Army Air Forces in World War II*, volume VI, *Men and Planes* [Washington: Office of Air Force History, 1983], 523)

1 November: Fifty white-piloted P-38s landed at Sal Solo Field in Italy, where mechanics of the black 99th Fighter Squadron serviced them. (99th Fighter Squadron history, Nov 1943–Jan 1944)

1 November: Back in the United States, the 553rd Fighter Squadron was activated at Selfridge Field, Michigan, to receive from Tuskegee Army Air Field replacement pilots for the 332nd Fighter Group, which was preparing to move from Selfridge to a combat theater overseas, and for the 99th Fighter Squadron, which was already serving in combat in Italy. (organization record cards)

3 November: Twenty-nine pilots graduated from advanced pilot training at Tuskegee Army Air Field. Twenty of the graduates (SE-43-J) were single engine pilots, and nine (TE-43-J) were twin engine pilots. TE-43-J was the first class of twin engine aircraft pilots to graduate from advanced flight training at Tuskegee. They would eventually be assigned to fly medium B-25 bombers with the 477th Bombardment Group (which would be activated at Selfridge Field, Michigan after the 332d Fighter Group departed). (Craig Huntly and lists of graduates from advanced flight training at Tuskegee Army Air Field) After the twin engine pilots graduated from advanced flying training at Tuskegee Army Air Field, they went to Mather Field, California, for B-25 transition training. Many of those eliminated from twin engine flight training at Tuskegee were sent to Hondo, Texas, to be trained as navigators, or to Keesler Field, Mississippi, to be trained as bombardiers. (History of The Corps of Aviation Cadets, Tuskegee Army Air Field, Alabama, AFHRA call number K289.28–1, 1 Aug 1941–1 Mar 1944)

5 November: Lieutenants William A. Campbell, Span Watson, and Herbert V. Clark of the 99th Fighter Squadron departed for the United States after having served much combat time overseas, in north Africa, Sicily, and mainland Italy. (99th Fighter Squadron history, Nov 1943–Jan 1944)

7 November: Major General John K. Cannon, now commander of the XII Air Support Command, visited the 99th Fighter Squadron and presented

Air Medals to some of the black pilots. (99th Fighter Squadron history, Nov 1943–Jan 1944)

Early November: 121 men who had failed to complete pilot training at Tuskegee Army Air Field were sent to Keesler Field, Mississippi, for possible bombardier training. After psychological testing there, only 9 were accepted. (Thole, 18)

12 November: 1st Lt. Louis R. Purnell, a veteran of the 99th Fighter Squadron, still serving overseas in combat, was appointed commander of the 553rd Fighter Squadron at Selfridge Field, Michigan. (332nd Fighter Group history, Oct 1942–1947)

13 November: A night storm in Italy blew down several tents of the 99th Fighter Squadron. With the wind came much rain, turning dirt into mud and preventing squadron flights for several days. (99th Fighter Squadron history for Nov 1943–Jan 1944)

15 November: The AAF Pilot School (Basic-Advanced) at Tuskegee Army Air Field was assigned to the 28th Flying Training Wing, headquartered in Selma, Alabama. (organization record cards at AFHRA)

16 November: The 553rd Fighter Squadron moved from Selfridge Field, Michigan, to Oscoda Army Air Field, Michigan. (organization record card)

16 November: Class 43-2-J began B-25 transition flying training at Mather Field, California. It included 194 white male pilots, 20 white Women Army Service Pilots, and 14 black male pilots. This was probably the first class at Mather to include black members. (History of Mather Field, Jan 1943-Jan 1944, vol. I, AFHRA call number 286.24–3, 45). Of the fourteen black pilots who entered the training, twelve would eventually graduate from the transition training on 19 January 1944, and move to Selfridge Field, Michigan, home of the newly activated 477th Bombardment Group. (History of Mather Field B-25 Transition School, AFHRA call number 286.24-4, vol. 7, 2)

18 November: Captain (later Major) Harold C. Magoon assumed command of the primary flight school at Moton Field, succeeding Major William T. Smith. Magoon became commander of the 66th Flying Training Detachment. (Tuskegee Airmen National Historic Site)

19 November: 2nd Lt. Leon Purchase of the 302nd Fighter Squadron (332nd Fighter Group) was killed in an airplane crash 8 miles northeast of Selfridge Field, Michigan. (332nd Fighter Group history, Oct 1942–1947)

22 November: The 99th Fighter Squadron moved to Madna, Italy. (Maurer, *Combat Squadrons of the Air Force, World War II*)

29 November: After several days of not flying missions, the 99th Fighter Squadron flew five missions in Italy this day. (99th Fighter Squadron history, Nov 1943–Jan 1944)

29 November: Back in Michigan, 2nd Lt. William Edward Hill of the 302nd Fighter Squadron of the 332nd Fighter Group drowned in Lake Huron after parachuting from his P-39, which had caught fire. (332nd Fighter Group history, Oct 1942–1947)

30–31 November: The 99th Fighter Squadron took part with the 79th Fighter Group in attacks on ground targets in support of Field Marshall Bernard Montgomery's crossing of the Sangro River in Italy.

December: In Italy, 99th Fighter Squadron was flying close air support missions for elements of the British Eighth Army, along with three squadrons of the 79th Fighter Group. Several individual fighter pilots of the 99th flew with the other squadrons, and not separately. The 99th Fighter Squadron officers enjoyed flying with the 79th Fighter Group, and were upset later when assigned to another group. (99th Fighter Squadron history, Nov 1943–Jan 1944)

4 December: 1st Lt. Lee Rayford, 99th Fighter Squadron veteran, was reassigned to the 301st Fighter Squadron of the 332nd Fighter Group. (332nd Fighter Group history, Oct 1942–1947)

5 December: Thirty-one new black military pilots graduated from advanced flight training at Tuskegee Army Air Field, the largest class to graduate thus far. Sixteen were in class SE-43-K for single-engine pilots, and fifteen of the graduates were in class TE-43-K for twin-engine pilots.

7 December: The third class of liaison pilots (CL-43–3) graduated at Tuskegee Army Air Field. Some of the liaison pilots went on to serve with the 92nd and 93rd Infantry Divisions, which were Army ground organizations. The 92nd Division served in Italy, but the 93rd Division served in the South Pacific. (David G. Styles, *The Tuskegee Airmen and Beyond: The Road to Equality* [Deerfield, IL: Dalton Watson Fine Books, 2013], 259; correspondence with Karyn J. Taylor, whose father was one of the black liaison pilots during World War II)

9 December: General Henry H. Arnold, commander of the Army Air Forces, visited the 99th Fighter Squadron at Madna Airfield, Italy, accompanied by Lieutenant General Carl Spaatz, commander of the Twelfth Air Force, and Major General John Cannon, Deputy Commander of the Mediterranean Allied Tactical Air Force.

15 December: The 403rd Fighter Squadron, a white organization providing guidance for the 332nd Fighter Group at its squadrons, was disbanded at Selfridge Field, Michigan. (Maurer, *Combat Squadrons*) Some of the white officers transferred to the 553rd Fighter Squadron, which had been activated at Selfridge the previous month, but which was then stationed at Oscoda Army Air Field, Michigan. The 553rd Fighter Squadron had white leaders, but mostly black pilots who had graduated from advanced flight training at Tuskegee Army Air Field. Eventually the squadron also included black pilots who returned from combat duty overseas, who were expected to help train the new replacement pilots. (History of Selfridge Field, Jan–Dec 1944, AFHRA call number 288.52-4, appendix XIV, item 5)

16 December: Enlisted men of the 332nd Fighter Group enjoyed a farewell party at Selfridge Field, Michigan, knowing they would soon depart for overseas combat service. (332nd Fighter Group history, Oct 1942–1947)

18 December: Class 43-2-K began B-25 transition training at Mather Field, California. It included 287 white and 18 black pilots. The blacks were assigned to "Squadron # 11," indicating they were segregated from the white pilots at the field. This was the second class of pilots in transition training at Mather to include black members. (History of Mather Field, CA, Jan 1943-Jan 1944, vol. I, AFHRA call number 286.24–3, 33 and 45)

20 December: Officers of the 332nd Fighter Group enjoyed a farewell party at Detroit's Labor Temple. They would soon leave nearby Selfridge Field, Michigan, for overseas combat duty. (332nd Fighter Group history, Oct 1942–1947)

21 December: All 332nd Fighter Group personnel were restricted to Selfridge Field pending movement. (332nd Fighter Group history, Oct 1942–1947)

22 December: The 332d Fighter Group departed Selfridge Field, Michigan, for movement overseas. (332d Fighter Group lineage and honors history and Maurer, *Air Force Combat Units of World War II*) Group members boarded a train bound from Michigan to Virginia. (332nd Fighter Group history, Oct 1942–1947)

22 December: The same day that the 332nd Fighter Group departed Selfridge Field, Michigan, for movement overseas, the 366th Service Squadron departed Oscoda, Michigan, for its own movement overseas, because it would continue to service the airplanes of the 332nd Fighter Group.

22 December: Meanwhile, in Italy, Lt. James Wiley of Pittsburgh, Pennsylvania became the first 99th Fighter Squadron pilot to complete 50 sorties. (99th Fighter Squadron history, Nov 1943–Jan 1944)

December: The 99th Fighter Squadron flew many missions while attached to the 79th Fighter Group to provide close air cover for ground troops of the British Eighth Army in Italy. (99th Fighter Squadron history, Nov 1943–Jan 1944)

December: 1st Lt. Herbert V. Clark, 1st Lt. William Campbell, and 1st Lt. Spann Watson, combat veterans from the 99th Fighter Squadron in Italy, were assigned to the 553rd Fighter Squadron in Michigan to help in the training of replacement pilots. (332nd Fighter Group history, Oct 1942–1947; *Hawk's Cry,* vol. II, no. 40, dated 17 Dec 1943)

December: 1st Lt. Ray B. Ware was appointed historical officer of the 332nd Fighter Group, among other duties. (332nd Fighter Group history, Oct 1942–1947)

December: Members of the 100th Fighter Squadron, while awaiting deployment overseas, visited the Bell Aircraft Plant in Buffalo, New York, and saw where P-39 type "Airacobra" aircraft were being built. That was the type of fighter that the unit would fly in combat, along with the two other squad-

Tuskegee Army Air Field was the most important flying training base of the Tuskegee Airmen, where the basic and advanced flying training phases occurred, after primary flight training at Moton Field.

rons of the 332nd Fighter Group, once it completed its deployment to Italy.

24 December: The first train bearing members of the 332nd Fighter Group and the 100th Fighter Squadron arrived at Camp Patrick Henry, Virginia. (332nd Fighter Group history, Oct 1942–1947)

25 December: A second train, bearing members of the 301st and 302nd Fighter Squadrons arrived at Camp Patrick Henry, Virginia, completing the move of the 332nd Fighter Group and its squadrons from Selfridge Field in the Detroit area of Michigan. (332nd Fighter Group history, Oct 1942–1947)

27 December: Col. Earl Bates, commander of the 79th Fighter Group, to which the 99th Fighter Squadron was then attached, spoke to the pilots of the 99th Fighter Squadron. He inaugurated a new policy that allowed several of the black pilots of the 99th to fly with other squadrons of the 79th Fighter Group. No longer would the black pilots be restricted to flying only with other black pilots, and white pilots be restricted to flying only with other white pilots. (99th Fighter Squadron history for Nov 1943–Jan 1944)

27 December: The 553rd Fighter Squadron moved from Oscoda Army Air Field, Michigan, back to Selfridge Field, Michigan, which had just been vacated by the 332d Fighter Group when it moved overseas. (organization record card)

30 December: Lt. Col. Charles A. Gayle, a white officer, assumed command of the 553rd Fighter Squadron at Selfridge Field, which consisted of African American pilots who had completed advanced flying training at Tuskegee, and were training to replace pilots of the 99th Fighter Squadron, already in Italy, and the 332nd Fighter Group, which had recently departed for eventual deployment to Italy. (History of Selfridge Field, Michigan, 1944, AFHRA call number 288.52-4, 195–196)

Late December: 332nd Fighter Group personnel at Camp Patrick Henry, Virginia, wrote letters and prepared packages to send home to their families, knowing that they would soon be departing overseas for combat duty.

1944

January: By this month, the Tuskegee Army Air Field had 1,890 enlisted personnel, 700 full-time civilian employees, 303 officers, and 293 students. Of the officers, 80 were white, but none lived on the base. Thirteen of the white officers were flight instructors. Black flying instructors did not begin serving at the base until May. For advanced single engine pilot training, the base had

36 AT-6s. The base had no gym. (Thole, 11, 14–15, 18)

January: The 79th Fighter Group included several pilots of the 99th Fighter Squadron among its own squadrons on certain missions. (99th Fighter Squadron history, Nov 1943–Jan 1944)

1–5 January: Several black officers of the 553rd Fighter Squadron, mostly graduates of advanced pilot training at Tuskegee Army Air Field, but also some veterans who returned from service with the 99th Fighter Squadron overseas, attempted to enter Lufberry Hall, the officers' club at Selfridge Field, Michigan. Selfridge was where replacement pilots for the 99th Fighter Squadron and for the deploying 332nd Fighter Group were being trained. On each of the five nights the African American officers tried to enter the club, either Col. William L. Boyd, the white base commander, or Lt. Col. Charles Gayle, the white commander of the 553nd Fighter Squadron, ordered them to leave, and they complied after being told it was a direct order. Since a War Department regulation 210–10, paragraph 19c authorized all officers at a base to be eligible to belong to the officers' club, Boyd and Gayle did not court martial any of the African American officers who had tried to enter the club, but they closed the club on January 6. A few weeks later, Brig. Gen. Benjamin O. Davis Sr., the first black general in the Army, visited Selfridge, to investigate the early January incident. Boyd and Gayle were replaced, but the officers' club remained off limits to blacks, by order of Maj. Gen. Frank O'Driscoll Hunter, commander of the First Air Force. Hunter favored construction of a separate officers' club at Selfridge for the African American officers. (Charles W. Dryden, *A-Train: Memoirs of a Tuskegee Airman* [Tuscaloosa: University of Alabama Press, 1997], 167–171)

2 January: 1 Lt. John H. Morgan of the 99th Fighter Squadron died while serving overseas. (American Battle Monuments Commission)

2 January: Back in the United States, Colonel Charles Gayle, commander of the 553rd Fighter Squadron, told black officers that they would be court-martialed if they entered the officers' club at Selfridge Field, Michigan, where they were based. (Lawrence P. Schott and William M. Womack Sr., *Double V: The Civil Rights Struggle of the Tuskegee Airmen* [East Lansing: Michigan State University Press, 1994], 200)

3 January: 332d Fighter Group and its three fighter squadrons, the 100th, 301st, and 302d, departed Hampton Roads, Virginia, on four ships in a convoy to cross the Atlantic Ocean. The 332d Fighter Group headquarters squadron voyaged on the SS *William Few* (HR-814), which group members nicknamed the "Billy Foo." (332d Fighter Group History, Oct 1942–1947;

organization record card, and lineage and honors folder) Squadrons of the group traveled on other ships in the convoy. The 100th Fighter Squadron rode aboard the SS *John M. Morehead* (HR-810); the 301st Fighter Squadron rode aboard the SS *Clark Mills* (HR-812); and the 302d Fighter Squadron rode aboard the SS *Thomas B. Robertson* (HR-811). (Information from Craig Huntly, organization record cards of the squadrons, and lineage and honors history folders for each squadron). On the same date, the 96th Service Group departed Hampton Roads Port of Embarkation, Virginia, for overseas duty. It sailed on ship 6122 (U.S.S. *Josiah Bartlett*) for the Mediterranean Sea. The 96th Service Group's 366th and 367th Air Service Squadrons also rode on the same ship. (Lineage and honors history of the 96th Logistics Group, organization record cards of the organization, and information supplied by Craig Huntly)

4 January: The 366th Service Squadron departed Newport News, Virginia, on the ship *SS Josiah Bartlett,* bound for Italy. It would continue to service the airplanes of the 332nd Fighter Group, which had departed from Hampton Roads, Virginia, the day before. (366th Service Squadron history, call number SQ-SV-366-HI)

7 January: Class SE-44-A graduated from advanced pilot training at Tuskegee Army Air Field. There were 10 in the class. On the same day, class TE-44-A graduated. There were 15 in the class. SE meant single-engine, for fighter pilots, and TE meant twin-engine, for bomber pilots. A total of 25 new pilots graduated that day at Tuskegee Army Air Field.

8 January: 1 Lt. Thomas J. Collins succeeded Maj. John G. Cooke Jr. as Commandant of Cadets at Tuskegee Army Air Field. (History of The Corps of Aviation Cadets, Tuskegee Army Air Field, Alabama, AFHRA call number K289.28-1, 1 Aug 1941–1 Mar 1944)

15 January: The 477th Bombardment Group, Medium, which had formerly been an all-white group before it had been inactivated, was activated again at Selfridge Field, Michigan, along with the 616th Bombardment Squadron. This time most of its personnel would be black. The group was equipped with B-25 medium bombers. Despite the activation of the bombardment group at Selfridge, the 553rd Fighter Squadron continued serving at the same base, training replacement P-39 pilots for the 332nd Fighter Group, which had moved overseas. (Maurer, *Air Force Combat Units of World War II*)

15 January: Meanwhile, back in Italy, 2d Lt. William E. Griffin of the 99th Fighter Squadron was last seen in a smoking and diving P-40 at 2,000 feet during an attack on a target in the town of San Valentino, Italy. He was listed as missing in action. (99th Fighter Squadron history, Nov 1943–Jan 1944)

16 January: The 99th Fighter Squadron headquarters moved from Madna to Capodichino Airdrome near Naples, Italy. From there it began flying tactical missions south of Rome. (Maurer, *Combat Squadrons of the Air Force, World War II;* 99th Fighter Squadron history)

19 January: Class 43–2-J of B-25 twin engine bomber transition training at Mather Field, California graduated. Among the graduates were twelve black pilots, who were reassigned to Selfridge Field, Michigan, where the 477th Bombardment Group had been activated four days earlier. (History of B-25 Transition School, Mather Field, California, 1 Jan-29 Feb 1944, p. 2, AF-HRA call number 286.24-4, vol. 7)

20 January: The 99th Fighter Squadron completed its third month of operations in Italy. (99th Fighter Squadron history for Nov 1943–Jan 1944)

21 January: The ship SS *William Few* that carried the headquarters squadron of the 332nd Fighter Group, along with other ships in a convoy, passed from the Atlantic Ocean into the Mediterranean Sea via the Strait of Gibraltar. (332nd Fighter Group history, Oct 1942–1947)

21 January: Back in the United States, Colonel Robert R. Selway Jr, a white officer who had commanded the 332d Fighter Group from 16 May to 8 Oct 1943, became commander of the 477th Bombardment Group at Selfridge Field, Michigan.

23 January-28 February: MSgt. William S. Surcey, Engineering Section Chief of AAF Service Detachment 99 at Madna Landing Ground, supervised third and fourth echelon repairs of seven P-40 Warhawk airplanes involved in crucial air operations over Anzio and Cassino. At the time the 99th Fighter Squadron was flying P-40s while attached to the 79th Fighter Group at nearby Capodichino, Italy. For this service, MSgt. Surcey later received, on 24 November 1944, the first Bronze Star awarded to an enlisted Tuskegee Airman. (confirming documentation supplied by Craig Huntly)

27 January: Captain Clarence C. Jamison, while leading a formation of 16 fighters of the 99th Fighter Squadron, spotted 15 FW-190s dive-bombing shipping off St. Peter's Beach near Anzio. During the ensuing engagement, 10 members of the 99th shot down a total of 10 enemy airplanes. The victors included 2d Lt. Clarence W. Allen (.5 credits), 1st Lt. Willie Ashley Jr. (1 credit), 2d Lt. Charles P. Bailey (1 credit), 1 Lt. Howard Baugh (1.5 credits), Capt Lemuel R. Custis (1 credit), 1st Lt. Robert W. Deiz (1 credit),

2d Lt. Wilson V. Eagleson (1 credit), 1st Lt. Leon C. Roberts (1 credit), 2d Lt. Lewis C. Smith (1 credit), 1st Lt. Edward L. Toppins (1 credit). All of the downed enemy airplanes were FW-190s. (Twelfth Air Force General Orders 66, 81, and 122, dated 24 May 1944, 22 Jun 1944, and 7 Aug 1944, respectively; 99th Fighter Squadron history, Nov 1943–Jan 1944). Lieutenant Samuel F. Bruce was killed in aerial combat with enemy FW-190s. He bailed out but his parachute did not fill. Lt. Lane (first name not given) was also shot down, but after he bailed out of his P-40, he was picked up by friendly Fifth Army troops on the ground. On the same mission, 99th Fighter Squadron commander Major George S. Roberts' airplane was hit by flak, which disabled three of his six machine guns. Still, he managed to silence an enemy machine gun nest on the way back to base. (99th Fighter Squadron history, Nov 1943–Jan 1944)

28 January: Following up the previous day's aerial victories, 2 members of the 99th Fighter Squadron shot down a total of 3 enemy airplanes that threatened American ground forces of the Fifth Army at Anzio. The victors were Capt. Charles B. Hall, who had been the first Tuskegee Airmen to shoot down an enemy airplane, and Lt. Robert W. Deiz. Captain Hall shot down two aircraft that day, raising his total to three. For his actions on this day, Hall earned the Distinguished Flying Cross. In two days, 27–28 January 1944, the Tuskegee Airmen shot down a total of 13 enemy airplanes over Anzio, Italy. (Twelfth Air Force General Orders 64 and 122, dated 22 May 1944 and 7 Aug 1944, respectively; 99th Fighter Squadron history, Nov 1943–Jan 1944). On the same day, the 96th Service Group arrived in North Africa. (Organization record card). On the same date, a multi-ship convoy carrying the 332d Fighter Group and the 100th, 301st, and 302nd Fighter Squadrons arrived in North Africa on the way to Italy. (organization record cards of the four organizations.

29 January: The 366th Service Group arrived at Bari, Italy, after having voyaged across the Atlantic Ocean and part of the Mediterranean Sea. (366th Service Squadron history, call number SQ-SV-366-HI)

January: A Department of Gunnery Training was organized at Tuskegee Army Air Field, under Captain James L. Wrathall, who became the Director of Gunnery Training. (History of Tuskegee Army Air Field, Mar-Jun 1944, AFHRA call number 289.28-4, vol. 1)

1–3 February: Ships carrying the 332d Fighter Group and its 100th, 301st, and 302nd Fighter Squadrons arrived on different ships at the mainland of Italy after stopping briefly in North Africa and Sicily on the way, after having crossed the Atlantic Ocean from Virginia. The organizations debarked at Bari, Taranto, and Naples, Italy. During the same week, the 96th Air Service Group debarked at Bari, Italy. (332d Fighter Group history, Oct 1942–1947; Craig Huntly; organization record cards of the four organizations, and their lineage and honors history folders)

1 February: The 821st Bombardment Squadron was activated as a B-25 training unit at Selfridge Field, Michigan, where the 477th Bombardment Group had been activated as a B-25 group for black crews the previous month. (organization record card)

2 February: The 99th Fighter Squadron dive-bombed a key bridge in the Anzio area to prevent escape of the enemy. The squadron flew two patrol missions from Capodichino, Italy. (99th Fighter Squadron history, Feb–Apr 1944; 99th Fighter Squadron War Diary for February 1944)

3 February: the 99th Fighter Squadron flew three combat missions. One encountered eight enemy FW-190 fighters and gave chase, but the enemy planes disappeared in the clouds before they could be intercepted. (99th Fighter Squadron War Diary for Feb 1944)

3 February: The 332d Fighter Group's 100th Fighter Squadron arrived at Montecorvino, Italy, the group's first overseas base of operations. (Maurer, *Air Force Combat Units of World War II*; Maurer, *Combat Squadrons of the Air Force, World War II*)

4 February: The 99th Fighter Squadron, still based at Capodichino, Italy, flew a patrol mission. (99th Fighter Squadron War Diary for Feb 1944)

5 February: The 332d Fighter Group's 100th Fighter Squadron began flying P-39s in Italy, but not yet on combat missions. (332d Fighter Group History, Oct 1942–1947; Maurer, *Air Force Combat Units of World War II;* Maurer, *Combat Squadrons of the Air Force, World War II*) The group flew with the 62d Fighter Wing.

5 February: The 99th Fighter Squadron in Italy (not yet assigned to the 332nd Fighter Group) flew multiple missions. On one of them, a patrol mission over the Allied beach head near Anzio and Nettuno, the squadron formation encountered more than ten enemy FW-190 fighters and an air battle commenced. Lt. Elwood T. Driver, flying a P-40 for the 99th Fighter Squadron (not yet assigned to the 332d Fighter Group), shot down one of the enemy airplanes. Captain Clarence Jamison was forced to belly-land after his airplane was hit, but he was able to return to the squadron later that day. Lt. George T. McCrumby went missing. (Twelfth Air Force General Order 66 dated 24 May 1944 and 99th Fighter Squadron War Diary for February 1944). On the same date, the 99th Fighter Squadron received ten more P-40s, bringing its inventory to 33 aircraft. (99th Fighter Squadron history, Feb–Apr 1944)

6 February: The 99th Fighter Squadron flew four missions, including two eight-plane patrols and one to escort A-20s bombing Raccasecca, Italy. (99th Fighter Squadron War Diary for February 1944)

7 February: The 99th Fighter Squadron in Italy flew three patrol missions, which put its total of combat missions beyond 300. (99th Fighter Squadron War Diary for February 1944) On these missions, three Tuskegee Airmen of the squadron, flying P-40s, shot down 3 FW-190s. The victors included 1st Lt. Clinton B. Mills and 2d Lts Wilson V. Eagleson and Leonard M. Jackson. (Twelfth Air Force General Orders 66 and 122, dated 24 May 1944 and 7 Aug 1944, respectively). On that same day, the 302d Fighter Squadron arrived at Montecorvino, where the 100th Fighter Squadron was already stationed. (Maurer, *Combat Squadrons of the Air Force, World War II*; 332d Fighter Group history, Mar–Apr 1944)

8 February: The 301st Fighter Squadron arrived at Montecorvino, Italy, where the 100th and 302d Fighter Squadrons were already stationed. All three of the 332d Fighter Group's squadrons were then stationed at the same base. (Maurer, *Combat Squadrons of the Air Force, World War II*)

8 February: Meanwhile, on the same date, six P-40s of the 99th Fighter Squadron escorted a DC-3 transport aircraft carrying Lieutenant General Mark Clark, commander of the Fifth Army, on a flight in Italy. Among the fighter escort pilots were Captain Charles B. Hall, who had been the first black pilot in the American military to shoot down an enemy airplane, and Captain Herbert Carter. The squadron flew two other missions that day, one of which was a dive bombing mission dropping 500-pound bombs on enemy targets. The other mission escorted three B-25 medium bombers to Porto Carbo, Italy. (99th Fighter Squadron history, Feb–Apr 1944)

8 February: Class SE-44-B graduated from advanced single-engine pilot training at Tuskegee Army Air Field. There were 20 in that class. On the same day, class TE-44-B graduated from advanced twin-engine pilot training at Tuskegee Army Air Field, with 8 in the class. A total of 28 pilots graduated at the field that day.

9 February: The 99th Fighter Squadron flew three patrol missions and one dive-bombing mission. On the bombing mission, eight P-40 pilots dropped 1,000-pound bombs on a road junction at Aquino, Italy. (99th Fighter Squadron War Diary for February 1944)

9 February: The 366th Service Group moved to Montecorvino, Italy, where it would continue to service the airplanes of the 332nd Fighter Group. (366th Service Squadron history, call number SQ-SV-366-HI)

10 February: The 96 Air Service Group arrived at Montecorvino to serve there with the 332d Fighter Group. (lineage and honors history of the 96th Logistics Group). On the same date, the 332nd Fighter Group was assigned to the 62nd Fighter Wing. Its duties would be convoy escort, harbor patrol, and point patrol. (332nd Fighter Group history, Oct 1942–1947)

13 February: The 99th Fighter Squadron flew three dive-bombing missions. On the same date, it received five replacement pilots, including 2nd Lieutenants George E. Gray, Charles F. Jamerson, John S. Sloan, Alva N. Temple, and John Daniels. (99th Fighter Squadron War Diary for February 1944) (The 332nd Fighter Group history, Oct 1942–1947 says the pilots arrived the next day)

14 February: The 99th Fighter Squadron flew one dive-bombing mission.

February: During the month, famous African American actress and singer and movie star Lena Horne visited the 320th College Training Detachment at Tuskegee. (320th College Training Detachment history, Tuskegee Institute, Alabama, March 1943-Mar 1944, Air Force Historical Research Agency call number 234.821, Mar 1943-Mar 1944)

15 February: The 332d Fighter Group's 301st Fighter Squadron became operational and started flying missions, from Montecorvino, Italy. (332nd Fighter Group history, Oct 1942–1947). Within days, all three of the group's squadrons, including the 100th and 302d Fighter Squadron, had also flown combat missions. For the first three months of its combat operations, the 332nd Fighter Group flew coastal patrol missions using P-39 airplanes. (Maurer, *Combat Squadrons of the Air Force, World War II*; B. O. Davis Jr. autobiography)

15 February: The 99th Fighter Squadron, not yet assigned to the 332nd Fighter Group, but also flying missions in Italy, flew a dive bombing mission during which twelve P-40s dropped 500-pound bombs on enemy supply dumps at Valmontove, Italy. Some flak damaged one of the fighters. Meanwhile, two American Red Cross women, Gretchen Alsmede and Jean Balby, served coffee and donuts to enlisted personnel of the 99th Fighter Squadron. Alsmede had visited the squadron earlier, when it was based in Sicily. (99th Fighter Squadron history, Feb–Apr 1944)

16 February: The 99th Fighter Squadron flew one dive bombing mission. On the same date, trucks took some of the enlisted squadron personnel to Naples to see a movie. (99th Fighter Squadron War Diary for February 1944)

16 February: The 366th Service Group moved from Montecorvino to Capod-ichino, Italy, where it would continue to service the airplanes of the 332nd Fighter Group. (366th Service Squadron history, call number SQ-SV-366-HI)

February: During the month, the majority of the missions of the 99th Fighter Squadron in Italy involved P-40s dropping 1,000-pound bombs in support of Allied ground troops. (99th Fighter Squadron history, Feb–Apr 1944)

February: The Commander of Mather Field, California, decided to end his policy of not allowing student officers to use the regular Mather Field Of-ficer's Club, and making them use their own student club. At the same time, he offered to let the black officers among the students have the old student club as their own separate club. The black officer students at Mather met and decided unanimously to turn down the offer, since they were opposed to having racially segregated facilities on the same base. (Mather Field History, February 1944, vol. I, AFHRA call number 286.24-4, 5)

17 February: the 99th Fighter Squadron flew three dive bombing missions, probably destroying a bridge in enemy territory on one of them. (99th Fighter Squadron War Diary, Feb 1944)

17 February: The 302nd Fighter Squadron flew its first operational mission (training), from its base at Montecorvino, Italy. On the same day, the 332nd Fighter Group received its first pay since leaving the United States. Mail also began to arrive for the group at Montecorvino on this date. (332nd Fighter Group history, Oct 1942–1947)

19 February: The 99th Fighter Squadron flew two combat missions. Captain Charles B. Hall and 1st Lieutenant James T. Wiley each flew his 80th sortie. (99th Fighter Squadron War Diary for Feb 1944)

19 February: Twelve P-39s of the 100th Fighter Squadron patrolled Allied shipping around Naples, Italy, completing the first 332d Fighter Group combat mission. On the same day, in the 99th Fighter Squadron, Captain Charles P. Hall and 1st Lieutenant James T. Wiley, each flew his 80th com-bat sortie, flying P-40s. The 99th was not yet assigned to the 332d Fighter Group. (Craig Huntly; Mission Report 1 of the 332d Fighter Group, 19 Feb 1944; 99th Fighter Squadron history, Feb–Apr 1944)

20 February: In the morning, twelve 99th Fighter Squadron P-40s dive bombed enemy troop concentrations and vehicles in the Anzio area, drop-ping 1,000-pound bombs from P-40s. That afternoon, two of the 99th Fighter Squadron pilots flew on missions with the 87th Fighter Squadron, a white unit, over the Anzio and Nettuno Allied beachheads. (99th Fighter

Squadron War Diary for Feb 1944)

20 February: Back at Mather Field, California, Class 43–2-K of B-25 transition training had a graduation ceremony. Eighteen black pilots had started the class on 18 December 1943, but how many of them graduated is not known. It is possible that the ones who were not eliminated were transferred to Class 44–2-A, which graduated on 24 March 1944, because that class had 10 black students. (History of B-25 Transition School at Mather Field, California, 1 Jan–29 Feb 1944, 2, AFHRA call number 286.24-4, vol. 7)

21 February: Class 44–2-B of B-25 transition training began at Mather Field, California. It included 159 white and 7 black pilots. How many graduated from that class on 25 April 1944 is not known. (History of B-25 Transition School, Mather Field, California, 1 Jan–29 Feb 1944, call number 286.24-4, vol. 7)

21 February: The 99th Fighter Squadron flew four patrol missions in Italy. On one of them, 2d Lt. Alwayne Dunlap overshot a landing field in the Anzio assault area and was killed. On the second mission, more than twenty enemy fighters attacked American troops in the same area, and the 99th Fighter Squadron engaged them until they departed. On the third mission, more than twelve enemy aircraft were seen, but they fled the area at the approach of the 99th Fighter Squadron P-40s. On the fourth 99th Fighter Squadron patrol mission, Lt. Heber C. Houston was forced to belly-land his fighter at Nettuno. 2d Lt. Pearlee E. Saunders was wounded in a crash landing of his P-40 at the Nettuno beachhead that day, and was hospitalized. Lt. Herbert Carter's fighter was hit by flak, but he survived uninjured. (99th Fighter Squadron War Diary for Feb 1944)

21 February: The 100th Fighter Squadron moved to Capodichino, Italy, but the other three squadrons of the 332d Fighter Group remained with group headquarters at Montecorvino. The squadrons would not all be located at the same base again until mid-April. (Maurer, *Combat Squadrons of the Air Force, World War II*) Meanwhile, the 99th Fighter Squadron, already at Capodichino, not yet assigned to the 332d Fighter Group, flew four patrol missions that day. 2nd Lt. Alwayne M. Dunlap of the 99th was killed in an aircraft crash after overshooting his landing field. (99th Fighter Squadron history, Feb–Apr 1944; American Battle Monuments Commission)

22 February: The 99th Fighter Squadron flew three more combat missions. On one of them, an oil leak obscured the windshield of one of the squadron's airplanes, but Lt. Elwood T. Driver escorted the pilot safely to home base. (99th Fighter Squadron War Diary for February 1944)

22 February: Nine pilots of the 332nd Fighter Group journeyed to Sidi Amor, Tunisia, to ferry P-39 airplanes from there to Montecorvino, Italy. (332nd Fighter Group history, Oct 1942–1947)

23 February: 2d Lieutenant Harry J. Daniels of the 332d Fighter Group's 301st Fighter Squadron was reported missing after flying into bad weather during a mission to Pompei, Italy. He was the first 332d Fighter Group pilot reported to have been killed overseas. (Craig Huntly; Missing Air Crew Report [not numbered] dated 24 Feb 1944) (332nd Fighter Group history, Oct 1942–1947)

24 February: The 99th Fighter Squadron, still not assigned to the 332nd Fighter Group, flew four patrol missions in Italy. One of its pilots was forced to crash-land his P-40 at Nettuno. (99th Fighter Squadron War Diary for Feb 1944)

24 February: The 332nd Fighter Group received a C-78 as a courier aircraft, to fly between Montecorvino, where the 301st and 302nd Fighter Squadrons were located with the headquarters of the group, and Capodichino, where the 100th Fighter Squadron was stationed. (332nd Fighter Group history, Oct 1942–1947)

26 February: The first black graduates completed navigator training at Hondo Field, Texas, which prepared them to serve eventually with the 477th Bombardment Group, which would fly B-25 medium bombers. (Craig Huntly message, and Lucille B. Milner, "Jim Crow in the Army," in *Reporting Civil Rights* [New York: The Library of America, 2003], 58). The latter source said bombardier when it should have read navigator.

28 February: The 99th Fighter Squadron flew a patrol mission over Allied lines. (99th Fighter Squadron War Diary for Feb 1944)

28 February: Capt. Lee Rayford assumed command of the 301st Fighter Squadron, succeeding Capt. Charles H. DeBow. (301st Fighter Squadron lineage and honors history). DeBow was relieved of command and temporarily suspended from flying because of physical disabilities. He was one of the first five black pilots in the Army. (332nd Fighter Group history, Oct 1942–1947)

29 February: 2d Lt. George T. McCrumby of the 99th Fighter Squadron disappeared with his P-40 on a mission to Anzio. His plane was last seen over water near Gaeta Point, about 3 miles off the west coast of Italy. The last two pilots to see McCrumby were 1st Lts. Howard Lee Baugh and Erwin B. Lawrence, also of the 99th Fighter Squadron. They supposed McCrumby left the formation to return to Capodichino because he had experienced engine trouble. The white commander of the 79th Fighter Group, Col. Earl E. Bates, flew in search of Lt. McCrumby because the 99th Fighter Squadron was attached to his group at the time. (99th Fighter Squadron history, Feb–Apr 1944; Missing Air Crew Report 2812)

February: During this month, the 99th Fighter Squadron flew 55 missions, mostly dive-bombing, but also patrol, while attached to the 79th Fighter Group of the Twelfth Air Force. (99th Fighter Squadron history, Feb–Apr 1944)

March: In Italy, Captain Charles H. DeBow was restored to full flying status. (332nd Fighter Group history, Oct 1942–1947)

1 March: Brig. Gen. Benjamin O. Davis Sr., the U.S. Army's first and only black general, visited Selfridge Field to investigate the treatment of African Americans there. He represented the Inspector General of the War Department. In early January, black officers were not allowed to enter the officers' club at Selfridge Field, after repeated attempts to integrate the club without violence, and the club was subsequently closed. (History of Selfridge Field, Jan–Dec 1944, AFHRA call number 288.52-4, 199)

2 March: At Selfridge AFB, Michigan, leaders contracted with the de Koning Company of Kalamazoo, Michigan, to build two new service clubs, a "Negro officer club" and a club for "Negro enlisted personnel." The contract was stopped the following month, since African American personnel were expected to be deployed elsewhere. (History of Selfridge Field, Jan–Dec 1944, AFHRA call number 288.52-4, 198)

2 March: The 99th Fighter Squadron in southern Italy flew three patrol missions. On one of them, members of the squadron witnessed the crash of a B-17 after its crew members bailed out. The 99th Fighter Squadron was not escorting the bomber. (99th Fighter Squadron war diary)

6 March: The 99th Fighter Squadron in Italy flew two dive-bombing missions against enemy positions, dropping a total of sixteen 1,000 pound bombs from its P-40 Warhawks, each fighter carrying one bomb. (99th Fighter Squadron War Diary)

6 March: The 302d Fighter Squadron moved from Montecorvino to Capodichino, Italy, where the 100th Fighter Squadron had already moved, but the 332d Fighter Group headquarters, and the 301st Fighter Squadron, remained at Montecorvino. (Maurer, *Combat Squadrons of the Air Force, World War II*; 332d Fighter Group history, Mar–Apr 1944)

6 March: Back at Selfridge Field, Michigan, Lt. Col. Sam P. Triffy, a white officer, assumed command of the 553rd Fighter Squadron, succeeding Lt.

Col. Charles A. Gayle, another white officer. Gayle had refused to allow African American officers to enter the officers' club at Selfridge Field. He was replaced a few days after a visit to the base by Brig. Gen. Benjamin O. Davis Sr., the first and then only black general in the U.S. Army, who had come to investigate the treatment of African American personnel. The 553rd Fighter Squadron included African American pilots who had trained at Tuskegee and who would eventually replace black pilots serving overseas. (History of Selfridge Field, Michigan, 1944, AFHRA call number 288.52-4, 195–196, 199)

Early March: Col. Benjamin O. Davis Jr. met with Lt. Gen. Ira C. Eaker,

Colonel Benjamin O. Davis Jr., commander of the 332nd Fighter Group in Italy, during a briefing in 1944.

commander of the Mediterranean Allied Air Forces, at Eaker's headquarters at Caserta, Italy. Eaker told Davis of his plans to change the 332nd Fighter Group's mission from coastal patrol with P-39s to fighter escort of heavy B-17 and B-24 bombers of the Fifteenth Air Force. The Fifteenth Air Force already had three P-38 fighter escort groups, and one P-47 fighter escort group. Eaker was planning to eventually have seven fighter escort groups for the Fifteenth Air Force. (B.O. Davis Jr. autobiography and Maurer, *Air Force Combat Units of World War II,* under 1st, 14th, 31st, 52nd, 82nd, and 325th Fighter Groups)

6 March: In a letter to Major General Barney Giles at Headquarters, Army Air Forces, Lt. Gen. Ira C. Eaker, commander of the Mediterranean Allied Air Forces, recommended that the 332d Fighter Group be equipped with P-47 fighters instead of P-39s so that the group could begin to escort heavy bombers as its primary mission. However, the group had to wait until June to begin flying heavy bomber escort missions for the Fifteenth Air Force. In the meantime, two other fighter escort groups, the 31st and the 52nd, were assigned to the Fifteenth Air Force for fighter escort duties, to help the four fighter escort groups the Fifteenth Air Force had by the beginning of the year.

7 March: In Italy, 99th Fighter Squadron P-40s dropped 1,000 pound bombs on enemy positions, as they had done the previous day. (99th Fighter Squadron War Diary for March 1944)

8 March: One 99th Fighter Squadron mission patrolled the Allied beach-head at Anzio. The squadron also received three P-47 aircraft that day, suggesting that the squadron might one day fly Thunderbolts like the ones flown by the 79th Fighter Group, to which it was attached, instead of only P-40s Warhawks. (99th Fighter Squadron War Diary for March 1944)

9 March: The 99th Fighter Squadron flew two dive-bombing missions against enemy positions in the Anzio area of Italy. Lt. Heber C. Houston's P-40 was damaged by flak. (99th Fighter Squadron War Diary for March 1944)

9 March: Lt. Wayne Vincent Liggins of the 301st Fighter Squadron was killed while on a training mission. His engine failed. (332d Fighter Group summary history, Oct 1942–1947) Meanwhile, in the 99th Fighter Squadron, not yet assigned to the 332d Fighter Group, 2d Lt. John Hamilton was wounded in the leg by flak during a dive-bombing mission in the Anzio area. (99th Fighter Squadron history, Feb–Apr 1944)

10 March: The 99th Fighter Squadron in Italy flew two dive-bombing missions, one to hit an enemy heavy gun position, and the other to attack enemy tanks and 88mm guns. (99th Fighter Squadron War Diary for March 1944)

11 March: the 99th Fighter Squadron flew three dive-bombing missions against enemy positions, each of the P-40s on the mission dropping one 1,000 pound bomb. (99th Fighter Squadron War Diary for March 1944)

12 March: Class SE-44-C graduated from advanced single-engine pilot training at Tuskegee Army Air Field. There were 22 in that class. On the same day, class TE-44-C graduated from advanced twin-engine pilot training at the same field. There were 5 in that class. A total of 27 pilots graduated at Tuskegee Army Air Field that day.

13 March: The 99th Fighter Squadron flew three missions. The first of these dive-bombed two heavy gun positions with 1000-pound bombs, with five hits recorded. The other missions targeted other gun positions and a fuel depot. (99th Fighter Squadron history, Feb–Apr 1944)

14 March: The 99th Fighter Squadron in Italy flew two dive-bombing missions before noon, one against an enemy gun position and one against a supply dump. (99th Fighter Squadron War Diary for March 1944)

15 March: Enemy aircraft bombed the 99th Fighter Squadron area before dawn, but none of the bombs hit the school building housing most of the squadron personnel. The operations tent was destroyed. Despite that, the 99th Fighter Squadron flew two dive-bombing missions that day on targets in the Cassino area of Italy. (99th Fighter Squadron history, Feb–Apr 1944)

16–17 March: The 99th Fighter Squadron temporarily acquired three P-47 fighter aircraft and began transition training with them, but continued to fly P-40 aircraft in combat. (99th Fighter Squadron history, Feb–Apr 1944)

17 March: The 99th Fighter Squadron acquired two more P-47s, raising its total of that kind of aircraft to five (the other three acquired on 8 March). Some of the pilots began flying P-47s for transition training. Despite that, the squadron continued to fly P-40s on dive-bombing missions against enemy positions. There were two such missions that day. (99th Fighter Squadron War Diary for March 1944)

18 March: 2d Lt. Clemenceau McAdoo Givins of the 100th Fighter Squadron was killed on a routine flying mission when his plane crashed into the sea. (332d Fighter Group summary history, Oct 1942–1947; American Battle Monuments Commission)

18 March: The 99th Fighter Squadron, in another part of Italy, witnessed the eruption of Mount Vesuvius, which was not far away from the squadron's base. The squadron flew two more dive-bombing missions against enemy gun positions that day. (99th Fighter Squadron history, Feb–Apr 1944)

19 March: Eight P-40s of the 99th Fighter Squadron, each dropping a 1,000 pound bomb, attacked an enemy gun position, and also strafed the enemy. (99th Fighter Squadron War Diary)

20 March: The 99th Fighter Squadron dive-bombed an enemy gun position and supply dump in Italy. (99th Fighter Squadron War Diary for March 1944)

21 March: Back at Selfridge Field, Michigan, 2nd Lt. Milton R. Henry of the 553rd Fighter Squadron, with African American pilots preparing to replace those overseas, was charged with a series of court martial offenses, including being absent without leave, disrespect of superior officers, and failure to report for duty. Most of the incidents occurred earlier that same month. Back in early January, Henry had attempted to enter the officers' club at Selfridge Field, since he was an officer. Colonel Boyd, the base commander, had ordered him to leave, and he complied then. The January incident was not directly connected with his court martial trial. (History of Selfridge Field, 1944, AFHRA call number 288.52-4, 204)

22 March: Mount Vesuvius continued erupting near Naples, Italy, spreading ash over the 332d Fighter Group at Montecorvino the rest of the day and the next. (332d Fighter Group History, Oct 1942–1947) Members of the 332nd Fighter Group wore gas masks to deal with the ash. (B. O. Davis Jr. autobiography)

23 March: Enlisted members of the 99th Fighter Squadron assisted in the evacuation of areas threatened by the eruption of nearby Mount Vesuvius. The 99th Fighter Squadron flew one dive-bombing mission against an enemy artillery position, dropping eight 1,000 pound bombs. (99th Fighter Squadron War Diary for March 1944)

24 March: A shift in the wind relieved the 332nd Fighter Group at Montecorvino, Italy, from ash falling from the continuing eruption of Mount Vesuvius. (332nd Fighter Group history, Oct 1942–1947) Ash from the eruption began falling on Capodichino, Italy, home of the 366th Service Group. (366th Service Squadron history, call number SQ-SV-366-HI)

24 March: The 99th Fighter Squadron dive-bombed an enemy artillery position, using twelve P-40s, each carrying a 1,000 pound bomb. (99th Fighter Squadron War Diary, March 1944)

24 March: Class 44–2-A of B-25 transition school at Mather Field, California, graduated. Among the graduates were 9 of the 10 black pilots who started the class in January. They were transferred to Selfridge Field, Michigan, where the 477th Bombardment Group was based. (Mather Field History, Mar–Apr 1944, vol. I, AFHRA call number 286.24-5, 6; History of B-25 Transition School at Mather Field, California, 1 Jan-29 Feb 1944, AFHRA call number 286.24-4, vol, 7, 2)

25 March: At night an enemy air raid struck the area of the 99th Fighter Squadron, at least the second such raid during the month. (99th Fighter Squadron War Diary, March 1944)

26 March: The 99th Fighter Squadron flew one dive-bombing and three patrol missions. (99th Fighter Squadron War Diary, March 1944)

26 March: Mount Vesuvius became calm again, after several days erupting. (332nd Fighter Group history, Oct 1942–1947) Its ash fall had crippled B-25s stationed near it.

27 March: The 99th Fighter Squadron flew another dive-bombing mission against enemy targets in Italy. Two P-40s were damaged by flak. (99th Fighter Squadron War Diary for March 1944)

28 March: The 99th Fighter Squadron flew one patrol mission in Italy. (99th Fighter Squadron War Diary, March 1944)

28 March: Two P-39s of the 332nd Fighter Group's 302nd Fighter Squadron, flying a patrol mission with 38 other P-39s along the coast of Italy, chased and fired at a German Ju-88 airplane. Although they saw it smoking, they did not see it go down. (report on incident, sent by Dr. Frank Olynyk)

29 March: 99th Fighter Squadron P-40 pilots flew two dive-bombing missions against enemy artillery positions. (99th Fighter Squadron War Diary, March 1944)

29 March: Sgt. Jenkins H. Bluitt of the 332nd Fighter Group was killed in a collision between a truck and a train in Italy. In the same accident, Sgt. Cathedral H. Smith of the group was injured. (332nd Fighter Group history, Oct 1942–1947)

30 March: The 99th Fighter Squadron flew two missions. On the second one, squadron P-40s dropped eight 1,000 pound bombs on an enemy command post. One of the P-40 pilots, after his fighter was hit by flak, crash-landed in a friendly area of southern Italy, and was rescued by Allied forces from New Zealand. The pilot was Lt. John S. Sloan. (99th Fighter Squadron War Diary, March 1944)

30 March: The Statistical Control Division, Office of Management Control, issued a report on "Operations of the 99th Fighter Squadron Compared with Other P-40 Aircraft Squadrons in the MTO (Mediterranean Theater of Operations), 3 July 1943–31 January 1944." The report noted that the black 99th Fighter Squadron had performed as well as other squadrons with which it served, implying that the letter of General House dated 16 September 1943, which had called the squadron inferior, had been wrong. (AFHRA call number 134.65-496; IRIS number 112858)

31 March: The 99th Fighter Squadron flew one dive-bombing mission. By the end of the month, the 99th had flown 379 missions since it started flying in the Mediterranean Theater of Operations. (99th Fighter Squadron War Diary, March 1944)

31 March: 2d Lt. Norvel Stoudmire in one of the squadrons of the 332d Fighter Group was killed while flying on a harbor patrol mission. His aircraft caught on fire and he was not able to bail out safely. (332d Fighter Group summary history, Oct 1942–1947)

March: During the month of March 1944, the 99th Fighter Squadron flew 39 missions, mostly dive-bombing enemy targets on the ground. During the month, squadron Lieutenants John Hamilton and John S. Sloan received purple hearts for having been wounded. (99th Fighter Squadron, Feb–Apr 1944)

April: The 99th Fighter Squadron flew a series of missions during which each of up to twelve P-40s dropped a 1,000 pound bomb on an enemy target. The airplanes flew despite enemy antiaircraft fire from the ground. (99th Fighter Squadron history, April 1944)

April: Maj. Gen. Frank O. D. Hunter, commander of the First Air Force, visited Selfridge Field, Michigan, home of the 477th Bombardment Group, in response to an attempt by Lt. Milton Henry to enter the "white only" officers' club there. Instead of rebuking base commander Col. William Boyd, Hunter arranged for the building of a separate new officers' club for blacks at Selfridge, but it was not completed before the group was transferred to Kentucky, farther from racially charged Detroit, in early May. (Moye, *Freedom Flyers*.pp. 126–127)

1 April: The 99th Fighter Squadron was attached again to the 324th Fighter Group after having been attached for five and a half months to the 79th Fighter Group. At the same time, it transferred the few P-47s it had acquired the previous month to one of the 79th Fighter Group's assigned squadrons. The 99th Fighter Squadron had been attached to the 324th Fighter Group before, between the end of June 1943 and 19 July 1943. The commander of the 324th Fighter Group in April 1944 was Col. Leonard C. Lydon. Some of the squadron members complained about the move, since they had grown to like their association with the 79th Fighter Group and its commander, Col. Earl Bates. (99th Fighter Squadron history, Feb–Apr 1944; Maurer, *Combat Squadrons of the Air Force, World War II*)

2 April: The first anniversary of the squadron's departure from Tuskegee for overseas duty. The 99th Fighter Squadron moved from Capodichino, a base it had shared with the 100th Fighter Squadron, to Cercola, Italy, home base of the 324th Fighter Group, to which it was attached. (99th Fighter Squadron history, Feb–Apr 1944)

3 April: SSgt. Eugene Pickett of the 99th Fighter Squadron's engineering section was shot, and died while being taken to the local hospital. Authorities launched an investigation, and details are not known. (99th Fighter Squadron War Diary for April 1944)

4 April: The 99th Fighter Squadron flew its first mission from Cercola, while attached to the 324th Fighter Group, also stationed there. During the mission, twelve P-40s dive bombed an enemy motor transport park near Frascati, Italy. (99th Fighter Squadron War Diary for April 1944)

5 April: The 99th Fighter Squadron flew another dive bombing mission in Italy. (99th Fighter Squadron War Diary for April 1944)

8 April: Lt. Ray B. Ware, public relations officer for the 332nd Fighter Group, visited the public relations office of the Mediterranean Allied Air Forces at Caserta, Italy. The commander of the Mediterranean Allied Air Forces, Lt. Gen. Ira C. Eaker, would visit the 332nd Fighter Group later that month and give it a new mission. (332nd Fighter Group history, Oct 1942–1947)

9 April: The 99th Fighter Squadron flew two dive bombing missions against enemy targets, despite the fact that it was Easter Sunday. Some of the squadron's enlisted men were invited to dinner by local Italians. (99th Fighter Squadron War Diary for April 1944)

10 April: The 115th Army Air Forces Base Unit was organized at Selfridge Field, Michigan, home of the 477th Bombardment Group. (115th AAF Base Unit organization record card). At the same time, the 821st Bombardment Squadron, a B-25 training unit, was disbanded at Selfridge.

11 April: In Italy, the 99th Fighter Squadron flew a dive bombing mission that involved seven P-40s dropping bombs on an enemy artillery position. The same day word arrived that squadron commander Major George S. Roberts would be returning to the United States soon, and would be replaced with another commander. (99th Fighter Squadron War Diary for April 1944)

11 April: 2nd Lt. Frank Moody, while flying a P-39 on a training mission with the 553rd Fighter Squadron at Selfridge Field, Michigan, crashed into Lake Huron and was killed. The 553rd trained replacement pilots for service with the 332nd Fighter Group in Italy. (Bob Gross, "Divers Discover Wreck of World War II Plane," *Times Herald*, Port Huron, Michigan, 29 July 2014. Article discovered by Ron Brewington. Unit information from organization record card.)

11 April: Col. William L. Boyd, commander of Selfridge Field, was transferred to another base. During his command at Selfridge, he had attempted to maintain an all-white officers' club, with the support of Maj. Gen. Frank O. D. Hunter, commander of the First Air Force. The War Department reprimanded Boyd for failure to enforce regulations that allowed all officers at a base to use its officers' club, but Boyd's new position was Air Inspector for First Air Force. (History of Selfridge Field, 1944, AFHRA call number 288.52-4, p. 203; Alan Gropman, *The Air Force Integrates*, p. 18)

12 April: Captain Leon C. Roberts succeeded Captain Lemuel R. Custis as operations officer of the 99th Fighter Squadron. (99th Fighter Squadron history, April 1944)

13 April: The 99th Fighter Squadron in Italy flew one dive bombing mission. That same day, Captain Erwin B. Lawrence succeeded Major George S. Roberts as commander of the 99th Fighter Squadron. Major Roberts soon returned to the United States for rest and recuperation, but he would eventually return to command the squadron again, for the third time. (99th Fighter Squadron history, April 1944; 99th Fighter Squadron lineage and honors history)

14 April: The 99th Fighter Squadron flew two combat missions. During the same day, recently arrived pilots flew transition flights, learning how to fly the squadron's P-40s in preparation for combat. (99th Fighter Squadron War Diary for April 1944)

15 April: The 99th Fighter Squadron flew two dive bombing missions against enemy targets in Italy. Newer pilots continued transition flights. (99th Fighter Squadron War Diary for April 1944)

15 April: The 332d Fighter Group and the 301st Fighter Squadron moved from Montecorvino, Italy, to Capodichino, Italy, to which the 100th and 302d Fighter Squadrons had already moved. For the first time since early February 1944, when the 332d Fighter Group and its three squadrons were all stationed at Montecorvino, the units were all stationed at the same base. (Maurer, *Air Force Combat Units of World War II;* Maurer, *Combat Squadrons of the Air Force, World War II*). On the same day, back in the United States, the 617th Bombardment Squadron was activated again and assigned to the 477th Bombardment Group, Medium. (Maurer, *Combat Squadrons of the*

Air Force, World War II)

15 April: 34 new pilots graduated from advanced pilot training at Tuskegee Army Air Field. They included 23 single engine pilots in class SE-44-D, and 11 twin-engine pilots in class TE-44-D.

16 April: The 99th Fighter Squadron band and SSgt. Plummer Alexander performed at the 324th Fighter Group radio station at Cercola Field, Italy, which broadcast their music. (99th Fighter Squadron War Diary for April 1944)

17 April: The 99th Fighter Squadron in Italy flew its 400th mission, and its 2592nd sortie. The mission involved the dropping of eight 500-pound bombs and 96 twenty-pound fragmentation bombs on enemy motor transport targets, from an altitude ranging from 2,000 to 9,500 feet. (99th Fighter Squadron history, April 1944). Newer pilots of the squadron continued transition training, despite a dust storm. (99th Fighter Squadron War Diary for April 1944)

17 April: Back in Michigan, Col. Robert Selway Jr. assumed command of Selfridge Field. He was already commander of the 477th Bombardment Group there. The former commander, Colonel William L. Boyd, had been reprimanded and transferred because of his failure to provide black officers with a club on base. (History of Selfridge Field, 1944, AFHRA call number 288.52-4, 194–195)

18 April: The 99th Fighter Squadron in Italy flew a dive bombing mission against enemy targets at Itri, Italy.

19 April: Major George S. Roberts, Captain Lemuel R. Custis, and Captain Herbert "Gene" Carter bade farewell to the enlisted personnel of the 99th Fighter Squadron as they prepared to return from Italy to the United States. Major Roberts and Captain Custis had been in the first class of five Tuskegee Airmen pilots. Other squadron personnel departing were Captain Charles B. Hall, who had scored the first aerial victory by a black American military pilot, Captain James T. Wiley, and Lieutenants Willie Ashley and Willie Fuller. (99th Fighter Squadron history, Feb–Apr 1944)

19 April: Elsewhere in Italy, 2d Lieutenant Beryl Wyatt of the 100th Fighter Squadron died from injuries suffered in an aircraft crash. (332d Fighter Group history, Mar–Apr 1944)

20 April: The 99th Fighter Squadron flew one dive bombing mission against an enemy artillery target.

20 April: Lieutenant General Ira C. Eaker, Commanding General, Mediterranean Allied Air Forces, visited the 332d Fighter Group at Capodichino,

Italy. On the same day, Lieutenant Ray B. Ware, the 332d Fighter Group public relations officer, announced that the group would soon be converting from P-39 to P-47 aircraft and move to the east coast of Italy, presumably for bomber escort duty. (332d Fighter Group history, Mar–Apr 1944; 332d Fighter Group War Diary, April 1944) Later that day, General Eaker, accompanied by Lt. Col. Benjamin O. Davis Jr., commander of the 332d Fighter Group, visited the 99th Fighter Squadron at Cercola, where it was serving with the 324th Fighter Group, to which it was attached but not assigned. The 99th Fighter Squadron, which Colonel Davis had commanded earlier, would eventually be assigned to the 332d Fighter Group for the bomber escort duty. On the same day, the 99th Fighter Squadron flew its 200th mission in Italy. (99th Fighter Squadron history, Feb–Apr 1944)

22 April: Capt. Melvin T. Jackson assumed command of the 302nd Fighter Squadron, succeeding 1st Lt. Edward C. Gleed. (302nd Fighter Squadron lineage and honors history)

23 April: The 99th Fighter Squadron flew two dive bombing missions in Italy. (99th Fighter Squadron War Diary for April 1944)

24 April: The 99th Fighter Squadron celebrated the first anniversary of its arrival overseas. On the same day, it flew two combat missions, at least one of which involved dive bombing an enemy artillery position. That night, enemy aircraft raided the Cercola area, using flares. (99th Fighter Squadron War Diary for April 1944)

24 April: 2d Lieutenant Edgar L. Jones was killed in an aircraft crash on takeoff for a strafing mission for the 332nd Fighter Group. That night, thirty to forty German JU-88 airplanes raided the 332d Fighter Group area, wounding one enlisted man, Staff Sergeant Alvin H. Kent, who earned the Purple Heart. (332d Fighter Group history, Mar–Apr 1944; 332d Fighter Group War Diary, April 1944)

25 April: The 332d Fighter Group received its first six P-47 airplanes, two of which were assigned to each of the group's fighter squadrons, the 100th, 301st, and 302d. P-47s eventually replaced all of the P-39 fighters the group had flown. (332d Fighter Group history, Mar–Apr 1944) The P-47 was more capable of engaging in aerial combat, and had a range long enough to escort bombers on long missions. (332nd Fighter Group history, Oct 1942–1947)

25 April: Back at Selfridge Field, Michigan, 2nd Lt. Milton R. Henry, an African American officer in the 553rd Fighter Squadron, was convicted in a court martial and dishonorably discharged from the service. The charges had been repeated absences without leave in March, failure to report, also in March, and disrespect for superior officers on 15 February. (History of Selfridge Field, 1944, AFHRA call number 288.52-4, pp 203–204.

26 April: Selfridge Air Force Base leaders canceled a contract to build service clubs for African American personnel, including an officers' club and an enlisted club, because they expected the black organizations to be transferred to other locations. (History of Selfridge Field, Jan–Dec 1944, AFHRA call number 288.52-4, appendix XIV, item 8)

27 April: On one of the days that rain prevented 99th Fighter Squadron combat missions in Italy, groups of enlisted men from the squadron traveled by truck to Caserta to see a production of "This is the Army." (99th Fighter Squadron War Diary for April 1944)

28 April: The 99th Fighter Squadron flew two combat missions. One of them dive bombed an enemy artillery position. Eight P-40s dropped 500 and 20-pound bombs. Only three of the 99th Fighter Squadron pilots who deployed with the squadron when it left the United States over a year earlier were still assigned to the squadron. (99th Fighter Squadron War Diary for April 1944)

29 April: The 99th Fighter Squadron flew another dive bombing mission in Italy, dropping demolition and fragmentation bombs from P-40s on an enemy target. (99th Fighter Squadron War Diary for April 1944)

30 April: The 320th College Training Detachment (Aircrew) was disbanded at Tuskegee Institute, Alabama. On the same day, the 318th Base Headquarters and Air Base Squadron (Colored) the 889th Basic Flying Training Squadron, the 890th Single Engine Flying Training Squadron, the 1155th Single Engine Flying Training Squadron, the 941st Guard Squadron, the 309th Sub-Depot, and the 1451st Quartermaster Company, Aviation Service, were disbanded at Tuskegee Army Air Field. (organization record cards) Their personnel transferred to elements of the 2143d Army Air Forces Base Unit. (history of the 318th Base Headquarters and Air Base Squadron for Mar–Apr 1944 and histories of Tuskegee Army Air Field at the Air Force Historical Research Agency) At the same time, the 66th Army Air Forces Flying Training Detachment, which supervised the primary flight training at Moton Field of Tuskegee Institute, was disbanded, and its functions were taken over by the 2164th AAF Base Unit, which was organized at the same field the next day.

30 April: In Italy, 99th Fighter Squadron P-40s dropped seven 500-pound bombs and 14 clusters of six 20-pound fragmentation bombs on an enemy supply dump southeast of Avezzano, Italy. The attack produced spectacular explosions that sent flames and smoke a thousand feet into the air. It was the most memorable mission of the squadron for the month. (99th Fighter Squadron history, April 1944)

April: During the month of April, the 99th Fighter Squadron flew 32 missions, mostly dive-bombing enemy targets. (99th Fighter Squadron history, Feb–Apr 1944)

May: 1st Lt. Ray B. Ware was appointed photo interpreter of the 332nd Fighter Group, and 1st Lt. Robert G. Pitts was appointed as group historian. (332nd Fighter Group history, May 1944)

Spring: Captain Clarence C. Jamison and 1st Lt. Allen G. Lane became the first black flying instructors at Tuskegee Army Air Field. They served in the P-40 transitional school. Both of them had graduated from advanced flying training at Tuskegee in 1942, and had much flying experience since then. (History of Tuskegee Army Air Field, Mar-Jun 1944, AFHRA call number 289.28-4, vol. 1)

1 May: The 99th Fighter Squadron in Italy was assigned to the 332d Fighter Group but remained attached to the 324th Fighter Group for combat operations. (Maurer, *Combat Squadrons of the Air Force, World War II*). It flew one mission, launching eight P-40s armed with 500-pound demolition and 20-pound fragmentation cluster bombs to dive bomb the Frosinone railroad station. Each P-40 carried one of the 500-pound bombs and twelve of the smaller bombs. (324th Fighter Group history for May 1944)

1 May: On the same day, back at Tuskegee Army Air Field in Alabama, the 2143d AAF Base Unit was activated. It operated the pilot school for basic and advanced training there. (unit's organization record card) The 318th Base Headquarters and Air Base Squadron was disbanded on 30 Apr 1944, as were the 889th Basic Flying Training Squadron and the 890th Single Engine Flying Training Squadron. The 613th Army Air Force Band remained active. (History of Tuskegee Army Air Field, Mar-Jun 1944, AFHRA call number 289.28-4, vol. 1). On the same date, the 2164th AAF Base Unit (Contract Pilot School Primary) was organized at Moton Field of Tuskegee Institute, for military supervision of the primary flight training that had been handled previously by the 66th AAF Flying Training Detachment, which had been disbanded the previous day.

2 May: The 99th Fighter Squadron, still attached to the 324th Fighter Group, flew two missions. On the first, it launched seven P-40s armed with 500-pound demolition and 20-pound fragmentation cluster bombs against an enemy heavy gun position. On the second mission, the squadron launched eight P-40s, similarly armed, against a similar target. (324th Fighter Group history for May 1944)

3 May: The 99th Fighter Squadron launched two 8-plane missions, flying P-40s armed with 500-pound demolition and smaller fragmentation or cluster bombs. One attacked enemy guns while the other targeted enemy motor vehicles. Lt. Wilson (first name not specified) was forced to bail out of his fighter on one of the missions, but he returned safely to his unit. (324 Fighter Group history for May 1944)

4 May: The 99th Fighter Squadron, still attached to the 324th Fighter Group, launched two 11-plane missions. One dropped 500-pound bombs on a railroad marshalling yard at Collefero. The other one dropped the same kind of bombs on enemy motor vehicles and a supply dump. (324 Fighter Group history for May 1944)

5 May: Lt. James R. Polkinghorne Jr. of the 301st Fighter Squadron was reported lost with his P-39 near Teragina, Italy while on a strafing mission. The cause was unknown. (Missing Air Crew Report 4518; 332nd Fighter Group history, May 1944)

5 May: Back in Michigan, the Army Air Forces ordered the major African American units at Selfridge Field to move to other bases. The 477th Bombardment Group and its white commander, Col. Robert Selway Jr., were transferred to Godman Field, Kentucky, while the 553rd Fighter Squadron, and its white commander, were transferred to Walterboro, South Carolina. The probable cause was the racial trouble at Selfridge, which came to a head during the controversial court martial trial and conviction of an African American pilot in April, and the reprimand of the Selfridge Field commander for failure to provide black officers with a club on base, for which he was transferred, also in April. Another reason might have been the proximity of Selfridge to racially charged Detroit, Michigan. (History of Selfridge Field, 1944, AFHRA call number 288.52-4, 203–204)

6 May: An advance party of the 99th Fighter Squadron moved to Pignataro Airfield in Italy. (99th Fighter Squadron history, Jun 1944) That same day, the 99th Fighter Squadron flew three missions, each one launching eight P-40s to drop 500-pound bombs on enemy guns (artillery). Some of the P-40s also dropped 20-pound fragmentation bombs in clusters. (324 Fighter Group history for May 1944)

6 May: Back in the United States, the 477th Bombardment Group, Medium, arrived at Godman Field, Kentucky. (Maurer, *Air Force Combat Units of*

World War II). Unlike the situation at Selfridge, black officers of the group were allowed to use the base officer's club. White officers used another officer's club at neighboring Fort Knox. (Lawrence P. Schott and William M. Womack Sr., *Double V: The Civil Rights Struggle of the Tuskegee Airmen* [East Lansing: Michigan State University Press, 1994], 210). The 115th Army Air Forces Base Unit moved from Selfridge Field, Michigan, to Godman Field, Kentucky, along with the 477th Bombardment Group with which it served. (115 AAF Base Unit organization record card)

6 May: The 126th Army Air Forces Base Unit was organized at Walterboro Army Air Field in South Carolina, to prepare for the movement of the 553rd Fighter Squadron from Selfridge Field, Michigan, to Walterboro. (organization record card)

7 May: The 553rd Fighter Squadron, which trained replacement pilots for the 332nd Fighter Group, which was serving in Italy, completed its move from Selfridge Field, Michigan, to Walterboro Army Air Field, South Carolina. On the same day, the unit was disbanded. The 126th Army Air Forces Base Unit continued active at Walterboro. Pilots who graduated from single-engine flight training at Tuskegee Army Air Field transferred to the unit to serve as replacement fighter pilots who would eventually deploy overseas to serve with the 332nd Fighter Group. (organization record cards) The unit could use the officer's club at Walterboro, because white officers rented another club off base for themselves. (Lawrence P. Schott and William M. Womack Sr., *Double V: The Civil Rights Struggle of the Tuskegee Airmen* [East Lansing: Michigan State University Press, 1994], 200)

9 May: The 99th Fighter Squadron, still attached to the 324th Fighter Group, flew one dive bombing mission, involving eight P-40s dropping 500-pound bombs on a building identified as an enemy military headquarters. (324th Fighter Group history for May 1944)

10 May: The main body of the 99th Fighter Squadron moved to Pignataro, near Capua, Italy. (99th Fighter Squadron history, Jun 1944; Maurer, *Combat Squadrons of the Air Force, World War II*) Despite the move, the squadron still was able to fly one mission, with eight P-40s dropping 500-pound demolition and 20-pound cluster bombs on a building identified as an enemy barracks. (324 Fighter Group history for May 1944)

11 May: The 99th Fighter Squadron, still attached to the 324th Fighter Group, launched one mission, with eight P-40s armed with 500-pound demolition and 20-pound fragmentation bombs, but the mission was aborted. The reason was not given, but bad weather could have been the cause. (324

Fighter Group history for May 1944)

12 May: The 99th Fighter Squadron flew three missions, using P-40s to drop 1,000-pound bombs on enemy-held road bridges. The first one involved 12 fighters, and Lt. Neal V. Nelson went missing. Each of the other two missions involved eight P-40s. (324 Fighter Group history for May 1944). Capt. Howard L. Baugh of the 99th Fighter Squadron earned the Distinguished Flying Cross for his heroism on a mission on this date. (Fifteenth Air Force General Order 4041 dated 19 Oct 1944)

12–14 May: The 99th Fighter Squadron earned its second Distinguished Unit Citation for missions over Cassino, Italy, an honor it shared with the 324th Fighter Group to which it was attached. (Maurer, *Combat Squadrons of the Air Force, World War II*)

13 May: The 99th Fighter Squadron flew two missions, each involving eight P-40s dropping 1,000-pound bombs. One of the missions targeted Esperia, while the other attacked Marandola, Italy. (324 Fighter Group history for May 1944)

14 May: The 99th Fighter Squadron, still attached to the white 324th Fighter Group, flew two 8-plane missions, each dropping 1,000 pound bombs, one mission targeting Trivio and the other attacking Marandola. (324 Fighter Group history for May 1944)

15 May: Using P-40s, 99th Fighter Squadron fighter pilots dive-bombed and strafed the towns of Itri and San Olivia, enemy-held roads, and enemy vehicles on those roads. Two of the missions, each involving eight P-40s, dropped 500-pound bombs. On the third mission, six P-40s, each carrying a 1,000-pound bomb, targeted enemy motor vehicles. (324 Fighter Group history for May 1944)

15 May: Back in the United States, the 618th Bombardment Squadron was activated again and assigned to the 477th Bombardment Group, Medium. (Maurer, *Combat Squadrons of the Air Force, World War II*)

16 May: 99th Fighter Squadron P-40 pilots armed with 500-pound bombs and small cluster bombs attacked various enemy targets, including the town of Itri, motor vehicles on roads, and an enemy-held bridge. Some of the P-40 pilots also strafed their targets. (324 Fighter Group history for May 1944)

17 May: The 99th Fighter Squadron, still attached to the white 324th Fighter Group, flew three missions, all involving P-40s armed with 500-pound bombs. On the first one, seven fighters dive bombed the town of Vallecorsa. One the second mission, eight fighter pilots attacked an enemy-held bridge and a truck on that bridge. On the third mission, seven fighters dive bombed and strafed enemy motor transports on a road, also using cluster bombs. (324 Fighter Group history for May 1944)

18 May: The 99th Fighter Squadron flew three missions, each involving eight P-40s armed with 500-pound bombs and strafing bullets. They targeted enemy-held roads, motor vehicles on those roads, and the town of San Giovanni. (324 Fighter Group history for May 1944)

19 May: The 99th Fighter Squadron, still attached to the 324th Fighter Group, launched three missions, armed with 500-lb bombs and machine gun bullets for strafing. One 8-plane mission targeted Vallecorsa, Italy, and another 4-plane mission struck Terracina. The third mission was aborted, and the four P-40s returned, because of weather. (324 Fighter Group history for May 1944)

19 May: The 332nd Fighter Group received ten new P-47 airplanes. (332nd Fighter Group history, May 1944)

20 May: The 332nd Fighter Group learned that it would be reassigned from the Twelfth to the Fifteenth Air Force and would move to Ramitelli for primarily bomber escort duties. (XV Air Force Service Command weekly activity report dated 20 May 1944)

20 May: The 99th Fighter Squadron, still attached to the white 324th Fighter Group, flew one armed reconnaissance mission, during which eight P-40s dropped 500-pound bombs on enemy-held Vallecorsa, Italy. (324th Fighter Group history for May 1944)

21 May: The 99th Fighter Squadron flew three missions. On each of them, eight P-40s cropped 500-pound bombs on enemy targets, including motor vehicles and a bridge, and the enemy-held towns of Ceccano and San Giovanni. (324th Fighter Group history for May 1944). 1st Lt. Charles W. Tate of the 99th Fighter Squadron earned the Distinguished Flying Cross for his heroic actions on this date. (Fifteenth Air Force General Order 449 dated 31 Jan 1945)

22 May: The 99th Fighter Squadron, still attached to the white 324th Fighter Group, flew three missions. On each of two of them, seven or eight P-40s dropped 1,000-pound bombs near Alatri, Italy in an attempt to create road blocks. On the other mission, eight P-40s dropped 100-pound phosphorus and 260-pound fragmentation bombs on enemy motor vehicles near the town of Priverno, Italy. (324th Fighter Group history for May 1944)

22 May: 2d Lt. Henry Pollard Jr. of the 302d Fighter Squadron was lost while flying a training mission from Capodichino. (American Battle Monuments

Commission; 332nd Fighter Group history, May 1944). The 332d Fighter Group was reassigned from the XII Fighter Command of the Twelfth Air Force to the Fifteenth Air Force. (Twelfth Air Force General Order 70, dated 31 May 1944; Army Air Forces, Mediterranean Theater of Operations General Order 28 dated 22 May 1944; Maurer, *Air Force Combat Units of World War II*). The group came under the operational control of the 306th Fighter Wing, which administered the fighter escort groups of the Fifteenth Air Force. The commander of the 306th Fighter Wing at the time was Brigadier General Dean C. Strother. At the same time, the 99th Fighter Squadron was relieved from attachment to the XII Tactical Air Command, although it remained assigned to the 332d Fighter Group and attached for operational control to the 324th Fighter Group. (Twelfth Air Force General Order 70 dated 31 May 1944 and Maurer, *Combat Squadrons of the Air Force, World War II*, p. 329). At the same time, the 96th Service Group and the 366th and 367th Service Squadrons were reassigned from the XII Air Force Service Command of the Twelfth Air Force to the Fifteenth Air Force. (organization record card of the group and Twelfth Air Force General Order 70 dated 31 May 1944) Other organizations reassigned from XII Air Force Service Command to the Fifteenth Air Force that day included the 99th Army Air Forces Service Detachment, the 99th Aviation Ordnance Detachment, the 1765th Ordnance Supply and Maintenance Company, the 1901st Quartermaster Truck Company, Aviation, the 1000th Signal Company Service Group, and the 1051st Quartermaster Company, Service Group, Aviation. (Twelfth Air Force General Order 70, dated 31 May 1944). While the effective date of all these organizational changes was 22 May, the order that authorized them was dated 31 May.

23 May: The 99th Fighter Squadron flew three missions, dropping 260-pound fragmentation and 500-pound demolition bombs on enemy gun and artillery positions in Italy. Each mission involved seven or eight P-40s. (324th Fighter Group history for May 1944)

23 May: Class SE-44-E graduated from advanced single-engine pilot training at Tuskegee Army Air Field. There were 30 in the class.

24 May: The 99th Fighter Squadron flew three missions. On each of two of them, eight P-40s dive bombed enemy installations and gun positions, dropping 260-pound fragmentation and 100-pound phosphorus bombs. The pilots also strafed enemy targets in the area. On the other mission, eight P-40s dropped 500-pound bombs on enemy transportation targets on roads. Lt. Clarence W. Dart was forced to belly-land when he returned from one of the missions that day. (324th Fighter Group history for May 1944)

24 May: 1st Lt. John H. Prowell of the 301st Fighter Squadron was reported lost with his P-39 over the Mediterranean Sea, with possible engine failure, while flying a convoy protection mission. (Missing Air Crew Report 13687; 332nd Fighter Group history, May 1944)

25 May: The 99th Fighter Squadron flew four missions. Two of them dropped 260-pound fragmentation and 100-pound phosphorus bombs on enemy motor vehicles, and the other two dropped 500-pound demolition bombs on enemy vehicles on roads in and near Frascati, Italy. Each mission involved seven or eight P-40s. (324th Fighter Group history for May 1944)

26 May: The 99th Fighter Squadron flew three missions, dropping 500-pound bombs on enemy transportation targets on roads near Ferentino, Italy. Each mission involved eight P-40s. (324th Fighter Group history for May 1944)

26–29 May: The 332nd Fighter Group moved from Capodichino, Italy, to Ramitelli Air Field, on the east coast of Italy, next to the Adriatic Sea. It was not far from the bases of other fighter escort groups of the Fifteenth Air Force, and just north of the bomber bases. By then, the group completed its transition from P-39 to P-47 airplanes. (332nd Fighter Group history, May 1944)

27 May: The 99th Fighter Squadron flew three dive-bombing missions, dropping 500-pound bombs against enemy motor vehicles in and around Ferentino, Italy. Each mission involved seven or eight P-40s. (324th Fighter Group history for May 1944). 1st Lt. Clarence W. Dart of the 99th Fighter Squadron in Italy earned the Distinguished Flying Cross for his heroism on this date. (Fifteenth Air Force General Order 449 dated 31 Jan 1945) On the same date, the 99th Fighter Squadron reported losing 2nd Lt. James B. Brown and his P-40 near Prossinone, Italy. The cause was not known. (Missing Air Crew Report 5372)

27 May: Back in the United States, the 619th Bombardment Squadron was activated again and assigned to the 477th Bombardment Group, Medium. The group now had all of its original squadrons active again under it, this time at Godman Field, Kentucky. (Maurer, *Combat Squadrons of the Air Force, World War II*)

27–30 May: The 366th Service Squadron, which serviced and repaired the airplanes of the 332nd Fighter Group, moved in three echelons from Capodichino Air Field to Ramitelli Air Field in Italy. This was in accordance with a 24 May 1944 order that also transferred the squadron from XII Air Force Service Command to XV Air Force Service Command. The commander of the squadron at the time was Capt. Elmer E. Jones Jr. (366 Service Squadron history, May 1944)

28 May: Still attached to the white 324th Fighter Group, the 99th Fighter Group flew three dive bombing missions, dropping 500-pound bombs on enemy motor vehicles on roads. Each mission involved seven or eight P-40s. (324th Fighter Group history for May 1944)

29 May: The 96th Air Service Group was assigned to the XV Air Force Service Command of the Fifteenth Air Force. On the same date, a great many P-47 fighter airplanes landed at Ramitelli, home of the 332nd Fighter Group, to replace the group's P-39s. The P-47s came from the 325th Fighter Group, which was acquiring P-51 fighter airplanes. (38th Service Group history, Dec 1943-Jun 1944). A 301st Fighter Squadron pilot, 2nd Lt. Lloyd S. Hathcock, disappeared on a flight to ferry a P-47 that day from Foggia Main Airport to Ramitelli. He reportedly overshot his target and landed accidentally at another airfield held by the enemy. He was captured and held as a prisoner of war in a German stalag. (Missing Air Crew Report 6921; Alexander Jefferson, *Red Tail Captured, Red Tail Free* [New York: Fordham University Press, 2005], v; Craig Huntly e-mail to Daniel Haulman dated 26 October 2012)

29 May: Benjamin O. Davis Jr., commander of the 332nd Fighter Group, was promoted from lieutenant colonel to colonel rank. (B.O. Davis autobiography)

29 May: The 99th Fighter Squadron flew two dive bombing missions against enemy transportation targets in Italy, each mission involving eight P-40s. (324th Fighter Group history for May 1944)

30 May: The 99th Fighter Squadron flew three dive bombing missions against enemy transportation targets in and around Alatri, Italy, each mission involving eight P-40s. (324th Fighter Group history for May 1944)

31 May: The 99th Fighter Squadron flew six dive-bombing missions against enemy targets in and around Marino, Italy, most missions involving a set of four P-40s. (324th Fighter Group history for May 1944)

31 May: An outdoor amphitheater opened at the northern edge of Tuskegee Army Air Field with a performance by Ella Fitzgerald and the Inkspots. Entertainers who performed at the base later included Louis Armstrong and Lena Horne. (Thole, p. 15) Overseas, the 332nd Fighter Group was assigned to the 306th Fighter Wing, which included six other fighter escort groups (31st, 52nd, 325th, 1st, 14th, and 82nd). (332nd Fighter Group history, May 1944; 306 Fighter Wing General Order 70 dated 31 May 1944)

May: By the end of this month, the grassy field at Moton Field had been marked with chert to delineate four runways, one each running N-S, E-W, NW-SE, and NE-SW. The primary flight school at Moton Field was also regularly using, by this time, another airstrip called Calibee Strip.

1 June: The 99th Fighter Squadron flew seven 4-plane missions, dive bombing enemy supply lines, supply dumps, and road junctions. (99th Fighter Squadron War Diary for June 1944)

2 June: The 99th Fighter Squadron flew seven combat missions (26 sorties). The 99th Fighter Squadron celebrated the first anniversary of its first combat mission. That same day it flew its 500th combat mission, led by squadron commander Capt. Erwin B. Lawrence. The same mission was the 298th the squadron had flown in Italy. (99th Fighter Squadron history, Jun 1944)

2 June: MSgt. William M. Harris, line chief, of the 302d Fighter Squadron of the 332d Fighter Group, was killed during an aircraft take-off. 2d Lt. Elmer Taylor, a pilot also of the 302d Fighter Squadron, was killed in a crash during a training mission. (332d Fighter Group history for June 1944)

3 June: The 99th Fighter Squadron in Italy flew four missions, attacking Tivoli, near Rome, and enemy-held bridges over the Tiber River. (99th Fighter Squadron War Diary for June 1944)

4 June: The 99th Fighter Squadron flew two 12-plane reconnaissance missions over roads north of Rome and destroyed ten enemy motor vehicles and damaged 34 more. Captains Edward L. Toppins and Leonard M. Jackson each earned the Distinguished Flying Cross for heroic actions on this date. (Fifteenth Air Force General Order 4041 dated 19 Oct 1944 and Fifteenth Air Force General Order 4876 dated 5 Dec 1944)

5 June: The 99th Fighter Squadron flew three 8-plane missions that targeted enemy vehicles near Rome. (99th Fighter Squadron War Diary for June 1944). The squadron's Captain Elwood T. Driver earned the Distinguished Flying Cross for his heroic actions on this date. (Fifteenth Air Force General Order 449 dated 31 Jan 1945) The 99th Fighter Squadron was detached from the white 324th Fighter Group and attached directly to the XII Tactical Air Command of the Twelfth Air Force. (99th Fighter Squadron history, Jun 1944)

5 June: The 96th Air Service Group moved from Montecorvino Air Field to Foggia, Italy, very near Ramitelli. Serving under the 96th Air Service Group were the 366th Service Squadron at Ramitelli and the 367th Service Squadron, at first at Foggia and later at Vasto and Falconara. (Organization record cards of the organizations)

5–9 June: The 100th Fighter Squadron moved from Capodichino, Italy, to

Ramitelli Air Field. (332nd Fighter Group history, June 1944)

6 June: The 99th Fighter Squadron in Italy flew six 4-plane missions and destroyed 11 enemy motor vehicles, while damaging 29 others. Lt. Clarence W. Dart crash-landed in friendly territory, and Lt. Leonard M. Jackson crash-landed on no-man's land between enemy and Allied lines. He returned the next day with two captured Germans. (99th Fighter Squadron history, Jun 1944)

7 June: The 332d Fighter Group flew its first mission with the Fifteenth Air Force, from Ramitelli. The mission was a fighter sweep of the Ferrara-Bologna area. 2d Lt. Carroll N. Langston Jr. of the 301st Fighter Squadron was reported lost with his P-47 near San Benedetti, Italy. The cause was probable engine failure. On the same mission, Captain Lee Rayford was wounded by flak. (332d Fighter Group mission report number 1; Missing Air Crew Report 5639; 332d Fighter Group summary history, Oct 1942–1947)

7 June: The 99th Fighter Squadron, not yet flying with the 332d Fighter Group, flew four 4-ship strafing missions to destroy 24 motor vehicles, damage 47 others, and destroy one self-propelled gun, with no friendly aircraft lost. (99th Fighter Squadron history, Jun 1944)

7 June: Captain William C. Boyd became director of the instrument flying school at Tuskegee Army Air Field. (History of Tuskegee Army Air Field, Mar-Jun 1944, AFHRA call number 289.28-4, vol. 1)

8 June: The 332d Fighter Group flew its first heavy bomber escort mission, protecting B-17s of the 5th Bombardment Wing on a mission to Pola, Italy. (332d Fighter Group mission report number 2)

8 June: The 99th Fighter Squadron flew six 6-plane missions, destroyed sixteen enemy motor vehicles, and damaged 28 more. 1st Lt. Lewis C. Smith fell out of his plane and went missing after being hit by flak on a dive-bombing mission with the 99th Fighter Squadron, which had not yet joined the 332d Fighter Group for bomber escort. (99th Fighter Squadron history, Jun 1944)

9 June: The 332d Fighter Group helped escort B-24s and B-17s of the 5th, 47th, 49th, 55th, and 304th Bombardment Wings on a raid to Munich, Germany, the group's first mission over Germany. (332d Fighter Group mission report number 3) Four Tuskegee Airmen shot down a total of five enemy Me-109 airplanes that day. The victors included 2d Lt. Frederick D. Funderburg, who shot down 2 Me-109s, and 1st Lts Charles M. Bussy, Melvin T. Jackson, and Wendell O. Pruitt, who each shot down one Me-109. (Fifteenth Air Force general order number 1473, issued 30 June 1944;

332d Fighter Group history for June 1944) These were the first aerial victories of the 332d Fighter Group (not counting the 99th Fighter Squadron). (332d Fighter Group history, December 1944 [summary of year's accomplishments]) For this mission, group commander Colonel Benjamin O. Davis Jr. earned a Distinguished Flying Cross for so skillfully handling his squadrons that "only a few bombers were lost." (Fifteenth Air Force General Order number 2972 dated 31 August 1944) Enemy airplanes actually shot down only two B-24s of the escorted wing's 459th Bombardment Group during the time the 332d Fighter Group was escorting them. (Missing Air Crew Reports 6317 and 6179) This was the first time 332d Fighter Group-escorted bombers fell to enemy airplanes. The losses were very understandable, given the fact that the number of bombers far exceeded the number of escort fighters to cover them. The group reported 2d Lt. Cornelius G. Rogers of the 301st Fighter Group lost with his P-47D to an unknown cause near Pols, Italy. (Missing Air Crew Report 5758). On the same date, 9 June 1944, a general from the XV Air Force Service Command visited Ramitelli Air Field, possibly to discuss the painting of the 332d Fighter Group aircraft for identification. (366 Service Squadron history, Jun 1944)

9 June: The 99th Fighter Squadron, still detached from the 332nd Fighter Group, flew 6 missions and 22 sorties. It destroyed 6 motor vehicles and damaged 15 others. It also destroyed 6 horse-drawn carts. (99th Fighter Squadron War Diary, June 1944)

10 June: The 99th Fighter Squadron in Italy flew five missions, destroying twelve motor vehicles and damaging eight others. (99th Fighter Squadron War Diary for June 1944)

11 June: The 99th Fighter Squadron moved to Ciampino, Italy. That same day it was attached to the white 86th Fighter Group under Col. Harold E. Kofahl, but remained assigned to the 332d Fighter Group. (99th Fighter Squadron lineage and honors history; 99th Fighter Squadron history, Jun 1944; Maurer, *Combat Squadrons of the Air Force, World War II*)

11 June: The 332d Fighter Group, from which the 99th Fighter Squadron was then still detached, escorted B-17 and B-24 bombers of the 5th and 55th Bombardment Wings to the Smedervo area. (99th Fighter Squadron lineage and honors history; 332d Fighter Group mission report number 4)

12 June: The 99th Fighter Squadron flew four missions, destroying 12 enemy motor vehicles and damaging 25 others. (99th Fighter Squadron War Diary for June 1944)

13 June: The 99th Fighter Squadron flew three missions, destroying five enemy motor transports and damaging ten others. (99th Fighter Squadron War Diary for June 1944)

13 June: The 332d Fighter Group escorted B-17 and B-24 bombers of the 5th and 49th Bombardment Wings to the Munich area. (332d Fighter Group mission report number 5) Enemy fighters shot down one of the B-24s over northern Italy (Missing Air Crew Report 6097)

14 June: The 332d Fighter Group escorted B-17 and B-24 bombers on a mission to the Budapest area of Hungary. (332d Fighter Group narrative mission report number 6) 2d Lt. Roger D. Brown of the 100th Fighter Squadron was reported missing, along with his P-47 airplane, southeast of Ramitelli Air Base, Italy. He experienced engine trouble on a training flight that day (Missing Air Crew Report 6922)

14 June: Meanwhile, the 99th Fighter Squadron flew four combat missions, attacking enemy railroad cars and motor vehicles. Lt. C. W. Allen went missing on a dive-bombing mission after his P-40 was hit by flak and he was forced to bail out. He returned two days later after evading the enemy. (99th Fighter Squadron history, Jun 1944)

15 June: The 99th Fighter Squadron flew six dive-bombing missions, targeting bridges, railroads, roads, and motor vehicles. One P-40 was hit by flak. The pilot belly-landed his damaged airplane. (99th Fighter Squadron history, Jun 1944)

15 June: Enlisted men of the 332nd Fighter Group and its squadrons organized an Enlisted Men's Club at Ramitelli Airfield, and elected SSgt. James Webb as its president. Webb was an accomplished piano player. (366 Service Squadron histories, Jun and Aug 1944)

16 June: For the second day in a row, the 99th Fighter Squadron flew six dive-bombing missions, targeting enemy-held bridges and enemy facilities in a town. (99th Fighter Squadron history, Jun 1944) Meanwhile, the 332d Fighter Group escorted Fifteenth Air Force heavy bombers to the Bratislava area of Slovakia. (332d Fighter Group mission report number 7)

17 June: The 99th Fighter Squadron moved to Orbetello, Italy. It flew one reconnaissance mission that day. (99th Fighter Squadron lineage and honors history; Maurer, *Combat Squadrons of the Air Force, World War II*; 99th Fighter War Diary for June 1944))

19 June: Workers from the 366th Service Squadron laid the framework for the Enlisted Men's Club building at Ramitelli. (366 Service Squadron history, Jun 1944)

20 June: The 99th Fighter Squadron in Italy flew two combat missions. It was still not flying with the 332nd Fighter Group, from which it was detached. (99th Fighter Squadron War Diary for June 1944)

21 June: On a 99th Fighter Squadron combat mission, one of the unit's P-40s was damaged by flak. (99th Fighter Squadron War Diary for June 1944)

22 June: P-47 fighters of the 332d Fighter Group embarked on a mission to strafe Airasca-Pinerole landing ground. Clouds and accidents prevented accomplishment of the mission. Captain Robert B. Tresville Jr., 2d Lieutenant Samuel Jefferson, and 2d Lieutenant Charles B. Johnson, all of the 100th Fighter Squadron, were reported missing after flying at extremely low altitudes over the Mediterranean Sea, near the coast of Corsica and northwestern Italy. Captain Tresville was a graduate of the U.S. Military Academy at West Point. (332d Fighter Group history for June 1944; 332d Fighter Group mission report number 8, and Missing Air Crew Reports numbered 6078 and 6079. The Missing Air Crew Reports note 22 June 1944, but the 332d Fighter Group narrative mission report 8 gives the date as 24 June 1944. The date of the mission report is probably wrong, since another mission, described in narrative mission report number 10, also has the 24 June 1944 date.)

22 June: Maj. Andrew D. Turner succeeded Capt. Robert B. Tresville as commander of the 100th Fighter Squadron. (100th Fighter Squadron lineage and honors history). On the same date, the XV Air Force Service Command learned that the 332nd Fighter Group would be trading in its P-47 fighters for P-51 Mustangs, by direction of Major General Nathan Twining, commander of the Fifteenth Air Force. (XV Air Force Service Command staff journal entry for 22 Jun 1944)

22 June: The 99th Fighter Squadron flew two missions. It strafed more than thirty enemy railroad cars at Bagni di Guiliano, Italy. (99th Fighter Squadron War Diary for June 1944)

23 June: The 332d Fighter Group escorted Fifteenth Air Force heavy bombers to the Bucharest-Giurgiu area of Rumania. (332d Fighter Group mission report number 9, number out of sequence with the date)

23 June: The 99th Fighter Squadron, not yet flying missions with the 332nd Fighter Group, flew two combat missions. Lt. Howard L. Baugh was hospitalized after accidentally shooting himself. (99th Fighter Squadron War Diary for June 1944)

24 June: The 99th Fighter Squadron, still detached from the 332nd Fighter Group, flew two combat missions. (99th Fighter Squadron War Diary for June 1944) On the same day, the emblem of the squadron was approved. It consisted of a gold-winged diving panther on a blue disk, with a background of 9 stars, 4 above and 5 below the panther (99th Fighter Squadron emblem folder)

25 June: In the morning, eight P-47 pilots of the 332d Fighter Group, including 2d Lt. Gwynne W. Pierson and Lieutenants Wendell O. Pruitt, Laurence D. Wilkins, and Freddie E. Hutchins, strafed a German warship in the Adriatic Sea (Gulf of Venice) near Pirano not far from Trieste, then in Italy. They reported the ship was a German destroyer and that they had sunk it. (332d Fighter Group mission report number 11 dated June 25, 1944; 332d Fighter Group history for June 1944; account by Gwynne Peirson in *The East Coast Chapter Newsletter* for Tuskegee Airmen Incorporated, vol. 4, no. 8) The ship was probably the TA-22, which had been converted into a German torpedo boat from the captured Italian warship *Giuseppe Missori*. The 240-foot-long ship might have appeared to be a German destroyer. No other German warship was reported hit by Allied aircraft that day, and the time and place agree. The TA-22 suffered so much damage that it was permanently taken out of service. It was reported scuttled on May 3, 1945 off Trieste. (Jurgen Rohwer, *Chronology of the War at Sea, 1939–1945: The Naval History of World War II* [London: Chatham Publishing, 2005], 338; David Brown, *Warship Losses of World War II* [Annapolis: Naval Institute Press, 1990], 95, 114, 149, 182)

25 June: The 99th Fighter Squadron, still detached from the 332nd Fighter Group, flew its P-40s on two dive-bombing missions. (99th Fighter Squadron War Diary for June 1944)

25 June: The 99th Service Detachment of the 38th Service Group was disbanded, and most of its men, who were already at Ramitelli, were reassigned to the 366th Service Squadron. (366 Service Squadron history, Jun 1944) The detachment had once served with the 99th Fighter Squadron, which was now a part of the 332nd Fighter Group.

26 June: The 332d Fighter Group flew a bomber escort mission to the Lake Balaton area of Hungary. (332d Fighter Group mission report number 12) Capt. Andrew Maples Jr. and 1st Lt. Maurice V. Esters, both of the 301st Fighter Squadron, suffered engine failure or mechanical trouble, and bailed out of their P-47D airplanes. (Missing Air Crew Reports 7061 and 7062) On the same date, the first P-51s arrived at Ramitelli Air Field, Italy, home base of the 332nd Fighter Group. There were thirteen of them. (332nd Fighter Group history, June 1944)

26 June: Captain Thomas J. Collins became Commandant of Cadets at

Tuskegee Army Air Field, back in Alabama. (History of Tuskegee Army Air Field, Mar-Jun 1944, AFHRA call number 289.28-4, vol. 1)

26 June: The 99th Fighter Squadron in Italy, not yet flying with the 332nd Fighter Group, flew dive bombing missions against enemy railroad targets. (99th Fighter Squadron War Diary for June 1944)

27 June: The 332d Fighter Group escorted B-17 bombers of the 5th Bombardment Wing and B-24 bombers of the 47th Bombardment Wing to the Budapest area of Hungary and reported no losses. (332d Fighter Group mission report number 13) On the same date, eighteen more P-51 Mustangs arrived at Ramitelli. (332nd Fighter Group history, June 1944)

27 June: Class SE-44-F graduated from advanced single-engine pilot training at Tuskegee Army Air Field. There were 19 members of the class. On the same day, class TE-44-F graduated from advanced twin-engine pilot training at the same base. A total of 26 new black military pilots graduated at Tuskegee Army Air Field that day.

27 June: The 99th Fighter Squadron in Italy flew one mission, target not specified. (99th Fighter Squadron War Diary for June 1944)

28 June: The 332d Fighter Group escorted B-17 bombers of the 304th Bombardment Wing to the Ferdinand area. Lt. Edward Laird of the 100th Fighter Squadron crashed and was killed on takeoff. (332d Fighter Group mission report number 14) 2d Lt. Othel Dickson of the 301st Fighter Squadron was also killed in a crash that same day while on a transition mission. (332d Fighter Group history for June 1944)

28 June: The 99th Fighter Squadron received orders to move to Ramitelli Air Field, Italy, where the 332d Fighter Group was already based. The move did not take place immediately. (99th Fighter Squadron history, June 1944)

29 June: The 99th Fighter Squadron flew two combat missions, targeting enemy railroad cars. It was the last mission the squadron flew before it moved to Ramitelli. 2d Lt. Floyd A. Thompson of the 99th Fighter Squadron was hit by flak and bailed out of his plane near Spescia, Italy. He was listed as missing. (99th Fighter Squadron history, Jun 1944)

29–30 June: Anticipating its move to Ramitelli Air Field, where the rest of the 332nd Fighter Group was stationed, the 99th Fighter Squadron gave up its P-40 airplanes, sending 10 of them to the 324th Fighter Group (to which it was formerly attached), 9 to a replacement center at Capodichino Airfield, and the remainder to a service squadron. (99th Fighter Squadron history, Jun 1944)

30 June: The 332d Fighter Group escorted heavy bombers of the Fifteenth Air

Force to the Vienna area. (332d Fighter Group mission report number 15) This was the last P-47 mission of the 332nd Fighter Group. (B. O. Davis autobiography). Five of the bombers were shot down by enemy aircraft, but probably after the 332d Fighter Group's escort duty had finished. (Missing Air Crew Reports 6335, 6394, 6395, and 6396) On the same date, the 99th Fighter Squadron transferred most of its remaining P-40 fighter aircraft and prepared to move to Ramitelli Air Field, home of the 332d Fighter Group, to which it was assigned. (99 Fighter Squadron history, June 1944)

3 July: Major General Nathan Twining, commander of the Fifteenth Air Force, and Brigadier General Dean C. Strother, commander of the 306th Fighter Wing, visited the 332nd Fighter Group at Ramitelli. (332nd Fighter Group history, July 1944)

4 July: The 332d Fighter Group flew its first mission in the P-51 Mustang aircraft, which replaced the P-47s the group had been flying. (332d Fighter Group history, July 1944) The group was assigned to escort B-17s of the 5th Bombardment Wing and B-17s of the 47th Bombardment Wing, but the 332d Fighter Group and the bombers failed to rendezvous as planned. (332d Fighter Group mission report number 16)

5 July: The 332d Fighter Group escorted Fifteenth Air Force heavy bombers on their way to an enemy target. (332d Fighter Group mission report number 17)

5–6 July: The 99th Fighter Squadron moved from Orbetello, Italy, to Ramitelli Airfield, Italy, with the help of the 2236th Quartermaster Truck Company. Elements of the squadron spend the night outside Caserta, Italy. (332nd Fighter Group history, July 1944)

6 July: At Ramitelli, the 99th Fighter Squadron joined the rest of the 332d Fighter Group, which already included the 100th, 301st, and 302nd Fighter Squadrons. The 332nd Fighter Group was the only one with four fighter squadrons. The other fighter groups had only three. As a result, the 332d Fighter Group had more pilots and planes than any of the other fighter groups. (Maurer, *Combat Squadrons of the Air Force, World War II;* 332d Fighter Group History, July 1944; War Diary of 99th Fighter Squadron). Although the 99th Fighter Squadron had been assigned to the 332d Fighter Group since 1 May, it had flown combat missions while attached to other fighter groups stationed in other parts of Italy. (99th Fighter Squadron lineage and honors history; 332d Fighter Group history for July 1944) Other squadrons of the 332d Fighter Group escorted B-24 bombers of the 47th Bombardment Wing to Latisana and Tagilamento-Casarsa. (332d Fighter

Group mission report number 18)

7 July: The 332d Fighter Group failed to rendezvous with bombers of the Fifteenth Air Force, probably because the 332nd Fighter group followed plan B and the bombers followed plan A, which took them to Blechhammer, Germany, instead of Vienna, Austria, with a different rendezvous time. Apparently the 332nd Fighter Group did not receive the Fifteenth Air Force message to go with plan A. (332d Fighter Group mission report number 19 and Fifteenth Air Force mission folder for that day)

8 July: The 99th Fighter Squadron received its first P-51 Mustang aircraft, which was far superior to the P-40s it had flown in the past. (99th Fighter Squadron lineage and honors history; 332d Fighter Group History, July 1944; 99th Fighter Squadron War Diary) Other squadrons of the 332d Fighter Group escorted B-24 bombers of the 304th Bombardment Wing to, over, and from Muchendorf Airdrome. Enemy fighters were reported to have attacked the escorted bombers. The 332d Fighter Group mission report number 20 for that day noted "2 B-24s destroyed over target area. 1 B-24 seen to disintegrate, 2 chutes seen to open from 2nd B-24." These bomber losses are not confirmed by Missing Air Crew Reports. On the same date, Captain Cornelius Vincent Jr. became the 332nd Fighter Group S-2 officer, and began serving as the group's historian. (332nd Fighter Group history, July 1944)

9 July: The 332d Fighter Group flew its first mission to Ploesti, escorting B-24s of the 47th Bombardment Wing on a raid on important petroleum refining facilities. (332d Fighter Group mission report number 21) The same week, the XV Air Force Service Command was busy modifying P-51s to use P-47 fuel tanks and bombs. (XV Air Force Service Command, weekly activity report dated 9 Jul 1944)

10 July: Captain Mac Ross, who was one of the first five Tuskegee Airmen pilots, in the first graduating class at Tuskegee Army Air Field, and who had been the 332nd Fighter Group operations officer, was killed in a crash while on a local transition flight during the squadron's conversion from P-40 to P-51 aircraft. Captain Alfonza Davis replaced Ross as group operations officer. (332d Fighter Group history for July 1944)

11 July: The 332d Fighter Group flew its first mission over occupied France, escorting B-24 bombers of the 47th Bombardment Wing to, over, and from Toulon. (332d Fighter Group narrative mission report number 22) Meanwhile, Captain Leon C. Roberts of the 99th Fighter Squadron was killed in a crash on a transition flight as his squadron was converting from P-40 to

P-51 aircraft. Captain Roberts had been 99th Fighter Squadron operations officer, and had a total of 116 combat sorties. (332d Fighter Group history for July 1944)

12 July: The 332d Fighter Group escorted the B-24s of the 49th Bomb Wing to raid the marshalling yards at Nimes in southern France and downed four enemy airplanes. (332d Fighter Group mission report number 23; 332d Fighter Group history for July 1944) 1st Lt. Harold E. Sawyer shot down one FW-190 (the first 332d Fighter Group victory in the P-51 Mustang), while 1 Lt. Joseph Elsberry shot down three of them, earning a Distinguished Flying Cross for the achievement. (Fifteenth Air Force General Orders numbered 2032 and 2466, dated 23 Jul and 10 Aug 1944 respectively) Enemy airplanes shot down 3 of the escorted B-24s. (Missing Air Crew Reports 6894, 6895, and 7034; 461 Bombardment Group mission report for 12 July 1944; Fifteenth Air Force mission folder for 12 July 1944)

13 July: The 332d Fighter Group escorted two B-17 groups of the 5th Bombardment Wing to bomb the Pinzano railroad bridge and the Vinzone viaduct in northern Italy. (332d Fighter Group mission report number 24)

13 July: Six P-51s of the 332nd Fighter Group flew a mission to escort a Catalina flying boat to and over Lake Lesina, Italy, on an air-sea rescue mission. The mission failed to find any survivors. This mission was covered in the same narrative mission report that described the bomber escort mission of the same date.

14 July: A "rest camp for colored enlisted men," located between Termoli and Vasto, Italy, was expected to be in operation by 31 July 1944. (XV Air Force Service Command staff journal entry for 14 Jul 1944)

15 July: The 99th Fighter Squadron flew its first combat mission for the Fifteenth Air Force, and its first combat mission with the other three squadrons of the 332d Fighter Group. (332d Fighter Group History, July 1944; 99th Fighter Squadron War Diary) This was the second group mission to Ploesti. The 332d Fighter Group escorted B-24 bombers of the 55th Bombardment Group, and encountered enemy aircraft, but reported no losses that day. (332d Fighter Group mission report number 25)

16 July: The 332d Fighter Group conducted a fighter sweep in the Vienna area of Austria. (332d Fighter Group mission report number 26) Two Tuskegee Airmen shot down 2 enemy airplanes. The victors included 1st Lt. Alfonza W. Davis and 2d Lt. William W. Green Jr. (Fifteenth Air Force General Orders 2029 and 2030, both issued on 23 July 1944) They each earned a Distinguished Flying Cross for their heroic actions on this date. (Fifteenth

Air Force General Order 3541 dated 22 Sep 1944 and Fifteenth Air Force General Order 49 dated 3 Jan 1945)

17 July: 3 members of the 302d Fighter Squadron each shot down 1 Me-109 during a mission to escort B-24s of the 304th Bombardment Wing to Avignon, France. (332d Fighter Group mission report number 27) The victors included 1st Lts. Luther H. Smith Jr., Laurence D. Wilkins and 2d Lt. Robert H. Smith. All of the downed airplanes were ME-109s. (Fifteenth Air Force General Order 2350 dated 6 Aug 1944) For their heroic actions on this date, 1st Lts. Luther H. Smith and Laurence D. Wilkins, both of the 302nd Fighter Squadron, each earned a Distinguished Flying Cross. (Fifteenth Air Force General Order 5068 dated 18 Dec 1944 and Fifteenth Air Force General Order 49 dated 3 Jan 1945)

18 July: The 332d Fighter Group escorted B-17s of the 5th Bombardment Wing on a raid against an airfield at Memmingen, Germany. (332d Fighter Group mission report number 28) Nine Tuskegee Airmen shot down 12 enemy airplanes on this mission in air battles over northeastern Italy and then near the target. 2d Lt. Clarence Lester shot down 3 Me-109s, and 1st Lt. Jack D. Holsclaw shot down 2. Other victors that day included Capt Edward L. Toppins, 1st Lt. Charles P. Bailey and Weldon K. Groves, and 2d Lts Lee A. Archer, Walter J. A. Palmer, Roger Romine, and Hugh S. Warner. (Fifteenth Air Force General Orders 2202, 2350, and 2484, issued on 31 Jul 1944, 6 Aug 1944, and 11 Aug 1944, respectively; 332d Fighter Group history for July 1944) Three of the 332d Fighter Group P-51C pilots, including 2d Lt. Gene C. Browne and 2d Lt. Wellington G. Irving of the 301st Fighter Squadron, were shot down by enemy aircraft near the target area. (Missing Air Crew Reports 6973 and 7027 and 332d Fighter Group history for July 1944) Lieutenant Browne became a prisoner of war in Germany, but Lieutenant Irving was killed. P-51 pilot Lt. Oscar Hutton of the 100th Fighter Squadron was also reported lost that day. (332d Fighter Group narrative mission report 28) 21 of the 332d Fighter Group's fighters had returned to base after the air battle over northern Italy, leaving only 36 of the group's fighters to escort the bombardment groups of the 5th Bombardment Wing. Unfortunately, enemy aircraft shot down 15 of the B-17 bombers in the last two groups of the 5th Bombardment Wing to arrive in the Memmingen target area. (Missing Air Crew Reports 6856, 6953–6954, 6975–6981, 7097–7099, 7153, 7310; Fifteenth Air Force mission folder for 18 July 1944) For their heroism on the Memmingen mission this day, the following five members of the 332d Fighter Group each earned the Distinguished Flying Cross: 2nd Lt. Clarence D. Lester (100th Fighter Squadron); 1st Lt. Jack D. Holsclaw (100th Fighter Squadron); Capt. Andrew D. Turner (100th Fighter Squadron); 1st Lt. Walter J. A. Palmer (100th Fighter Squadron); and 1st Lt. Charles P. Bailey (99th Fighter Squadron). (Fifteenth Air Force General Order 3617 dated 6 Sep 1944; Fifteenth Air Force General Order 4009 dated 17 Oct 1944; Fifteenth Air Force General Order 654 dated 13 Feb 1945; Fifteenth Air Force General Order 3484 dated 29 May 1945) The order awarding Distinguished Flying Crosses to Lts. Lester and Holsclaw noted that the bomber formation they guarded was attacked by "300 enemy fighters" on this date. Given the very large number of bombers to escort and the very many enemy fighters that attacked them, relative to the number of escort fighters, it is understandable that many of the bombers were shot down by enemy aircraft. (Fifteenth Air Force General Order 3617 dated 6 Sep 1944)

19 July: The 332d Fighter Group escorted B-24 bombers of the 49th Bombardment Wing to Munich/Schleiszheim Airdrome. (332d Fighter Group mission report number 29)

20 July: The 332d Fighter Group escorted bombers to the Friedrichshafen area of Germany. (332d Fighter Group mission report number 30) Four Tuskegee Airmen shot down four Me-109s. The victors included Capts Joseph D. Elsberry, Armour G. McDaniel, and Edward L. Toppins, and 1st Lt. Langdon E. Johnson. Elsberry became the first Tuskegee Airmen to earn four aerial victory credits. (Fifteenth Air Force General Orders 2202, 2284, and 2484, dated 31 Jul 1944, 3 Aug 1944, and 11 Aug 1944, respectively) Unfortunately, two of the escorted B-24s were shot down by enemy aircraft. (Missing Air Crew Reports 6914 and 6919) The same day, 20 July 1944, the 332d Fighter Group flew two air-sea rescue missions over the Adriatic Sea. (332d Fighter Group mission reports numbered 31 and 32) Capt. Henry B. Perry of the 99th Fighter Squadron earned the Distinguished Flying Cross for his heroic actions on this date. (Fifteenth Air Force General Order 4993 dated 14 Dec 1944)

21 July: The 332d Fighter Group escorted B-17 bombers of the 5th Bombardment Wing home after they had bombed the Brux synthetic oil refinery in Bohemia (German-held Czechoslovakia). The group reported losing one pilot on the mission, Lt. William F. Williams of the 301st Fighter Squadron, near Linz, Austria. (332d Fighter Group mission report number 33 and 332d Fighter Group history for July 1944; Missing Air Crew Report number 6965)

22 July: The 332d Fighter Group escorted B-24 bombers of the 55th Bomb Wing to and from Ploesti, Rumania. (332d Fighter Group mission report number 34) 1st Lt. James Alonza Walker of the 302d Fighter Squadron was reported lost with his P-51C over the Kraljevo area of Yugoslavia, probably as a result of enemy antiaircraft artillery fire (Missing Air Crew Report 6852). He returned safely on 28 Aug 1944 after having evaded enemy forces in Yugoslavia. (Escape, Evasion, and Repatriation Reports, 332d Fighter Group)

24 July: The 332d Fighter Group escorted B-24 bombers of the 47th Bombardment Group on a raid to Genoa harbor in northwestern Italy. (332d Fighter Group mission report number 35)

25 July: Lt. Harold Sawyer of the 301st Fighter Squadron shot down 1 Me-109 German fighter during a mission to escort B-24s of the 55th Bombardment Wing to Linz, Austria. (332d Fighter Group mission report number 36; Fifteenth Air Force General Order 2284 dated 3 Aug 1944) For his heroic actions on this date, Capt. Sawyer earned the Distinguished Flying Cross. (Fifteenth Air Force General Order 4876 dated 5 Dec 1944) On the same mission, the 301st Fighter Squadron reported two of its pilots missing in action, Lieutenants Starling B. Penn and Lt. Alfred Q. Carrol. (332d Fighter Group history for July 1944)

25 July: 387 Service Group (later 387 Air Service Group) was activated at Daniel Field, Georgia, which ultimately became the "housekeeping" group to support the 477th Bombardment Group. It was composed of primarily black personnel, but the first commander, who served until 21 June 1945, was a white officer named Lt. Col. David H. Thomas. The 590th Air Materiel Squadron and the 602d Air Engineering Squadron were eventually assigned to the group. (387th Air Service Group organization record card and 387th Air Service Group history for the period 25 July-31 December 1944)

26 July: Four Tuskegee Airmen each shot down 1 Me-109 during a mission to escort B-24s of the 47th Bombardment Wing to Markendorf Airdrome. (332d Fighter Group mission report number 37) The victors included Capt Edward L. Toppins, 1st Lts Freddie E. Hutchins and Leonard M. Jackson, and 2d Lt. Roger Romine. (Fifteenth Air Force General Orders 2350 and 2482, dated 6 Aug 1944 and 11 Aug 1944, respectively) Toppins earned his fourth aerial victory credit that day. Unfortunately, 2d Lt. Charles S. Jackson Jr. of the 100th Fighter Squadron was reported lost that day with his P-51B after experiencing engine trouble 25 miles northwest of Zagreb, Yugoslavia. He bailed out. He later returned safely, on 27 August 1944, after evading enemy forces for more than a month. (Missing Air Crew Report 7007 and Escape, Evasion, and Repatriation Reports, 332d Fighter Group). The 332d Fighter Group mission report for that day also noted "1 B-24 spiraling out of formation after attack by enemy aircraft," but there is no corresponding Missing Air Crew Report for the bomber.

27 July: The 332d Fighter Group escorted B-24s of the 47th Bombardment Wing raiding an arms factory in the Budapest area of Hungary. (332d Fighter Group mission report number 38) North of Lake Balaton they encountered enemy aircraft and six Tuskegee Airmen shot down a total of 8 enemy airplanes. 1st Lt. Edward C. Gleed and 2d Lt. Alfred M. Gorham each shot down 2 FW-190s. Other victors, who each shot down one Me-109, included Capt Claude B. Govan, 1st Lts Leonard M. Jackson and Felix J. Kirkpatrick, and 2d Lt. Richard W. Hall. (Fifteenth Air Force General Orders 2284, 2350, 2484, and 2485, dated 3 Aug 1944, 6 Aug 1944, 11 Aug 1944, and 11 Aug 1944, respectively) 2d Lt. Emory L. Robbins Jr. of the 302d Fighter Squadron was reported missing that day with his P-51C in the area of the air combat (Missing Air Crew Report 7151). 1st Lt. Edward C. Gleed earned the Distinguished Flying Cross for his heroism on this date. (Fifteenth Air Force General Order 3106 dated 4 Sep 1944)

28 July: The 332d Fighter Group escorted B-24 bombers of the 55th Bombardment Wing to, over, and from Ploesti, Rumania. Three B-24s were seen to go down in flames. (332d Fighter Group mission report number 39) The bomber losses are not confirmed by corresponding Missing Air Crew Reports.

28 July: Captain Ranz of the 11th Air Depot Group telephoned XV Air Force Service Command headquarters asking the command's policy regarding "white and colored E.M. [enlisted men] attending the same dance at the group club. He was informed that "the policy of this command is no discrimination" and the no was underlined. (XV Air Force Service Command staff journal dated 28 July 1944.)

30 July: 2d Lt. Carl Johnson shot down an enemy airplane during a mission to escort B-17 bombers of the 5th Bombardment Wing to Budapest, Hungary. (332d Fighter Group mission report number 40; Fifteenth Air Force General Order 2485 dated 11 Aug 1944)

July: During the month of July 1944, members of the 332d Fighter Group and its squadrons shot down 39 enemy aircraft, more for them than in any other month of the war.

August: During the month, Lt. Edward Gleed was promoted to captain and named operations officer of the 332d Fighter Group in place of Captain Alfonza Davis, who became the group's deputy commander. Major George S. Roberts, who had been in the first class of pilot graduates from Tuskegee

Army Air Field, who had served as commander of the 99th Fighter Squadron, and who had returned to the United States in April 1944 to take part in War Bond fund drives, arrived at Ramitelli Air Field, Italy, to serve the 332nd Fighter Group. (332nd Fighter Group history, August 1944). During the same month, August 1944, Roscoe Brown arrived at Ramitelli, and was assigned to the 100th Fighter Squadron. He would later be one of the three Tuskegee Airmen who shot down German jet aircraft. Capt. Ray B. Ware succeeded Capt. Cornelius Vincent Jr. as 332nd Fighter Group historian. (332nd Fighter Group history, August 1944)

2 August: The 332d Fighter Group escorted B-17s of the 5th Bombardment Wing to bomb Le Pousin Oil Storage and Portes Le Valences, France. The 332d Fighter Group mission report for that day (number 42) noted that "Formation of bombers was spread out over area of approximately 50 miles . . . It was impossible to cover all groups or afford desired protection from E/A (enemy aircraft)."

3 August: The 332d Fighter Group again escorted B-17 bombers of the 5th Bombardment Wing, this time to raid Ober Raderach Chemical Works in Germany. Although four Me-109s were seen in the Udine area on the way, the group reported no encounters and no attacks on the bombers. (332d Fighter Group mission report number 43)

3 August: Twelve black officers led by Captain Willard B. Ransom entered the west dining room of the Tuskegee Army Air Field post exchange restaurant, which had been reserved for white officers, and demanded service. When 2nd Lt. George D Frye, Assistant Exchange Officer, asked the black officers to go to the larger east dining room reserved for them, Captain Ransom showed Frye two War Department letters that noted service at base recreational facilities and post exchanges would not be denied any personnel because of race. With Col. Noel Parrish's support, Lt. Frye agreed to let the black officers be served in the west dining room, effectively integrating the restaurant without violence. Many white officers stopped eating at the facility. The elimination rate for black cadets increased. Some white officers asked for transfers, and within two months, Tuskegee Army Air Field received its first black flight instructors. Col. Parrish assured the white leadership of nearby towns that integration of the base facilities would not affect areas outside the base. Parrish's handling of the integration crisis at Tuskegee Army Air Field contrasted sharply with the later Freeman Field Mutiny of April 1945. (History of Tuskegee Army Air Field, 1 July to 31 August 1944, 12–15, call number 289.28-5 at the Air Force Historical Research Agency)

4 August: A total of 37 new black military pilots graduated from advanced pilot training at Tuskegee Army Air Field. Twenty-three of them belonged to class SE-44-G, for single-engine pilots, and fourteen belonged to class TE-44-G, for twin-engine pilots. The single engine pilots would go on to fly fighter aircraft, while the twin-engine pilots would go on to fly medium bombers.

6 August: The 332d Fighter Group escorted B-24 bombers of the 55th Bombardment Wing to the Avignon area of southern France. (332d Fighter Group mission report number 44) One B-24 was shot down by enemy antiaircraft artillery fire.

6 August: The 332d Fighter Group flew a second mission on 6 August, this time to escort a single B-25 over Yugoslavia. (332d Fighter Group mission report number 45)

6 August: The Enlisted Men's Club building opened at Ramitelli Air Field. It was named "Club Exotic." (366 Service Squadron history, Aug 1944)

7 August: The 332d Fighter Group escorted B-24s of the 55th Bombardment Wing and B-17s of the 5th Bombardment Wing to raid enemy oil refineries at Blechhammer. One Me-109 dove through the bombers during the raid. Bombers were shot down that day, but after the 332d Fighter Group had finished escorting them. (332d Fighter Group mission report number 46 and Missing Air Crew Reports for 7 August 1944) Lt. Alfred Gorham of the 301st Fighter Squadron, 332nd Fighter Group, got lost while returning from the Blechhammer mission. After dark, he attempted to land at Lesina Airfield, home of the 325th Fighter Group not far from Ramitelli, but the field was not equipped with airfield lights. Gorham undershot the runway and crashed into a Lake Lesina. The P-51 caught fire when it hit the water, but Gorham survived. (Aircraft accident report 45–8–7–527 at Air Force Historical Research Agency)

9 August: The 332d Fighter Group escorted B-17s of the 5th Bomb Wing on a mission to Gyor, Hungary. (332d Fighter Group mission report number 47) 2d Lt. Alphonso Simmons of the 100th Fighter Squadron was reported missing with his P-51C about 10 miles south of Banja Luka, Yugoslavia (Missing Air Crew Report 7327). He evaded enemy forces in Yugoslavia for almost a month, returning on 8 September 1944. (Escape, Evasion, and Repatriation Reports, 332d Fighter Group)

9 August: Back in Alabama, Tuskegee Army Air Field held a third anniversary celebration, which was filmed and broadcast. Part of the celebration film footage was later used in the film *Wings for This Man*, a War Department public relations movie. (History of Tuskegee Army Air Field, Jul-Aug 1944,

AFHRA call number 289.28-5)

10 August: The 332d Fighter Group escorted B-24 bombers of the 304th Bombardment Wing against the Campina Stevea Romana Oil Refineries. (332d Fighter Group mission report number 48)

12 August: The 332d Fighter Group attacked radar stations in southern France on a strafing mission in preparation for the Allied invasion of southern France (scheduled for 15 August). (332d Fighter Group mission report number 49) 1st Lt. Langdon E. Johnson of the 100th Fighter Squadron was seen crashing into the Mediterranean Sea with his P-51C that day after being hit by flak, in the area 10 miles southeast of Marseilles, France (Missing Air Crew Report 7469 and 332d Fighter Group history for August 1944). Other 332d Fighter Group P-51 pilots reported shot down that day included Lieutenants Alexander Jefferson, Robert Daniels Jr., Richard Macon, and Joseph Gordon. (332d Fighter Group history for August 1944; Don Dodd and Amy Bartlett-Dodd, *Deep South Aviation*, 98) Lieutenants Jefferson, Daniels, and Macon all became prisoners of war in Germany. (Alexander Jefferson, *Red Tail Captured, Red Tail Free*) Lt. Gordon did not survive. (American Battle Monuments Commission). For their heroic actions on this date, the following six members of the 332d Fighter Group each earned the Distinguished Flying Cross: Capt. Lee Rayford (301st Fighter Squadron); Capt. Woodrow W. Crockett (100th Fighter Squadron); Capt. William T. Mattison (100th Fighter Squadron); 1st Lt. Freddie E. Hutchins (302nd Fighter Squadron); 1st Lt. Lawrence B. Jefferson (301st Fighter Squadron); and 1st Lt. Lowell C. Steward (100th Fighter Squadron). (Fifteenth Air Force General Order 5068 dated 18 Dec 1944; Fifteenth Air Force General Order 49 dated 3 Jan 1945; Fifteenth Air Force General Order 231 dated 15 Jan 1945)

13 August: The 332d Fighter Group escorted B-24s of the 304th Bombardment Wing on a mission to destroy railroad bridges in the vicinity of Avignon in southern France. (332d Fighter Group mission report number 50)

14 August: 2d Lt. George M. Rhodes Jr. of the 100th Fighter Squadron shot down 1 FW-190 enemy fighter during a strafing and fighter sweep mission in the Toulon area. (Fifteenth Air Force General Order 2831 dated 25 Aug 1944) 2d Lt. Robert O'Neil of the 100th Fighter Squadron was last seen in a spin over the Toulon area, and Lt. Allen was reported to have bailed out safely over the island of Elba. (332d Fighter Group mission report number 51 and 332d Fighter Group history for August 1944) O'Neil eventually returned to his unit after having evaded enemy forces in France for almost two weeks. (Escape, Evasion, and Repatriation Reports, 332d Fighter Group).

The strafing mission was in preparation for the Allied invasion of southern France. For their heroic actions on this date, the following four members of the 332nd Fighter Group each earned a Distinguished Flying Cross: Capt. Melvin T. Jackson (302nd Fighter Squadron); 1st Lt. Gwynne W. Pierson (302nd Fighter Squadron); Capt. Arnold W. Cisco (301st Fighter Squadron); and Capt. Alton F. Ballard (301st Fighter Squadron). (Fifteenth Air Force General Order 3689 dated 29 Sep 1944; Fifteenth Air Force General Order 287 dated 19 Jan 1945; Fifteenth Air Force General Order 839 dated 21 Feb 1945; Fifteenth Air Force General Order 1153 dated 5 Mar 1945)

15 August: The Allies invaded German-occupied southern France, and the 332d Fighter Group escorted the 55th Bombardment Wing to hit targets in southern France. (332d Fighter Group mission report number 52) Two Me-109 enemy airplanes were seen, but they did not appear to attack the bomber formation and were too distant for interception. One 332d Fighter Group pilot, Lt. Wilson V. Eagleson, was reported missing.

16 August: The 332d Fighter Group escorted B-24s of the 55th Bomb Wing on a mission to bomb the Ober Raderach Chemical Works in Germany. (332d Fighter Group mission report number 53) P-51C pilot 1st Lt. Herbert V. Clark of the 99th Fighter Squadron was shot down by enemy antiaircraft artillery over Italy that day (Missing Air Crew Report 7691 and 332d Fighter Group history for August 1944). He survived and returned in May 1945 after evading enemy forces in Italy for more than eight months. (Escape, Evasion, and Repatriation Reports, 332d Fighter Group)

17 August: The 332d Fighter Group escorted B-24 heavy bombers of the 304th Bombardment Wing to, over, and from Ploesti's oil refineries in Rumania. (332d Fighter Group mission report number 54) Nine bombers were shot down, according to Missing Air Crew Reports for that day, but the reason given was enemy antiaircraft artillery fire.

17 August: Back in the United States, a cadet named Edward S. Bishop stationed at Tuskegee Army Air Field in Alabama crashed in an AT-6C training aircraft near Roswell, Georgia. (Aircraft record card for aircraft serial number 42–48883, provided by Archangelo Difante)

18 August: The 332d Fighter Group returned to Ploesti a second day in a row, this time to escort B-17s of the 5th Bombardment Wing. No losses were reported. (332d Fighter Group mission report number 55)

19 August: The 332d Fighter Group completed its eighth mission escorting bombers to Ploesti, Rumania, and its third in a row to that target. That was its last mission to that target during the war. This time the group escorted

B-24 bombers of the 47th Bombardment Wing. Lt. Thomas was reported to have crash landed on Pianosa Island, but was reported safe. (332d Fighter Group mission report number 56 and 332d Fighter Group history for August 1944)

19 August: Back at Tuskegee Army Air Field, fourteen black officers entered a section of a dining facility reserved for white officers, and demanded service. They were served, but white officers complained to the field's commander, Col. Noel Parrish. Parrish reluctantly refused to restore segregation at the dining facility because such an action would have violated a 1940 War Department regulation entitling all officers at an Army base to use its facilities. (Benjamin O. Davis Jr., *Benjamin O. Davis, Jr., American* [Washington: Smithsonian Institution Press, 1991], 129.)

20 August: The 332d Fighter Group escorted B-17 heavy bombers of the 5th Bombardment Wing to raid the Oswiecim Oil Refinery. The mission encountered some sixteen Me-109 and FW-190 enemy fighter airplanes, but did not report any attack on the bombers. (332d Fighter Group narrative mission report number 57)

22 August: the 332d Fighter Group escorted B-24s of the 55th Bombardment Wing to, over, and from the Korneuburg Oil Refineries in Vienna, Austria. (332d Fighter Group mission report number 58) They encountered enemy Me-109 fighters over Lake Balaton in Hungary. According to Missing Air Crew Reports for that day, two bombers were lost on the mission, one to enemy antiaircraft artillery, and one to an unknown cause. The 332d Fighter Group flew a second mission on this day, this time to provide escort cover for six C-47s over Yugoslavia. (332d Fighter Group mission report number 59) Those C-47s apparently carried former prisoners of war, most of them American airmen, from Yugoslavia to Italy, and at least three other fighter groups of the Fifteenth Air Force, besides the 332d, were also assigned to escort them. On the same day, the 96th Air Service Group moved from Foggia to Iesi (Jesi), Italy. (Lineage and honors history of the 96th Logistics Group)

22 August: In the afternoon, Staff Sergeant Joe Louis, the heavyweight boxing champion of the world, visited Ramitelli Air Field, home of the only black Army Air Forces flying units in combat. (366 Service Squadron history, Aug 1944)

23 August: Flight Officer William L. Hill of the 302d Fighter Squadron shot down 1 Me-109 during a mission to escort B-24 bombers of the 55th Bombardment Wing to Markersdorf Airdrome, Germany. (332d Fighter Group mission report number 60; Fifteenth Air Force General Order 3538 dated

21 Sep 1944) Fourteen enemy Me-109 fighters were encountered in the target area. The mission report also noted "1 B-24 seen to go down in flames in T/A (target area)." There was no corresponding Missing Air Crew Report.

24 August: Three Tuskegee Airmen each shot down an enemy aircraft during a mission to escort B-17s of the 5th Bombardment Wing to Pardubice Airdrome, Czechoslovakia. (332d Fighter Group mission report number 61) The victors included 1st Lts. Charles E. McGee and William H. Thomas, who each shot down a FW-190, and 1st Lt. John F. Briggs, who shot down an Me-109. (Fifteenth Air Force General Orders 3153, 3174, and 449, dated 6 Sep 1944, 7 Sep 1944, and 31 Jan 1945, respectively) Enemy aircraft shot down one of the escorted B-17 bombers after flak had crippled it and forced it to drop out of the formation (Missing Air Crew Report 7971). 1st Lt. John F. Briggs of the 100th Fighter Squadron and 1st Lt. William H. Thomas of the 302nd Fighter Squadron each earned a Distinguished Flying Cross for their heroic actions on this date. (Fifteenth Air Force General Order 49 dated 3 Jan 1945 and Fifteenth Air Force General Order 449 dated 31 Jan 1945)

25 August: The 332d Fighter Group escorted B-17s of the 5th Bombardment Wing on a raid against Brno Airdrome. Four enemy Me-109 aircraft were seen on the mission, but there was no apparent aerial combat. (332d Fighter Group mission report number 62) 2d Lt. Robert O'Neil, who was reported Missing in Action on 14 August, returned after having evaded enemy forces in France for eleven days. French partisans had helped him remain hidden from the Germans, and helped him get back to his unit. (332nd Fighter Group history, August 1944; Escape and evasion reports give the date as 26 August for the return)

26 August: The 332d Fighter Group provided close escort to B-24 bombers of the 304th Bombardment Wing to Banasea Airdrome. 2d Lt. Henry A. Wise is reported to have bailed out of his P-51 during the mission, and to have landed safely near Krujino, Yugoslavia. (332d Fighter Group mission report number 63; 332d Fighter Group history for August 1944)

27 August: While returning from a mission to escort B-24s of the 304th and 55th Bombardment Wings to Blechhammer, Germany, units of the 332d Fighter Group attacked airfields in Czechoslovakia, destroying 22 enemy aircraft on the ground. (332d Fighter Group mission report number 64) On the same day, 2d Lt. Charles S. Jackson returned safely after evading enemy forces in Yugoslavia for more than a month. (Escape, Evasion, and Repatriation Reports, 332d Fighter Group). For heroic actions on this date, the following three members of the 332nd Fighter Group each earned the Distinguished Flying Cross: Capt. Wendell O. Pruitt (302nd Fighter Squadron); Capt. Dudley M. Watson (302nd Fighter Squadron); 1st Lt. Roger Romine (302d Fighter Squadron). (Fifteenth Air Force General Order 3950 dated 15 Oct 1944; Fifteenth Air Force General Order 4009 dated 17 Oct 1944; Fifteenth Air Force General Order 5068 dated 18 Dec 1944)

28 August: The 332d Fighter Group escorted B-24s of the 47th Bombardment Wing against Miskolc Min marshalling yards. (332d Fighter Group mission report number 65) On the same day, 1st Lt. James Alonza Walker, who had been reported missing in action on 22 July 1944, returned safely after having evaded enemy forces in Yugoslavia for more than a month. (Escape, Evasion, and Repatriation Reports, 332d Fighter Group). Lt. Charles S. Jackson also returned to the group, after having been shot down over Yugoslavia on 26 August. (332nd Fighter Group history, July 1944)

29 August: The 332d Fighter Group were assigned to escort B-17s of the 5th Bombardment Wing to, over, and from Bohumin, Privoser, and Morvaska Main. (332d Fighter Group mission report number 66) The bombers were early, and when the 332nd Fighter Group finally caught up with them at about 1100 hours near the target, enemy fighters had already shot down nine of the B-17s of the 2nd Bombardment Group and were departing the scene. On the mission, 2d Lt. Emile G. Clifton Jr. of the 99th Fighter Squadron bailed out of his P-51B after losing coolant while flying over the area of Zgon, Yugoslavia. (332d Fighter Group mission report 66; Missing Air Crew Report 8101; 332d Fighter Group history for July 1944) Clifton returned on 9 September 1944 after successfully evading enemy forces in Italy for eleven days. (Escape, Evasion, and Repatriation Reports, 332d Fighter Group)

30 August: The 332d Fighter Group strafed Grosswardein Airdrome in Rumania and claimed to have destroyed 83 enemy aircraft on the ground and to have damaged another 31. (332d Fighter Group mission report number 67 and its supplement) 2d Lt. Charles T. Williams of the 301st Fighter Squadron was reported lost with his P-51 over Yugoslavia during the mission (Missing Air Crew Report 8332). He became a prisoner of war. Capt. Clarence H. Bradford of the 301st Fighter Squadron earned the Distinguished Flying Cross for his heroic actions on this date. (Fifteenth Air Force General Order 1811 dated 27 Mar 1945)

31 August: The 332d Fighter Group escorted B-17s of the second wave of 5th Bombardment Wing bombers to and over Popesti Airdrome. (332d Fighter Group mission report number 68) On a second mission that day, fighters of the 332d Fighter Group escorted B-17s of the third wave to Popesti

Airdrome. (332d Fighter Group mission report number 69) These bombers were not on a bombing mission, but on an air evacuation mission, to carry former prisoners of war out of Rumania to Italy. The B-17s had been modified temporarily to serve as troop transports for this special series of missions. The same day the 366th and 367th Service Squadrons at Ramitelli and Vasta were redesignated as the 366th and 367th Air Service Squadrons. They were still assigned to the 96th Air Service Group, headquartered in Foggia. (Organization record cards of the three organizations)

Late August: Major Feetwood M. McCoy, president of the Tuskegee Army Air Field Officers' Club, announced that the club would donate all of the funds it had left over at the end of the war to the Negro College Fund and the National Association for the Advancement of Colored People (NAACP). Half of the money would go to each. (*Hawk's Cry*, vol. III, no. 34, dated 26 Aug 1944)

1 September: The 332d Fighter Group escorted B-17s of the 5th Bombardment Wing to Popesti for a second day (332d Fighter Group mission report number 70), for a continuation of the air evacuation of former prisoners of war from Rumania to Italy. On the same day, Major George S. Roberts replaced Captain Erwin B. Lawrence Jr. as commander of the 99th Fighter Squadron. Major Roberts had commanded the squadron twice previously, and had been the first black commander of the squadron. (99th Fighter Squadron lineage and honors history)

31 August and 1 September: The 332d Fighter Group, along with five other fighter groups of the Fifteenth Air Force, escorted more than 50 B-17s bombers of the 5th Bombardment Wing's 2d and 97th Bombardment Groups that flew to Rumania's Popesti Airdrome to carry more than 1,000 American airmen who had been held as prisoners of war from Rumania to Italy. Operation Reunion, as it was called, involved B-17s that had been modified to carry up to 20 personnel each in their bomb bays.

September: Back at Tuskegee Army Air Field in Alabama, a Basic Instructors School was set up to train black flying instructors who had served in the primary flying training phase at Moton Field to become flight instructors in the basic flight training phase at Tuskegee Army Air Field. (History of Tuskegee Army Air Field, Nov–Dec 1944, AFHRA call number 289.28–7)

2 September: the 332d Fighter Group conducted a strafing mission to Stalac, Cuprija, and Osipaonica Road in Yugoslavia. (332d Fighter Group mission report number 71)

3 September: The 332d Fighter Group escorted B-24 bombers of the 304th

Bombardment Wing to Szolnok and Szeged, Hungary. (332d Fighter Group mission report number 72) On the same day, Brig. Gen. Yantis H. Taylor replaced Brigadier General Dean C. Strother as commander of the 306th Fighter Wing, under which had served the seven fighter squadrons (6 white and 1 black) of the XV Fighter Command of the Fifteenth Air Force. Strother at the same time became commander of the new XV Fighter Command. At the same time, the Fifteenth Air Force organized a provisional 305th Fighter Wing, which assumed management of the three P-38 groups, while the 306th Fighter Wing retained direct control of the four P-51 fighter groups, including the 332d. (Maurer, *Air Force Combat Units of World War II*; Organization record card of 305 Fighter Wing (P))

4 September: The 332d Fighter Group escorted B-24 bombers of the 304th Bombardment Wing again, this time to Tagliamento Casarsa and Latisana, Italy. (332d Fighter Group mission report number 73)

5 September: The 332d Fighter Group escorted B-17s of the 5th Bombardment Wing to Budapest, Hungary, and back. (332d Fighter Group mission report number 74)

6 September: The 332d Fighter Group escorted B-17s of the 5th Bombardment Wing for a second day in a row, but this time to the Oradea Main marshalling yards in Rumania. (332d Fighter Group mission report number 75)

7 September: the 67th AAF Base Unit took the place of the Tuskegee Weather Detachment at Tuskegee Army Air Field. (History of Tuskegee Army Air Field, Jul-Aug 1944, AFHRA call number 289.28-5 and organization record card)

8 September: The 332d Fighter Group claimed to have destroyed 36 enemy airplanes on the ground at two airfields during a strafing mission to Yugoslavia. P-51 pilot Lt. James A. Calhoun crashed and was killed in the target area. (332d Fighter Group narrative mission report 76; Missing Air Crew Report 8261; American Battle Monuments Commission) 2d Lt. Alphonso Simmons, who went Missing in Action on 9 August 1944, returned after having evaded enemy forces in Yugoslavia for a month. (Escape, Evasion, and Repatriation Reports, 332d Fighter Group). Maj. George S. Roberts of the 332d Fighter Group and 1st Lt. Heber C. Houston of the 99th Fighter Squadron each earned a Distinguished Flying Cross for his heroic actions on this date. (Fifteenth Air Force General Order 137 dated 8 Jan 1945; Fifteenth Air Force General Order 3484 dated 29 May 1945)

8 September: Thirty-two new black military pilots graduated from advanced pilot training at Tuskegee Army Air Field. Twenty-three of them belonged

Brig. Gen. Benjamin O. Davis Sr., first African American general in the U.S. Army, pinning a Distinguished Flying Cross on his son, Col. Benjamin O. Davis Jr., at a ceremony in September 1944. The younger Davis later became the first African American USAF general.

to class SE-44-H, for single-engine pilots destined to fly fighters, and nine of them belonged to class TE-44-H, for twin-engine pilots destined to fly medium bombers.

10 September: Lt. Gen. Ira C. Eaker, commander of the Mediterranean Allied Air Force; Maj. Gen. Nathan F. Twining, commander of the Fifteenth Air Force; Brig. Gen. Dean C. Strother, commander of the XV Fighter Command; and Brig. Gen. Benjamin O. Davis Sr., Inspector General's Department, attended an impressive awards ceremony for members of the 332d Fighter Group at Ramitelli Airfield in Italy. At that ceremony, General Davis presented the Distinguished Flying Cross to his son, Colonel Benjamin O. Davis Jr., commander of the group, for an escort mission he led on 9 June 1944. (332d Fighter Group history, Oct 1942–1947; 332d Fighter Group history, September 1944) The elder Davis was the first black general in the U.S. Army, and Captain Joseph D. Elsberry, Lieutenant Jack D.

Holsclaw, and Lieutenant Clarence D. "Lucky" Lester were also awarded Distinguished Flying Crosses in the same ceremony that day. Elsberry was recognized for shooting down three enemy aircraft on 12 July 1944 on a mission over France; Lester was honored for shooting down three enemy aircraft on 18 July 1944 on an escort mission to Memmingen; Holsclaw was honored for shooting down two enemy aircraft on the 18 July 1944 mission to Memmingen. (Benjamin O. Davis Jr., *Benjamin O. Davis, Jr, American* Washington: Smithsonian Institution Press, 1991)

12 September: The 332d Fighter Group escorted B-17 bombers of the 5th Bombardment Wing on a mission to an unspecified target. The group mission report states "10 Me 109s attacked rear of bomber formation from below . . . 1 B-17 was left burning. 6 chutes seen to open." (332d Fighter Group mission report number 77) The 301st and 463d Bombardment Groups of the 5th Bombardment Wing each reported a bomber lost. (Fifteenth Air Force daily mission folder for 12 September 1944) Missing Air Crew Reports do not confirm these bombers were lost to enemy aircraft. Members of the 332d Fighter Group claimed to have damaged 4 enemy aircraft during the mission.

13 September: The 332d Fighter Group escorted B-24 and B-17 bombers of the 304th and 5th Bombardment Wings to Blechhammer North Oil Refinery. The mission report notes "Two B-24s hit by flak seen to explode and crash. No chutes seen." Lt. Wilbur Long and his P-51 were reported missing near Szombathely. (332d Fighter Group mission report number 78; Missing Air Crew Report 8626) Lt. Long became a prisoner of war in Germany. (Jefferson, *Red Tail Captured, Red Tail Free*)

17 September: The 332d Fighter Group escorted B-17s of the 5th Bombardment Wing to raid the Rakos marshalling yards of north Budapest, Hungary. (332d Fighter Group mission report number 79)

18 September: The 332d Fighter Group escorted B-24 bombers of the 304th Bombardment Wing to raid the Shell Oil Refinery and railroad bridges in Budapest, Hungary. The group reported seeing a B-24 hit by flak in the target area, and 7 men parachuting from it. (332d Fighter Group mission report number 80)

20 September: The 332d Fighter Group escorted B-24s of the 304th Bombardment Wing again, this time to attck the Makacky Airdrome in Czechoslovakia. (332d Fighter Group mission report number 81)

21 September: The 332d Fighter Group escorted B-17 bombers of the 5th Bombardment Wing to raid the Debreczen Marshalling Yards in Hungary.

(332d Fighter Group mission report number 82)

22 September: The 332d Fighter Group escorted B-17 bombers of the 5th Bomb Wing to hit the Allach BMW Engine Works in Munich, Germany. (332d Fighter Group mission report number 83) Flight Officer Leonard R. Willette of the 99th Fighter Squadron and his P-51 were reported lost near Lake Chien, Germany, on the mission. (Missing Air Crew Report 8947)

23 September: The 332d Fighter Group escorted B-17s of the 5th Bombardment Wing to bomb the Brux synthetic oil plant. (332d Fighter Group mission report number 84)

24 September: The 332d Fighter Group escorted B-24 bombers of the 304th Bombardment Wing as they raided enemy targets in Athens, Greece. (332d Fighter Group mission report number 85)

24 September: Twenty-two black officers training to be bombardiers at Midland Army Air Field, Texas, (most of whom were already navigators) signed a letter to the Inspector General of the War Department protesting a racial discrimination policy that forbid them from using the base Officer's Club and requiring them to use a segregated section of the Officer's cafeteria. They demanded the base policy be changed to conform to Army regulations. Nine of the black officers who signed the letter were later arrested in the "Freeman Field Mutiny" in Indiana in April 1945, which also involved resistance to segregation on Army Air Force installations. The nine were: Robert Payton, Coleman Young, Carl O. Roach, Roger V. Pines, Marcel Clyne, Glen L. Head, Leonard E. Williams, Edward V. Hipps, and James C. Warren.

Late September: A new Basic Instructor School opened at Tuskegee Army Air Field, designed to train black pilots to teach basic flying training at the field. Some of the first graduates had taught primary flight training at Moton Field.

Autumn: During this time period, 1st Lt. Willie Fuller, a veteran pilot with 76 combat missions with the 99th Fighter Squadron overseas, became the first black flight instructor in the advanced single-engine flying school at Tuskegee Army Air Field, and remained the only black flight instructor in that phase through the end of December 1944. Captain James T. Wiley became the first black flight instructor in the advanced twin engine flying school at Tuskegee Army Air Field, and remained the only black flight instructor in that phase through the end of the year. Flight Officers James O. Plinton Jr. and Adolph J. Moret Jr. became the first black flight instructors in the basic flying training school at Tuskegee Army Air Field. Three other black pilots began working as instructors in the fighter transition school at the same field. By the end of the year, there were seven black flying instructors at Tuskegee Army Air Field, and more were on the way. (Histories of Tuskegee Army Air Field, Sep–Oct 1944 and Nov–Dec 1944, call numbers 289.28–6 and 289.28–7 at the Air Force Historical Research Agency)

4 October: The 332d Fighter Group took part in three missions, two to escort C-47 transport aircraft to Sofia, Bulgaria and Bucharest, Rumania, and one to strafe targets in Tatoi, Kalamaki, and Eleusis, Greece. In Greece, the group reported destroying 9 enemy aircraft on the ground. Captains Erwin B. Lawrence and Kenneth I. Williams, both of the 99th Fighter Squadron, were reported lost or missing in the Athens area on the mission to Greece. (332d Fighter Group mission reports numbered 86, 87, and 88; Missing Air Crew Reports 8981 and 8982) For their heroic actions on this date, the following five members of the 332d Fighter Group each earned the Distinguished Flying Cross: 1st Lt. Samuel L. Curtis (100th Fighter Squadron); 1st Lt. Dempsey Morgan (100th Fighter Squadron); Capt. Claude B. Govan (301st Fighter Squadron); 1st Lt. Herman A. Lawson (99th Fighter Squadron); 1st Lt. Willard L. Woods (100th Fighter Squadron). (Fifteenth Air Force General Order 158 dated 10 Jan 1945; Fifteenth Air Force General Order 231 dated 15 Jan 1945; Fifteenth Air Force General Order 255 dated 16 Jan 1945; Fifteenth Air Force General Order 449 dated 31 Jan 1945)

6 October: The 332d Fighter Group strafed enemy airdromes in Tatoi, Kalamaki, Eleusis, and Megara Airdromes in Greece, similar to the mission two days earlier. (332d Fighter Group mission report number 89) This was in preparation for the Allied invasion of Greece. Four 332d Fighter Group pilots were reported missing on this mission, including 1st Lt. Freddie E. Hutchins of the 302d Fighter Squadron, who was seen to crash about 3 miles west of Megara after the explosion of an ammunition dump; 1st Lt. Carroll S. Woods of the 100th Fighter Squadron, whose P-51 was seen flaming in the area of Kalamaki Airdrome; 2d Lt. Joe A. Lewis of the 301st Fighter Squadron, who was seen to crash near Athens after being hit by antiaircraft artillery fire; and 2d Lt. Andrew D. Marshall of the 301st Fighter Squadron. (Missing Air Crew reports 8980, 8983, and 9035) Marshall returned on 14 October 1944 after evading enemy forces in Greece for eight days. Hutchins also returned from Greece, but not until 25 October. (Escape, Evasion, and Repatriation Reports, 332d Fighter Group). For their heroic actions on this date, the following five members of the 332d Fighter Group each earned a Distinguished Flying Cross: 1st Lt. Alva N. Temple (99th Fighter Squadron); Capt. Lawrence E. Dickson (100th Fighter Squadron); 1st Lt. Edward M. Thomas (99th Fighter Squadron); 1st Lt. Robert L. Martin (100th Fighter Squadron); and Capt. Robert J. Friend (301st Fighter Squadron). (Fifteenth Air Force General Order 231 dated 15 Jan 1945; Fifteenth Air Force General Order 287 dated 19 Jan 1945; Fifteenth Air Force General Order 517 dated 6 Feb 1945; Fifteenth Air Force General Order 839 dated 21 Feb 1945; Fifteenth Air Force General Order 1811 dated 27 Mar 1945)

7 October: The 332d Fighter Group returned to escorting bombers, this time protecting B-17s of the 5th Bombardment Wing on a raid against the Lobau Oil Refineries at Vienna, Austria. Lieutenant Robert Wiggins, 2d Lt. Roosevelt Stiger of the 302d Fighter Squadron and Flight Officer Carl J. Woods of the 100th Fighter Squadron were reported lost on this mission. Stiger and Woods were last seen over the Adriatic Sea. (Missing Air Crew Reports 9029 and 9034) One B-17 was reported hit at 30,000 feet, but there is no corresponding Missing Air Crew Report. (332d Fighter Group mission report number 90)

7 October: Back in Alabama, Tuskegee Army Air Field's football team, the Warhawks, defeated Alabama State College's football team by a score of 21–0. 2nd Lt. William M. Bell, who had played as an All-American tackle at Ohio State University, coached the Warhawks. (Tuskegee Army Air Field history, Sep-Oct 1944, AFHRA call number 289.28–6)

11 October: The 332d Fighter Group strafed railroad and river traffic along the Danube Riber from Budapest to Bratislava, and reported destroying 17 enemy airplanes on the ground. Lt. Rhodes was reported to have crash landed at Ramitelli. The airplane was destroyed, but the pilot survived. (332d Fighter Group mission report number 91) Capt. William A. Campbell, 1st George E. Gray, and 1st Lt. Richard S. Harder of the 99th Fighter Squadron and 1st Lt. Felix J. Kirkpatrick of the 302nd Fighter Squadron, each earned a Distinguished Flying Cross for his heroic actions on this day. (Fifteenth Air Force General Order 4215 dated 28 Oct 1944; Fifteenth Air Force General Order 4425 dated 10 Nov 1944; Fifteenth Air Force General Order 4876 dated 5 Dec 1944; and Fifteenth Air Force General Order 836 dated 21 Feb 1945)

12 October: The 332d Fighter Group strafed railroad traffic from Budapest to Bratislava for a second day in a row. (332d Fighter Group mission report number 92) Six members of the 332d Fighter Group's 302d Fighter Squadron shot down a total of 9 enemy airplanes. 1 Lt. Lee Archer shot down 3 Me-109s, bringing his total aerial victories score to 4. Capt Wendell O. Pruitt shot down 2 enemy airplanes that day, including an He-111 and an Me-109. Other victors included Capt Milton R. Brooks, 1st Lts William W. Green, Jr, Roger Romine, and Luther H. Smith Jr. (Fifteenth Air Force General Orders 4287 and 4604, dated 1 Nov 1944 and 21 Nov 1944, respectively). Enemy antiaircraft artillery shot down 1st Lt. Walter L. Mc-Creary of the 100th Fighter Squadron that day about 25 miles southeast of Lake Balaton, Hungary, at approximately 2 p.m. (Missing Air Crew Report 9084). For their heroic actions on this day, the following nine pilots of the 332d Fighter Group each earned the Distinguished Flying Cross: 1st Lt. Lee Archer (302nd Fighter Squadron), Capt. Milton R. Brooks (302nd Fighter Squadron); 1st Lt. Frank E. Roberts (100th Fighter Squadron); 1st Lt. Spurgeon N. Ellington (100th Fighter Squadron); 1st Lt. Leonard F. Turner (301st Fighter Squadron); Capt. Armour G. McDaniel (301st Fighter Squadron); Capt. Stanley L. Harris (301st Fighter Squadron); 1st Lt. Marion R. Rodgers (99th Fighter Squadron); and 1st Lt. Quitman C. Walker (99th Fighter Squadron). (Fifteenth Air Force General Order 4876 dated 5 Dec 1944; Fifteenth Air Force General Order 255 dated 16 Jan 1945; Fifteenth Air Force General Order 287 dated 19 Jan 1945; Fifteenth Air Force General Order 449 dated 31 Jan 1945; Fifteenth Air Force General Order 836 dated 21 Feb 1945; Fifteenth Air Force General Order 1430 dated 15 Mar 1945; Fifteenth Air Force General Order 1811 dated 27 Mar 1945; and Fifteenth Air Force General Order 3484 dated 29 May 1945)

13 October: The 332d Fighter Group resumed bomber escort duty, protecting B-24s of the 304th Bombardment Wing to, over, and from Blechhammer South Oil Refinery. On the mission the group reported having destroyed 7 enemy airplanes on the ground. Enemy antiaircraft artillery fire shot down three of the 332d Fighter Group pilots, all of whom belonged to the 302d Fighter Squadron. They were 1st Lieutenants Walter D. Westmoreland, William W. Green Jr., and Luther A. Smith Jr. Westmoreland was seen to crash in Hungary, and Smith was seen to parachute over Yugoslavia. Lieutenant Smith was injured trying to abandon his burning P-51, and was captured. Green disappeared over Yugoslavia. (Missing Air Crew Reports 9085, 9086, and 9087) One B-24 was also seen to crash, probably also as result of flak. (332d Fighter Group mission report number 93) 1st Lt. Milton S. Hays of the 99th Fighter Squadron earned a Distinguished Flying Cross for his heroic actions on this day. (Fifteenth Air Force General Order 719 dated 16 Feb 1945)

14 October: The 332d Fighter Group escorted B-24s of the 49th Bombardment Wing on a raid against the Odertal Oil Refineries in Germany. Flight Officer Rual W. Bell of the 100th Fighter Squadron was seen to parachute out of his P-51C after engine trouble over Yugoslavia. (332d Fighter Group mission report number 94 and Missing Air Crew Report number 9140) Bell returned on 23 October after having evaded enemy forces in Yugoslavia for nine days. On 14 October 2d Lt. Andrew D. Marshall of the 301st Fighter Squadron, who went Missing in Action on 6 October, returned after having avoided enemy forces in Greece for eight days. (Escape, Evasion, and Repatriation Reports, 332d Fighter Group). 1st Lt. George M. Rhodes Jr. of the 100th Fighter Squadron earned a Distinguished Flying Cross for his heroic actions on this day. (Fifteenth Air Force General Order 49 dated 3 Jan 1945)

16 October. Thirty-five new black military pilots graduated from advanced pilot training at Tuskegee Army Air Field. Twenty of them belonged to class SE-44-I-1 for single engine pilots, and fifteen belonged to class TE-44-I-1 for twin engine pilots. The single engine pilots would fly fighters, and the twin engine pilots would fly medium bombers.

16 October. The 332d Fighter Group escorted B-17s of the 5th Bombardment Wing to bomb the Brux oil refineries. (332d Fighter Group mission report number 95)

17 October. The 332d Fighter Group conducted two missions, one to escort B-17s of the 5th Bombardment Wing to the Blechhammer South Oil Refinery, and one to escort a single B-17 of the same wing to Bucharest, Rumania. (332d Fighter Group mission report numbers 96 and 97)

20 October. The 332d Fighter Group conducted two missions, one to escort B-17s of the 5th Bombardment Wing to raid the Brux Oil Refineries (target cover and withdrawal) and one air-sea rescue escort to Rimini to protect a Catalina search and rescue aircraft. (332d Fighter Group mission report numbers 98 and 99) Captain Alfonza W. Davis assumed command of the 99th Fighter Squadron that same day, succeeding Major George S. Roberts. (99th Fighter Squadron lineage and honors history)

21 October. The 332d Fighter Group flew its 100th mission for the Fifteenth Air Force. It escorted B-24s of the 304th Bombardment Wing to, over, and from Gyor, Hungary. On the same day, the 332d Fighter Group flew its 101st mission, this one a search of the Venezia area. (332d Fighter Group mission report numbers 100 and 101) Capt. Vernon V. Haywood of the 302nd Fighter Squadron earned the Distinguished Flying Cross for his heroic actions on this day. (Fifteenth Air Force General Order 5068 dated 18 Dec 1944)

23 October. The 332d Fighter Group escorted B-24 bombers of the 304th Bombardment Wing to Regensburg and back. 1st Lieutenants Robert C. Chandler and Shelby F. Westbrook, both of the 99th Fighter Squadron, were reported missing with their P-51Cs. Chandler survived a crash that day, and eventually returned. (332d Fighter Group mission report number 102; Missing Air Crew Report numbers 9447 and 9448) Westbrook also returned, a month after he was reported Missing in Action, having evaded enemy forces in Yugoslavia for a month. Flight Officer Rual W. Bell, who was reported Missing in Action on 14 October, returned on 23 October, after having evaded enemy forces in Yugoslavia for 9 days. (Escape, Evasion, and Repatriation Reports, 332d Fighter Group)

25 October: 1st Lt. Freddie Hutchins of the 302nd Fighter Squadron, who went Missing in Action on 6 October, returned after having evaded enemy forces in Greece for nineteen days. (Escape, Evasion, and Repatriation Reports, 332d Fighter Group)

29 October: The 332d Fighter Group flew four missions. One escorted B-24 bombers of the 49th Bombardment Wing to and from Regensburg. (332d Fighter Group mission report number 103) Two members of the 332d Fighter Group, Captain Alfonza W. Davis, in a P-51D, and 2d Lieutenant Fred L. Brewer Jr. of the 100th Fighter Squadron in a P-51C, were reported missing that day, Davis over the Gulf of Trieste and Brewer over Germany. (Missing Air Crew Report numbers 9586 and 9600). Two other 29 October 1944 mission reports each noted that the group escorted a P-38 for reconnaissance of the Munich area. (332d Fighter Group mission report numbers 104 and 105) Finally, a fourth mission report for the day noted that the 332d Fighter Group escorted two B-25s on a mission to Bredgrad and Glina, Yugoslavia. (332d Fighter Group mission report number 106) On the same day, Major William A. Campbell assumed command of the 99th Fighter Squadron, succeeding Captain Alfonza W. Davis. (99th Fighter Squadron lineage and honors history)

1 November: The 332d Fighter Group reported flying three missions, one to escort 2 B-25s to Yugoslavia (duplicate of mission 106?), one to escort B-24 bombers of the 304th Bombardment Wing to Vienna, Austria, and back, and one to escort one C-47 transport aircraft to Yugoslavia. (332d Fighter Group mission reports numbered 107, 108, and 109)

2 November: The 302d Fighter Squadron emblem was approved. On a disk, it depicted a winged running red devil with a machine gun, over a cloud. (Unit emblem folder)

3 November: Major George S. Roberts became commander of the 332d Fighter Group, temporarily replacing Colonel Benjamin O. Davis Jr., who returned to command the group on 24 December. (Maurer, *Air Force Com-*

bat Units of World War II)

4 November: The 332d Fighter Group escorted B-17 bombers of the 5th Bombardment Wing to Regensburg, Germany. On the same day, the 332d Fighter Group also flew two reconnaissance escort missions, each to escort a lone P-38, one over the Linz area of Austria (then part of Germany) and one over the Munich area of Germany. (332d Fighter Group mission reports numbered 110, 111 and 112)

5 November: The 332d Fighter Group flew three missions again in one day. One escorted B-17s of the 5th Bombardment Wing to and from Florisdorf, Austria (Germany), and two others each to escort a single P-38 reconnaissance aircraft over the Munich area. (332d Fighter Group mission reports numbered 113, 114, and 115)

6 November: The 332d Fighter Group escorted B-17s of the 5th Bombardment Wing to and from Mossbierbaum oil refinery in the Vienna area of Austria (Germany). Captain William J. Faulkner Jr. of the 301st Fighter Squadron was reported missing over Austria on that mission, possibly because of mechanical failure of his P-51C. (332d Fighter Group mission report number 116 and Missing Air Crew Report number 9681)

7 November: The 332d Fighter Group provided target cover for B-24s of the 55th Bombardment Wing raiding the Trento and Bolzano areas of northern Italy. (332d Fighter Group mission report number 117)

11 November: The 332d Fighter Group escorted B-17s of the 5th Bombardment Wing to and over the Brux oil refineries. At least one of the group pilots reported seeing a jet-propelled aircraft in the distance. Lt. Payne crash landed at Lesina. The airplane was destroyed, but he survived, while 2d. Lt. Elton H. Nightingale of the 301st Fighter Squadron was reported missing over Italy with his P-51B. (332d Fighter Group mission report number 118 and Missing Air Crew Report number 9697)

16 November: The 332d Fighter Group escorted B-24 bombers of the 304th Bombardment Wing to and from Munich West marshalling yards. During the mission, the group encountered several Me-109 enemy fighters that attempted to shoot down the bombers. Captain Luke J. Weathers of the 302d Fighter Squadron shot down 2 of the enemy fighters. The 52d Fighter Group also escorted the 304th Bombardment Wing that day. (332d Fighter Group mission report number 119 and Fifteenth Air Force General Order 4990 dated 13 Dec 1944) For his heroic actions following a take-off accident on this day, Capt. Woodrow W. Crockett of the 100th Fighter Squadron was awarded the Soldiers Medal. After two P-51s crashed into each other and caught fire, Captain Crockett, at the risk of his own life, entered the burning wreckage to aid the trapped pilots. He was able to rescue one of them, Lt. William Hill, before the burning planes exploded. Unfortunately, Lt. Roger Romine died in the accident. (Fifteenth Air Force General Order 2132 dated 6 Apr 1945, and Diary of Henry Peery Bowman, excerpt of which was sent by Craig Huntly) Capt. Luke J. Weathers of the 302nd Fighter Squadron earned the Distinguished Flying Cross for his heroic actions on this day. (Fifteenth Air Force General Order 5228 dated 28 Dec 1944)

17 November: The 332d Fighter Group escorted B-17s of the 5th Bombardment Wing back to Brux synthetic oil refinery. (332d Fighter Group mission report number 120)

18 November: The 332d Fighter Group escorted heavy bombers raiding the Vicenza-Villafranca area of northern Italy. Lt. Henry R. Peoples was reported missing. (332d Fighter Group mission report number 121)

19 November: The 332d Fighter Group conducted a strafing mission against enemy railway, highway, and river traffic targets in the Gyor-Vienna-Esztergom area of Austria. 1st Lieutenant Roger B. Gaiter of the 99th Fighter Squadron was seen to bail out of his P-51 after it was hit by enemy anti-aircraft fire (flak). 1st Lieutenant Quitman Walker, also of the 99th Fighter Squadron, was also reported missing after also being hit by flak. Both were lost near Lake Balaton, Hungary. For this mission, Fifteenth Air Force commander Major General Nathan F. Twining commended the 332d Fighter Group. (332d Fighter Group mission report number 122; Missing Air Crew Report numbers 9932 and 9933) For their heroic actions on this day, the following four members of the 332d Fighter Group each earned the Distinguished Flying Cross: Capt. Albert H. Manning (99th Fighter Squadron); Capt. John Daniels (99th Fighter Squadron); 1st Lt. William N. Alsbrook (99th Fighter Squadron); and 1st Lt. Norman W. Scales (100th Fighter Squadron). (Fifteenth Air Force General Order 4876 dated 5 Dec 1944; Fifteenth Air Force General Order 5068 dated 18 Dec 1944; and Fifteenth Air Force General Order 836 dated 21 Feb 1945)

20 November: The 332d Fighter Group escorted B-17 bombers of the 5th Bombardment Wing to and from Blechhammer South oil refinery. The group also escorted B-24s of the 55th Bombardment Wing to the same target. 1st Lieutenant Maceo A. Harris Jr. of the 100th Fighter Squadron was reported missing after his P-51C lost coolant over Germany. (332d Fighter Group mission report number 123 and Missing Air Crew Report number 9951)

20 November: Eugene G. Theodore graduated from pilot training at Tuskegee Army Air Field. Although he was originally from Trinidad, he belonged to the United States Army Air Forces, unlike the five Haitian pilots who trained at Tuskegee Army Air Field and then returned to Haiti to serve in its armed forces. (Zellie Rainey Orr, historian, Atlanta Chapter, Tuskegee Airmen, Incorporated; Lynn M. Homan and Thomas Reilly, *Black Knights: The Story of the Tuskegee Airmen* (Gretna: Pelican Publishing Company, 2006), 309; Craig Huntly.

20 November: Thirty-five new black military pilots graduated from advanced pilot training at Tuskegee Army Air Field. Twenty-one of them belonged to class SE-44-I for single engine pilots, and fourteen of them belonged to class TE-44-I for twin-engine pilots.

22 November: 332d Fighter Group fighters escorted two B-25 medium bombers to and from Pedgrad, Yugoslavia. (332nd Fighter Group mission report number 124)

24 November: Master Sergeant William S. Surcey, Chief Inspector, Engineering Section, 366th Air Service Squadron, was awarded the Bronze Star "for exceptionally meritorious conduct in performance of outstanding services from 23 January to 28 February 1944," during which time he supervised third and fourth echelon repairs of seven P-40 Warhawks involved in air operations over Anzio and Cassino. MSgt. Surcey had then been serving as Engineering Section Chief of AAF Service Detachment #99 at Madna Landing Ground. At the time, the 99th Fighter Squadron was flying P-40 missions while attached to the 79th Fighter Group, then stationed at nearby Capodichino, Italy. This was the first Bronze Star awarded to an enlisted Tuskegee Airman. The award was presented by Brig. Gen. James A. Mollison, Commanding General, XV Air Force Service Command. (confirming documentation supplied by Craig Huntly)

25 November: The 100th Fighter Squadron emblem was approved. It depicted, on a disk, a winged panther on a globe. (Unit emblem folder)

26 November: 332d Fighter Group P-51s escorted one reconnaissance P-38 aircraft to and from Grodenwoh and Nurnberg, Germany. (332d Fighter Group mission report number 125)

29 November: Four black officers completed a 10-week Basic Instructors' School at Tuskegee Army Air Field, in preparation for becoming flight instructors there. Among the graduates were Flight Officers James O. Plinton Jr., Adolph J. Moret Jr., Charles W. Stephens Jr., and 1st Lt. Archie F. Williams. The three flight officers had all been civilian flight instructors in the primary flying school at Moton Field. Plinton and Moret became the first black flight instructors in the basic flying training phase at Tuskegee Army Air Field, and at first they served with fourteen white flight instructors in that phase. The only black flight instructors at Tuskegee Army Air Field before them were 1st Lt. Willie Fuller, who taught in the advanced single engine flight training school, and Captain James T. Wiley, who taught in the advanced twin engine flight training school. (History of Tuskegee Army Air Field, Nov–Dec 1944, AFHRA call number 289.28–7)

November-December: Moton Field's PT-17s were replaced by PT-13D airplanes, which were virtually identical except for the engines and propellers.

December: By the beginning of this month, 1st Lt. Willie Fuller, who had returned from combat flying overseas with the 332nd Fighter Group, was the only black flight instructor in the advanced single engine flying training phase at Tuskegee Army Air Field. At the time, the twelve other flight instructors in that phase were white. More black flight instructors were expected for this school as more black pilots with combat experience returned from overseas. At the same time, there was only one black flight instructor in the advanced twin engine flying training phase. He was Captain James T. Wiley, who had also returned from overseas combat flying duty. The other seven instructors at that school, at the time, were white. By December 1944, there were also three black flight instructors in the fighter transition school at Tuskegee Army Air Field. They were Captain Charles B. Hall, 1st Lt. William R. Melton Jr., and 2nd Lt. Milton T. Hall. Captain Hall had been the first Tuskegee Airman to shoot down an enemy aircraft. There were two black flight instructors in the basic flying training phase at Tuskegee Army Air Field by the end of the year. Flight Officers James O. Plinton Jr. and Adolph J. Moret Jr. Two others, Flight Officer Charles W. Stephens Jr. and 1st Lt. Archie F. Williams were expecting to become flight instructors at the basic flying school at Tuskegee Army Air Field early the next year. By the end of 1944, seven of the 49 flying instructors at Tuskegee Army Air Field, or one in seven, was black. (History of Tuskegee Army Air Field, Nov–Dec 1944, AFHRA call number 289.28–7)

December: At least by the end of the week ending on 2 December 1944, the 366th Air Service Squadron at Ramitelli Airfield in Italy began issuing 110-gallon auxiliary fuel tanks to the 332d Fighter Group. The 332d Fighter Group had been using smaller 75-gallon wing tanks. The larger fuel tanks, also attached to the wings of the P-51 airplanes, allowed them to fly on longer missions, such as the famous one to Berlin almost four months later (24 March 1944). (38th Air Service Group histories for November and

December 1944)

2 December: The 332d Fighter Group escorted B-24s of the 49th and 55th Bombardment Wings on a raid to Blechhammer oil refinery (South). Lt. Cornelius P. Gould Jr. of the 301st Fighter Squadron was reported to have bailed safely out of his P-51B after experiencing engine trouble over Czechoslovakia. (332d Fighter Group mission report number 126 and Missing Air Crew Report number 10045)

3 December: The 332d Fighter Group escorted B-24 bombers of the 49th Bombardment Wing to and from the Udine Pass area of northern Italy. Lt. Marion R. Rodgers was reported to have crash-landed safely at Ramitelli Air Base, home base of the 332d. (332d Fighter Group mission report number 127)

9 December: The 332d Fighter Group escorted B-17s of the 5th Bombardment Wing to Brux, Germany. For the first time, they encountered some German Me-262 jet aircraft, two of which attacked the bomber formation. Lt. Rich and Lt. Brown were reported missing. (332d Fighter Group mission report number 128 and 332d Fighter Group history for December 1944; B. O. Davis Jr. autobiography)

9–10 December: Back in Alabama, famous black singer Lena Horne entertained airmen at Tuskegee Army Air Field. She had sung there on several previous occasions, greatly improving morale at the field. (History of Tuskegee Army Air Field, Nov–Dec 1944, AFHRA call number 289.28–7)

11 December: The 332d Fighter Group flew two missions, one to escort B-24s of the 47th Bombardment Wing to and from the Moosbierbaum oil refinery of Austria (Germany), and one to escort a reconnaissance aircraft to Praha, Czechoslovakia. On the Moosbierbaum mission, one B-24 was seen to explode in the Vienna area. (332d Fighter Group mission report numbers 129 and 130)

15 December: The 332d Fighter Group escorted B-24s of the 47th Bombardment Wing to and from Innsbruck, Austria (Germany). (332d Fighter Group mission report number 131)

16 December: The 332d Fighter Group flew two missions, one to escort B-17s of the 5th Bombardment Wing to and from Brux, Germany, and one to escort a single B-25 to Mrkoplj, Yugoslavia. (332d Fighter Group mission report numbers 132 and 133)

17 December: The 332d Fighter Group escorted B-17s of the 5th Bombardment Wing and B-24s of the 49th and 304th Bombardment Wings on withdrawal from a raid on Olomouc (Olmutz), Germany. (332d Fighter

Group mission report number 134)

18 December: The 332d Fighter Group flew two missions, one to escort B-24 Liberators of the 49th Bombardment Wing to and from oil refineries at Blechhammer, and one to escort a P-38 on a reconnaissance mission to Innsbruck, Austria (Germany). (332d Fighter Group mission report numbers 135 and 136)

19 December: The 332d Fighter Group again flew two missions, one to escort B-24s of the 55th Bombardment Wing to and from Blechhammer South oil refinery, and one to escort a P-38 on a reconnaissance mission to Praha (Prague), Czechoslovakia. (332d Fighter Group mission report numbers 137 and 138)

20 December: The 332d Fighter Group flew two missions, one to escort B-17 Flying Fortresses of the 5th Bombardment Wing to and from an oil refinery at Brux, and one to escort a single P-38 on a reconnaissance mission to Prague, Czechoslovakia. (332d Fighter Group mission report numbers 139 and 140)

22 December: After a day without a mission, the 332d Fighter Group escorted one P-38 on a reconnaissance mission to and from Ingolstadt, Germany. (332d Fighter Group mission report number 141)

23 December: The 332d Fighter Group again escorted a single P-38 on a reconnaissance mission, this time to Praha (Prague), Czechoslovakia. Captain Lawrence E. Dickson of the 100th Fighter Squadron was reported to have bailed out of his P-51D over Italy because of engine trouble. (332d Fighter Group mission report number 142 and Missing Air Crew Report number 10734)

24 December: Col. Benjamin O. Davis Jr. resumed command of the 332d Fighter Group, replacing Major George S. Roberts, who had commanded the group since 3 November. (Maurer, *Air Force Combat Units of World War II*)

25 December: After a day without a mission, the 332d Fighter Group escorted Fifteenth Air Force Bombers (number and wing not specified) during a raid on the Brux oil refinery, Germany. Although no enemy aircraft were encountered, Me-109 German fighters were seen chasing B-26 medium bombers in the distance. (332d Fighter Group mission report number 143)

26 December: The 332d Fighter Group escorted B-17s of the 5th Bombardment Wing and B-24s of the 55th Bombardment Wing on withdrawal from the Odertal and Blechhammer oil refineries of Germany. (332d Fighter Group mission report number 144)

27 December: The 332d Fighter Group escorted B-17s Flying Fortresses of the 5th Bombardment Wing to and from oil refineries in the Vienna area of Austria (Germany at the time). During the mission, a B-17 was seen to explode in the Linz area. (332d Fighter Group mission report number 145)

28 December: The 332d Fighter Group escorted B-24s of the 304th Bombardment Wing to and from the Kolin and Pardubice oil refineries in Czechoslovakia. (332d Fighter Group mission report number 146)

28 December: Thirty-five new black military pilots graduated from advanced pilot training at Tuskegee Army Air Field. Twenty of them belonged to class SE-44-J for single engine pilots, and fifteen of them belonged to class TE-44-J for twin engine pilots.

29 December: For the second day in a row, the 332d Fighter Group escorted B-24s of the 304th Bombardment Wing, this time to and from targets in Muhldorf and Lanshut, Germany. At noon, 1st Lt. Frederick D. Funderburg Jr. and 2d Lt. Andrew D. Marshall, both of the 301st Fighter Squadron, were reported missing with their P-51Cs over the Munich area of Germany. Lieutenants Robert J. Friend and Lewis Craig were reported to have bailed out of their P-51s. (332d Fighter Group mission report number 147, Missing Air Crew Report numbers 10931 and 10932, and Lynn M. Homan and Thomas Reilly, *Black Knights*) On the same day, bad weather forced many Fifteenth Air Force B-24 crews returning from their mission to land their bombers at alternative fields. Eighteen of the Liberators, seventeen from the 485th Bombardment Group and one from the 455th Bombardment Group, landed at Ramitelli Air Field, Italy, the home base of the 332d Fighter Group, where the white bomber crews spent five days enjoying the hospitality of the black Tuskegee Airmen. (Fifteenth Air Force mission folder for 29 December 1944; 485th Bombardment Group history for December 1944; 332d Fighter Group history for December 1944)

31 December: Military personnel at Tuskegee Army Air Field numbered 2144, including 369 officers and 1775 enlisted.

1945

January: Capt. Armour G. McDaniel assumed command of the 301st Fighter Squadron, succeeding Capt. Lee Rayford. (301st Fighter Squadron lineage and honors history). Capt. Vernon V. Haywood assumed command of the 302nd Fighter Squadron, succeeding Capt. Melvin T. Jackson. (302nd Fighter Squadron lineage and honors history)

January: German prisoners of war completed working on runways and taxiways at Tuskegee Army Air Field. (History of Tuskegee Army Air Field, Jan-Feb 1945, AFHRA call number 289.28–8, vol. 1)

1 January: Brigadier General Dean C. Strother, commander of the XV Fighter Command, awarded Distinguished Flying Crosses to seven 332d Fighter Group pilots, including Major Lee Rayford and Captains Andrew D. Turner, William A. Campbell, Melvin T. Jackson, Vernon Haywood, Dudley Watson, and George E. Gray. At the same ceremony, Bronze Stars were awarded to TSgt. Raymond Washington and SSgt. Professor Anderson. (332d Fighter Group history for January 1945)

2 January: Captain Leonard A. Crozier was appointed head of the Twin Engine School at Tuskegee Army Air Field. At the same time, 1st Lt. Richard C. Timberlake was appointed head of the fighter transition school there. The former head of both schools had been Major Clay Albright. All three men were white, although the number of black flying instructors under them was increasing.

3 January: 332d Fighter Group pilot strength was noted as 121, with overall personnel numbering 1250. After four days without missions, the 332d Fighter Group provided reconnaissance escort for a P-38 to the Munich and Linz areas of Germany and Austria. (332d Fighter Group mission report number 148)

5 January: The 332d Fighter Group escorted one Mosquito aircraft on a reconnaissance mission to the Munich area of Germany. (332d Fighter Group mission report number 149)

5 January: Back at Tuskegee Army Air Field, Captain Leroy Love, who had been head of the Instrument School there, succeeded Captain Raymond I. MacKinnon as Base Operations Officer. Captain Charles T. Hood succeeded Captain Love as head of the Instrument School. (2143d Army Air Forces Base Unit, Tuskegee Army Air Field history, Jan-Feb 1945, AFHRA call number 289.28–8, vol. 1)

8 January: After two days without missions, the 332d Fighter Group escorted B-24 Liberators of the 47th Bombardment Wing to and from the marshalling yards of Linz, Austria (Germany). (332d Fighter Group mission report number 150)

10 January: Major Clay Albright, who had served as Director of both the Twin Engine Advanced Flight School and the Fighter Transition School at Tuskegee Army Air Field, was succeeded by Captain Leonard A. Crozier, who became head of the Twin Engine Advanced Flight School, and 1st Lt.

332nd Fighter Group P-51 pilots at Ramitelli Air Field, Italy. Note the pierced steel planking airfield surface and the underwing fuel tank.

Richard C. Timberlake, who became head of the Fighter Transition School. Albright, Crozier, and Timberlake were all white. (2143d Army Air Forces Base Unit, Tuskegee Army Air Field, Jan-Feb 1945, AFHRA call number 289.28–8, vol. 1)

11 January: The 387th Air Service Group moved from Daniel Field, Georgia, to Godman Field, Kentucky, where it was welcomed by Colonel Robert R. Selway Jr., commander of Godman Field. (387th Air Service Group history for January 1945). According to the group history, "Recreational facilities at Godman were adequate to satisfy most of the men" under Colonel Selway. Selway was also commander of the 477th Bombardment Group. (387th Air Service Group history, February-April 1945)

15 January: After six days without missions, the 332d Fighter Group escorted B-24s of the 304th Bombardment Wing to and from a raid on targets in Vienna, Austria (Germany). (332d Fighter Group mission report number 151)

18 January: After two days without a mission, the 332d Fighter Group flew two missions, each to escort a single P-38 for reconnaissance photographs over Germany. One went to Stuttgart and the other went to Munich. (332d Fighter Group mission report numbers 152 and 153)

19 January: P-51s of the 332d Fighter Group escorted a P-38 toward Praha (Prague), Czechoslovakia for reconnaissance photographs. The P-38 suffered engine failure and the pilot had to bail out. (332d Fighter Group mission report number 154)

20 January: The 332d Fighter Group flew two missions, one that escorted B-17 Flying Fortresses of the 5th Bombardment Wing to oil storage targets at Regensburg, Germany, and one that escorted a single P-38 on a photographic reconnaissance mission to and from Praha (Prague), Czechoslovakia. On the latter mission, the escort formation ran into a snowstorm and became separated. (332d Fighter Group mission report numbers 155 and 156). On the same day, the 96th Service Group was officially redesignated as the 96th Air Service Group. (Organization Record Card)

21 January: the 332d Fighter Group escorted B-17s of the 5th Bombardment Wing for a second day in a row, but this time to and from Vienna Lobau Distillation Unit and Schwechat Oil Refinery. Two German fighter jet Me-262s were seen following the bomber formation. According to Missing Air Crew Reports, 3 of the bombers were lost, two because of mechanical difficulty, and one to an unknown cause. Two of the 332d Fighter Group P-51 pilots, both from the 100th Fighter Squadron, were also reported lost, both because of engine trouble. Flight Officer Samuel J. Foreman was reported missing over northern Yugoslavia at 1100 hours, and 2d Lt. Albert L. Young was reported missing at 1205 near Vienna, Austria. A Lt. Smith was hit by enemy antiaircraft artillery at Wiener Neustadt. (332d Fighter Group mission report number 157; Missing Air Crew Report numbers 11387, 11539, 11540, 11541, 11542)

22 January: Colonel Benjamin O. Davis Jr., commander of the 332d Fighter Group, presented Distinguished Flying Crosses to eleven 332d Fighter Group pilots, including Major George S. Roberts, Captains Woodrow W. Crockett, Samuel L. Curtis, Claude B. Govan, Freddie B. Hutchins, William T. Mattison, Gwynne W. Pierson, Lowell C. Steward, Alva N. Temple, Luke J. Weathers Jr., and 1st Lieutenant Frank Roberts. During the same awards ceremony, SSgt. Marshall L. Jones was awarded the Bronze Star. (332d Fighter Group history for January 1945)

31 January: After nine days without missions, because of bad winter weather that obscured targets, the 332d Fighter Group escorted B-24s of the 47th and 55th Bombardment Wings to and from the Moosbierbaum Oil Refinery in the Vienna area of Austria (then Germany). (332d Fighter Group mission report number 158)

January-February: Tuskegee Army Air Field had 112 white personnel assigned, including 97 officers and 15 enlisted personnel. Most of them lived not at the base or even in the town of Tuskegee, but at Auburn, and commuted to and from the base daily. The Basic Flight School at Tuskegee Army Air Field had 25 instructors, 14 of them black and 11 white. Some of the black flight instructors had come from the Primary Flight School at Moton Field. The Advanced Single Engine Flight School at Tuskegee Army Air Field had 18 instructors, 12 of them white and six of them black. There was also an Advanced Twin Engine Flight School at Tuskegee, with unknown numbers of black and white instructors during the period. (2143d Army Air Forces Base Unit, Tuskegee Army Air Field history, Jan-Feb 1945, AFHRA call number 289.28–8, vol. 1)

February: Tuskegee Army Air Field discarded its BT-13 aircraft, that it had been using for basic flying training, and began using AT-6 airplanes for that purpose. AT-6s continued to be used for the advanced single engine flying training. (History of Tuskegee Army Air Field, Jan-Feb 1945, AFHRA call number 289.28–8, vol. 1)

February: Tuskegee Army Air Field had 664 civil service employees, 214 of whom where women. (History of Tuskegee Army Air Field, 2143rd AAFBU, Mar–Apr 1945, vol. 1, AFHRA call number 289.28–9)

February: During this month, Captain Leonard A. Crozier, director of advanced twin engine training at Tuskegee Army Air Field, deployed temporarily to Moody Army Air Field for B-25 transition training, since B-25s were to replace the AT-10 twin engine airplanes that Tuskegee Army Air Field had been using for such training. (History of Tuskegee Army Air Field, 2143rd AAFBU, Mar–Apr 1945, vol. 1, AFHRA call number 289.28–9)

1 February: The 332d Fighter Group flew two different missions that day, one to escort B-24s of the 49th Bombardment Wing and one to escort B-24s of the 47th Bombardment Wing, but both wings with their escorts raided the same target: Moobierbaum Oil Refinery in the Vienna area of Austria (then Germany). (332d Fighter Group mission report numbers 159 and 160)

1 February: Twenty-three new black military pilots graduated from advanced pilot training at Tuskegee Army Air Field. Sixteen of them belonged to class SE-44-K for single engine pilots, and seven belonged to class TE-44-K for twin-engine pilots.

3 February: P-51 fighter pilots of the 332d Fighter Group escorted a single P-38 on a photographic reconnaissance mission over the Munich area of southern Germany. (332d Fighter Group mission report number 161)

5 February: The 332d Fighter Group escorted B-24 Liberators of the 47th Bombardment Wing to and from the marshalling yards and main railroad station at Salzburg, Austria (then Germany). (332d Fighter Group mission report number 162)

6 February: The 332d Fighter Group conducted a fighter sweep over Yugoslavia. (332d Fighter Group mission report number 163)

7 February: The 332d Fighter Group flew two different missions that day, one to escort B-24s of the 47th Bombardment Wing and one to escort B-24s of the 304th Bombardment Wing, but both wings raided the same target: Moosbierbaum Oil Refinery in the Vienna area of Austria (then Germany). The two missions were similar to those on February 1. (332d Fighter Group mission report numbers 164 and 165)

8 February: The 332d Fighter Group flew three missions on the same day. On one of the missions, P-51 fighters escorted a single P-38 aircraft on a photographic reconnaissance mission over Stuttgart, Germany. On a second mission, 332d Fighter Group pilots conducted a fighter sweep over Yugoslavia. On the third mission of the day, the 332d Fighter Group escorted B-24 bombers of the 55th Bombardment Wing to and from Vienna South depots in Austria (then Germany). (332d Fighter Group mission reports numbered 166, 167, and 168)

11 February: 2d Lt. Thomas C. Street of the 99th Fighter Squadron died while serving overseas. (American Battle Monuments Commission)

12 February: P-51 fighter pilots of the 332d Fighter Group escorted a single P-38 airplane on a photographic reconnaissance mission to and from Praha (Prague), Czechoslovakia. (332d Fighter Group mission report number 169)

13 February: The 332d Fighter Group flew three missions. On one mission, the group escorted a P-38 aircraft on a reconnaissance mission over Munich in southern Germany. On the second mission, the group escorted B-24 Liberators of the 49th Bombardment Wing to and from Vienna Central railroad repair shops in Austria (then Germany). On its third mission that day, the 332d Fighter Group escorted bombers over Zagreb, Maribor, and Graz. A pilot reported seeing an unidentified jet-propelled enemy aircraft in the distance. One of the 332d Fighter Group pilots also reported hearing a radio transmission from a bomber noting a jet-propelled aircraft had made a pass at the bombers. (332d Fighter Group mission reports numbered 170,

171, and 172)

14 February: The 332d Fighter Group flew two missions, one to escort B-17 Flying Fortresses of the 5th Bombardment Wing, and one to escort B-24 Liberators of the 55th Bombardment Wing, but both wings attacked the same targets: oil refineries in Vienna, Lobau, and Schwechat. On both missions, the 332d Fighter Group provided penetration, target cover, and withdrawal escort for the bombers. (332d Fighter Group mission report numbers 173 and 174)

15 February: The 332d Fighter Group flew two missions to escort two different sections of the B-24s of the 49th Bombardment Wing (Red Force and Blue Force) to and from the Penzinger marshalling yards in Vienna, Austria (then Germany). (332d Fighter Group mission report numbers 175 and 176)

16 February: The 332d Fighter Group flew three missions. The group escorted a Mosquito aircraft on a photographic reconnaissance mission over Munich and a P-38 aircraft on another photographic reconnaissance mission over Munich. On the third mission P-51 pilots of the 332d Fighter Group escorted B-17 Flying Fortresses of the 5th Bombardment Wing to and from the airdrome at Lechfeld, Germany. On this mission, 2d Lt. John M. Chavis of the 99th Fighter Squadron was reported lost with his P-51C at 1020 hours over Italy. On this mission, 332d Fighter Group pilots reported seeing three bombers explode in the air, including two B-17s near Bolzano, Italy, and a B-24 (not assigned to the 332d Fighter Group for escort that day) near Innsbruck, Austria (then Germany). (332d Fighter Group mission report numbers 177, 178, and 179) Capt. Emile G. Clifton of the 99th Fighter Squadron earned a Distinguished Flying Cross for his heroic actions on this day. (Fifteenth Air Force General Order 3484 dated 29 May 1945)

17 February: The 332d Fighter Group flew three missions in one day, again. The group escorted a P-38 on a reconnaissance mission to Nurnberg, Germany. The group also escorted a Mosquito aircraft on another reconnaissance mission, this one to Munich, Germany. A pilot reported seeing jet aircraft in the distance on this mission. On its third mission of the day, the group strafed railroad targets between Linz and Vienna, Austria (then Germany). (332d Fighter Group mission report numbers 180, 181, and 182) Capt. Louis G. Purnell of the 301st Fighter Squadron earned the Distinguished Flying Cross for his heroic actions on this day. (Fifteenth Air Force General Order 2362 dated 14 Apr 1945)

18 February: The 332d Fighter Group flew two missions, one to escort B-24 bombers of the 47th Bombardment Wing to and from the Wels marshalling yards in the Linz area of Austria (then Germany), and one to escort a single P-38 aircraft on a photographic reconnaissance mission in the Linz area. (332d Fighter Group mission report numbers 183 and 184)

19 February: The 332d Fighter Group escorted B-24 Liberator bombers of the 49th Bombardment Wing to and from the Vienna area of Austria (then Germany). A Spitfire with British markings was seen firing on the formation. (332d Fighter Group mission report number 185)

19 February: A Tuskegee Instructors School was set up at Tuskegee Army Air Field to train black combat pilots returning from overseas to become flight instructors for the basic and advanced flying training phases there. (History of Tuskegee Army Air Field, Jan-Feb 1945, AFHRA call number 289.28–8, vol. 1)

20 February: The 332d Fighter Group flew two missions, one to escort a single P-38 aircraft on a photographic reconnaissance mission over Nurnberg, Germany, and another to escort B-24s of the 47th Bombardment Wing to and from Vipitento and Brenner marshalling yards. The second mission report for the day noted that the "fighters had to leave bombers because of shortage of gas". (332d Fighter Group mission report numbers 186 and 187)

21 February: The 332d Fighter Group escorted B-24 Liberators of the 304th Bombardment Wing on a raid to Vienna's central marshalling yards. (332d Fighter Group mission report number 188)

22 February: The 332d Fighter Group flew three missions. The group escorted B-17 Flying Fortresses of the 5th Bombardment Wing to provide target cover during raids on marshalling yards in southeastern Germany. The other two missions escorted P-38s on photographic reconnaissance missions, one to Prague, Czechoslovakia and Linz, Austria (then Germany), and one to Stuttgart, Germany. (332d Fighter Group mission report numbers 189, 190, and 191)

23 February: The 332d Fighter Group escorted B-24 Liberator bombers of the 304th Bombardment Wing to Gmund West marshalling yards in Germany. (332d Fighter Group mission report number 192)

24 February: P-51 fighter pilots of the 332d Fighter Group escorted a Mosquito aircraft on a photographic reconnaissance mission over the Munich area of southern Germany. (332d Fighter Group mission report number 193)

25 February: The 332d Fighter Group flew two missions, one to strafe railroad traffic in southern Germany and Austria (then part of Germany), and one to escort a single P-38 aircraft on a photographic reconnaissance mission over the Munich area. Three of the 332d Fighter Group P-51C pilots were reported missing that day. 1st Lt. Alfred M. Gorham of the 301st Fighter Squadron was reported lost at 1145 hours east of Munich after experiencing mechanical failure. 2d Lt. Wendell W. Hockaday of the 99th Fighter Squadron was reported missing at 1225 over Uttendorf, Austria after suffering damage during a strafing attack. 2d Lt. George J. Iles, also of the 99th Fighter Squadron, was reported missing at 1245 hours over Augsburg, Germany after being hit by antiaircraft artillery fire. (332d Fighter Group mission report numbers 194 and 195 and Missing Air Crew Report numbers 12664, 12665, and 12670) 1st Lt. Roscoe C. Brown and 1st Lt. Reid E. Thompson, both of the 100th Fighter Squadron, each earned the Distinguished Flying Cross for his heroism on this day. (Fifteenth Air Force General Order 1430 dated 15 Mar 1945 and Fifteenth Air Force General Order 2270 dated 11 April 1945)

26 February: P-51 fighters of the 332d Fighter Group escorted a Mosquito aircraft on a photographic reconnaissance mission over Munich in southern Germany. (332d Fighter Group mission report number 196)

27 February: The 332d Fighter Group escorted B-24s of the 49th Bombardment Wing to and from the Augsburg marshalling yards in Germany. No enemy aircraft were encountered, but at least one pilot saw what he believed to be a German Me-163 in the distance. (332d Fighter Group mission report number 197)

28 February: The 332d Fighter Group flew three missions, two of them to escort P-38 airplanes on two separate photographic missions over Praha (Prague), Czechoslovakia, and one to escort B-17 Flying Fortresses of the 5th Bombardment Wing over Verona in northern Italy. The third mission of the day was the 200th mission of the 332d Fighter Group for the Fifteenth Air Force. Of those 200 missions, 138 had been to escort bombers. (332d Fighter Group mission reports numbered 198, 199, and 200)

28 February: By this date, there were 25 flight instructors in the basic flying training phase at Tuskegee Army Air Field, 14 of whom were black. Black flight instructors were beginning to outnumber white flying instructors in certain schools at the field. Most of the new black flight instructors were veterans returning from overseas combat duty with the 332nd Fighter Group. (History of Tuskegee Army Air Field, Jan-Feb 1945, AFHRA call number 289.28–8, vol. 1)

March: The First Air Force selected Freeman Field, Indiana, to be the new base for the 477th Bombardment Group, the 387th Air Service Group, and the Replacement Crew Training Program (for black bomber crews). Freeman Field was larger than Godman Field, Kentucky, which was not even large enough for all the 477th Bombardment Group's four squadrons. (History of Freeman Field, Indiana, 1 March-15 June 1945, AFHRA call number 283.28–6)

March: Lt. Col. Donald G. McPherson, who had been serving as Director of Flying Training at Tuskegee Army Air Field, became Deputy Commanding Officer of the 2143rd Army Air Forces Base Unit there, becoming second in command to Colonel Noel B. Parrish. Like Parrish, he was a white officer.

March: By the beginning of this month, 112 white military personnel, including 97 officers and 15 enlisted men, were still working at Tuskegee Army Air Field. None of them lived on the airfield. Most of them, in fact, commuted from Auburn. (History of Tuskegee Army Air Field, Jan-Feb 1945, AFHRA call number 289.28–8, vol. 1)

March: The swing band and glee club of Tuskegee Army Air Field (TAAF) took part in a musical show called "Roger," which had been written and produced by TAAF personnel. They performed at Napier Field, Alabama; Athens, Georgia; and Atlanta, Georgia. One of the places they performed was Lawson General Hospital in Atlanta. (History of Tuskegee Army Air Field, 2143rd AAFBU, Mar–Apr 1945, vol. 1, AFHRA call number 289.28–9)

1 March: The 332d Fighter Group flew four missions. One escorted a P-38 airplane on a photographic reconnaissance mission over Praha (Prague), Czechoslovakia, and two escorted P-38s on photographic reconnaissance missions over Stuttgart, Germany. The fourth mission escorted B-24 Liberator bombers of the 55th Bombardment Wing to and from the Moobierbaum oil refineries in the Vienna area of Austria (then part of Germany). (332d Fighter Group mission report numbers 201, 202, 203, and 204)

2 March: The 332d Fighter Group flew two missions, one to escort a single P-38 on a photographic reconnaissance mission over Praha (Prague), Czechoslovakia, and the the other to escort B-24 bombers of the 304th Bombardment Wing to, over, and from the marshalling yards of Linz, Austria (then part of Germany). (332d Fighter Group mission report numbers 205 and 206)

2 March: The 618th Bombardment Squadron moved from Atterbury Army Air Field, Indiana, to Freeman Field, Indiana, where it would at last be stationed with the other three squadrons of the 477th Bombardment Group.

(Maurer, *Combat Squadrons of World War II*)

3 March: The 332d Fighter Group conducted a strafing mission against railroad targets between Maribor, Bruck, and Weiner-Neustadt. First Lieutenants Robert L. Martin and Alphonso Simmons, both P-51D pilots of the 100th Fighter Squadron, were reported missing on that mission after having been hit by antiaircraft artillery fire at 1410 hours over Graz Airdrome, Austria. (332d Fighter Group mission report number 207 and Missing Air Crew Report Numbers 12827 and 12828) Simmons had been reported Missing in Action before, in August 1944, but had returned in September of that year. Martin later returned after his 3 March 1945 loss, after evading enemy forces in Yugoslavia for more than a month. (Escape, Evasion, and Repatriation Reports, 332d Fighter Group)

3 March: Back in Alabama, transition flying training using P-40 airplanes ceased at Tuskegee Army Air Field. That training, and the 8 airplanes used for it, were transferred to Walterboro in South Carolina. For some time, Walterboro had been the airfield to which graduates from single engine flying training at Tuskegee Army Air Field had gone, to be replacement pilots for the 332nd Fighter Group and its four squadrons overseas. P-40s were

Ground crew members of the 332nd Fighter Group loading a wing tank on a P-51 before a long-range mission. Most of the Tuskegee Airmen, like these crewmen, were not pilots.

more like the P-51s used by then in combat than the AT-6s used for the advanced single engine flying training. (History of Tuskegee Army Air Field, 2143rd AAFBU, Mar–Apr 1945, vol. 1, AFHRA call number 289.28–9)

4 March: The 332d Fighter Group flew two missions, one to escort B-24s of the 49th Bombardment Wing to, over, and from the marshalling yards of Graz. On that mission, one B-24 was seen going down, with six crew members parachuting out of the bomber. On the other mission, P-51 fighter pilots of the 332d Fighter Group escorted a Mosquito type aircraft on a photographic reconnaissance mission over Munich in southern Germany. (332d Fighter Group mission report numbers 208 and 209)

5 March: The 477th Bombardment Group moved from Godman Field, Kentucky, to Freeman Field, Indiana, a larger base which had recently been vacated as a twin-engine pilot training station. (477th Bombardment Group history for period 16 Jan-15 April 1945). The field consisted of more than 117 acres, and contained four large runways, each 150 by 5,500 feet. (Freeman Field history, 1 Mar-15 Jun 1945, AFHRA call number 283.28–6)

5–7 March: The 616th, 617th, and 619th Bombardment Squadrons moved from Godman Field, Kentucky, to Freeman Field, Indiana, the new home of their 477th Bombardment Group. The 618th Bombardment Squadron had already moved to the new base on 2 March. The commander of Freeman Field then was Major Wilmer E. McDowell. The commander of the 477th Bombardment Group, Col. Robert R. Selway, did not become commander of the field until April. (History of Freeman Field, Indiana, 1 March-15 June 1945, AFHRA call number 283.28–6; Maurer, *Combat Squadrons of the Air Force, World War II;* organization record card of the 477th Bombardment Group)

6 March: 332d Fighter Group pilots escorted a P-38 on a photographic reconnaissance mission over the Klagenfurt and Linz areas of Austria (Germany). (332d Fighter Group mission report number 210) On the same day, the 302d Fighter Squadron was inactivated, leaving the 332d Fighter Group with three fighters squadrons, the 99th, 100th, and 301st. This was the first time since July 1944 that the 332nd Fighter Group managed only three fighter squadrons, like the other fighter groups. (Maurer, *Combat Squadrons of the Air Force, World War II*). From then until the end of the war, the 332d Fighter Group had the same number of fighter squadrons as the other six fighter groups of the Fifteenth Air Force.

7 March: The 332d Fighter Group again escorted a P-38 on a photographic reconnaissance mission, this time over Munich, Germany. (332d Fighter

Group mission report number 211)

7 March: The 387th Air Service Group moved from Godman Field, Kentucky, to Freeman Field, Indiana, to which the 477th Bombardment Group, which the 387th Air Service Group supported, had already moved two days earlier. (387th Air Service Group history for the period February-April 1945)

7–9 March: Several black officers of the 477th Bombardment Group entered Freeman Field's Officers' Club 2, which was assigned to "base and supervisory" (white) personnel, instead of Officers' Club 1, which was assigned to them. They were told to leave and to use the other officers' club. After an argument, and being refused service there, they did. That desegregation attempt failed, but a later attempt in April achieved national attention. (History of Freeman Field, Indiana, 1 March-15 June 1945, AFHRA call number 283.28–6; Histories of Godman Field, KY for 1 Feb-15 Apr 1945, Atterbury Army Air Field, Indiana, 15 Jan-1 Mar 1945, and Freeman Field, Indiana, 1 Mar-15 Apr 1945, AFHRA call number 283.48–7)

9 March: The 332d Fighter Group flew three missions in one day. Two of them escorted P-38s on photographic reconnaissance missions, one to Linz, Austria (then part of Germany) and one to the Munich area of Germany. The third mission that day escorted B-17 Flying Fortress bombers of the 5th Bombardment Wing to, over, and from the marshalling yards at Bruck, Austria. (332d Fighter Group mission report numbers 212, 213, and 214)

9 March: Mr. Truman K. Gibson, civilian aide to the Secretary of War (Henry I. Stimson) visited the 332d Fighter Group at Ramitelli Air Field, accompanied by Maj. Gen. James M. Bevans, deputy commander of the Mediterranean Allied Air Forces. The visit reflected the War Department's interest in the success of the group. (332d Fighter Group history for March 1945)

10 March: An article by Roi Ottley entitled "Dark Angels of Doom" was published in *Liberty* Magazine. It suggested that members of the 332d Fighter Group had never lost a bomber in more than 100 missions, despite the fact some of the group's escorted bombers were shot down by enemy aircraft the previous summer. (Roi Ottley, "Dark Angels of Doom," *Liberty* Magazine, 10 March 1945)

11 March: Thirty-eight new black military pilots graduated from advanced pilot training at Tuskegee Army Air Field. Twenty-two of them belonged to class SE-45-A for single engine pilots, and sixteen belonged to class TE-45-A for twin engine pilots.

12 March: The 332d Fighter Group, after not flying missions for two days, flew three missions, as it had on 9 March. Two escorted P-38s on photographic reconnaissance missions, one to the Linz area of Austria (then part of Germany) and one to Munich, Germany. The third mission escorted B-24s of the 47th Bombardment Wing to, over, and from the Floridsdorf oil refinery in the Vienna area of Austria. During the mission, pilots reported having heard on the radio that an aircraft was being jumped by enemy aircraft. (332d Fighter Group mission report numbers 215, 216, and 217) Capt. Walter M. Downs of the 301st Fighter Squadron earned the Distinguished Flying Cross for his heroic actions on this date. (Fifteenth Air Force General Order 3484 dated 29 May 1945)

13 March: The 332d Fighter Group again flew three missions. Two escorted P-38s on photographic reconnaissance missions, one to Stuttgart, Germany, and the other to Nurnberg, Germany. The third mission escorted B-17 Flying Fortress bombers to, over, and from the marshalling yards at Regensburg, Germany. On two of the missions, enemy FW-190 fighter airplanes were seen. On the bomber escort mission, the bombers were early and the fighters were late to the rendezvous point. (332d Fighter Group mission reports 218, 219, and 220)

13 March: Back at Tuskegee Army Air Field, Major Gabe C. Hawkins Jr., who had served as director of basic flying training, was promoted to Director of Training and Operations at the field, taking the place of Lt. Col. Donald G. McPherson. McPherson became Deputy Commander of the 2143rd Army Air Force Base Unit, second in command only to Col. Noel Parrish, who remained the commander of Tuskegee Army Airfield. (History of Tuskegee Army Air Field, Mar–Apr 1945, vol. 1, call number 289.28–9 at the Air Force Historical Research Agency)

14 March: The 332d Fighter Group flew four missions. One strafed targets on the railroad line connecting Bruck, Leoben, and Steyr. One escorted B-24s of the 47th Bombardment Group to, over, and from a railroad bridge and marshalling yards at Varazdin, Yugoslavia. The other two missions escorted P-38 airplanes on photographic reconnaissance missions over Munich. On one of those missions, at least one pilot reported seeing a German Me-262 jet in the distance. 1st Lt. Harold H. Brown of the 99th Fighter Squadron was reported lost with his P-51C at 1115 hours east of Bruck, Austria after being damaged during a strafing attack. (332d Fighter Group mission report numbers 221, 222, 223, and 224; Missing Air Crew Report number 12996) For their heroic actions on this day, the following five members of the 332d Fighter Group and its 99th Fighter Squadron each earned a Distinguished Flying Cross: 1st Lt. Shelby F. Westbrook; 1st Lt. Hannibal M. Cox; 2nd Lt. Vincent I. Mitchell; 1st Lt. Thomas P. Braswell; and 2nd Lt. John W. Davis.

(Fifteenth Air Force General Order 2362 dated 14 Apr 1945; Fifteenth Air Force General Order 3031 dated 5 May 1945; Fifteenth Air Force General Order 3484 dated 29 May 1945)

14 March: Class 45-E graduated from primary flight training at Moton Field. Of the 83 students who began that training on 29 Dec 1944, 60 graduated and became eligible to move on to Tuskegee Army Air Field for the basic and advanced phases of flight training. (History of 2164 AAFBU at Moton Field, AFHRA call number 234.81, Mar–Apr 1945)

15 March: The 332d Fighter Group flew two missions, one to provide target cover for Fifteenth Air Force B-24s on raids in the area from Flotsam to Geisha, Yugoslavia, and one to escort B-17s of the 5th Bombardment Wing to Zittau, Germany. (332d Fighter Group mission report numbers 225 and 226)

16 March: Lt. William S. Price III of the 301st Fighter Squadron shot down an Me-109 during a strafing mission against railroad targets. (Fifteenth Air Force General Order 1734 from 1945, and 332d Fighter Group mission report number 227) This was the first day in four months that members of the 332d Fighter Group shot down enemy aircraft, reflecting the diminished enemy aircraft opposition during the winter. One 332d Fighter Group P-51B pilot, 1st Lt. Jimmie D. Wheeler of the 99th Fighter Squadron, was lost with his P-51B at 1320 hours over Muhldorf, Germany, after he struck a tree on the strafing mission. There were three other missions that day. Two escorted Mosquito type aircraft on photographic reconnaissance missions, one over Munich, Germany, and the other over Prague, Czechoslovakia. The fourth mission escorted Fifteenth Air Force B-24s over and from Monfalcone Harbor, Italy. (332d Fighter Group mission reports 228, 229, and 230 and Missing Air Crew Report number 13060) 1st Lts. Roland W. Moody, Henry R. Peoples, and William S. Price III, all of the 301st Fighter Squadron, each earned the Distinguished Flying Cross for their heroic actions on this day. (Fifteenth Air Force General Order 2834 dated 28 Apr 1945)

17 March: The 332d Fighter Group flew two missions to escort P-38s on photographic reconnaissance missions, one to Prague, Czechoslovakia, and the other to Linz, Austria (then part of Germany). (332d Fighter Group mission reports 231 and 232)

19 March: The 332d Fighter Group flew three missions, two to escort Mosquito type aircraft on photographic missions, one to the Linz and Munich areas of Austria and Germany, and the other to Linz. The third mission escorted B-24 Liberator bombers of the 55th Bombardment Wing to, over, and from the marshalling yards at Muhldorf. At least one of the pilots reported seeing an enemy jet-propelled aircraft over the Brenner Pass between Italy and Austria. (332d Fighter Group mission reports 233, 234, and 235)

19 March: Major Marvin A. Coleman succeeded Major Gabe C. Hawkins as director of the Basic Flying School. Like Hawkins, Coleman was white. (History of Tuskegee Army Air Field, 2143rd AAFBU, Mar–Apr 1945, vol. 1, AFHRA call number 289.28–9)

19 March: Twin engine advanced flying training at Tuskegee Army Air Field began using B-25 medium bombers in place of AT-10 airplanes. (History of Tuskegee Army Air Field, 2143rd AAFBU, Mar–Apr 1945, vol. 1, AFHRA call number 289.28–9)

20 March: The 332d Fighter Group flew three missions. One escorted a Mosquito type aircraft on a photographic reconnaissance mission over Linz, Austria and Munich, Germany, one to escort a C-47 transport type aircraft over Sanki Most, Yugoslavia, and one to escort B-24 bombers in the second wave of 304th Bombardment Wing bombers to Kralupy oil refinery in Czechoslovakia. On the bomber escort mission, Flight Officer Newman C. Golden of the 99th Fighter Squadron was reported missing after bailing out of his mechanically troubled P-51B aircraft at 1132 hours over Wels, Austria. (332d Fighter Group mission report numbers 236, 237, and 238 and Missing Air Crew Report number 13126)

20 March: Lt. Col. William R. Bradford succeeded Major Wilmer E. McDowell as commander of Freeman Field. Col. Robert R. Selway, commander of the 477th Bombardment Group at the field, was not yet commander of the field itself, but would take command at Freeman Field in early April. (Freeman Field history, 1 Mar-15 Jun 1945, AFHRA call number 283.28–6)

21 March: The 332d Fighter Group flew four missions. One escorted B-24 bombers of the 47th Bombardment Wing to an airdrome at Neuberg, Germany. The other three missions escorted P-38 aircraft on photographic reconnaissance missions over Linz, Austria; Munich, Germany; Nurnberg, Germany; and Prague, Czechoslovakia. (332d Fighter Group mission report numbers 239, 240, 241, and 242)

22 March: P-51 fighters of the 332d Fighter Group flew two missions, one to escort one P-38 airplane on a photographic reconnaissance mission over Ruhland, Germany. On that mission, one of the P-51s was damaged by enemy antiaircraft artillery fire. The other 332d Fighter Group mission that day escorted two waves of B-24 bombers of the 304th Bombardment Wing to, over, and from the Kralupy oil refinery in Czechoslovakia. (332d Fighter

Group mission report numbers 243 and 244)

23 March: The 332d Fighter Group escorted two waves of B-17s of the 5th Bombardment Wing to, over, and from the Ruhland oil refinery, Germany. 2d Lt. Lincoln T. Hudson of the 301st Fighter Squadron was reported missing with his P-51C at 1310 hours northeast of Vienna, Austria after suffering engine trouble. (332d Fighter Group mission report number 245 and Missing Air Crew Report number 13256)

23 March: Major Harold D. Martin, who had been serving as head of the ground school at Tuskegee Army Air Field, was killed in an airplane crash at Reidsville, North Carolina. Martin had served at Tuskegee Army Air Field since 29 May 1942 and as director of the ground school since 11 March 1943. Killed with him was the plane's pilot, Flight Officer Charles Walter Stephens, who had also been serving at Tuskegee Army Air Field, but as a flight instructor. (History of Tuskegee Army Air Field, 2143rd AAFBU, Mar–Apr 1945, vol. 1, AFHRA call number 289.28–9; e-mail from Ms Brooke Stephens to the Air Force Historical Research Agency dated 19 Jun 2014)

23 March: Back at Tuskegee Army Air Field, effective this date, many fighter pilots who had flown with the 332nd Fighter Group in combat overseas were assigned as basic and advanced flight instructors. Although some of the flight instructors at Tuskegee Army Air Field had been black since November 1944, most had moved from primary flight instruction duties at Moton Field. (Tuskegee Army Air Field Special Order 68 dated 21 Mar 1945, copy provided by Craig Huntly; Tuskegee Army Air Field history)

23–24 March: The 366th Air Service Squadron at Ramitelli was able to overcome a shortage of 110-gallon fuel tanks in order to supply them to the 332d Fighter Group for a long mission to Berlin on 24 March. Documents suggest that the 366th Air Service Squadron obtained the wing tanks from the 55th Air Service Squadron. (38th Air Service Group history for March 1945)

24 March: The 332d Fighter Group took part in the longest World War II raid of the Fifteenth Air Force. Along with other fighter groups of the Fifteenth Air Force, it escorted B-17 bombers of the 5th Bomb Wing on a mission to Berlin, the German capital. On the way the Tuskegee Airmen encountered German jet Me-262 fighters and shot down three of them. (332d Fighter Group mission report number 246) The three victors were 1st Lt. Roscoe Brown, 1st Lt. Earl R. Lane, and 2d Lt. Charles V. Brantley, all of whom belonged to the 100th Fighter Squadron. (Fifteenth Air Force

General Order 2293 dated 12 Apr 1945) For this mission, the 332d Fighter Group earned its only Distinguished Unit Citation of World War II. (332d Fighter Group lineage and honors history; Maurer, *Air Force Combat Units of World War II*) The group's 99th Fighter Squadron earned its third Distinguished Unit Citation for this mission. (99th Fighter Squadron lineage and honors history) Five members of the white 31st Fighter Group's 308th Fighter Squadron also each shot down a German jet that day. Missing Air Crew Reports indicate five 332d Fighter Group P-51 fighters as missing that day The pilots included Captain Armour G. McDaniel and Flight Officers James T. Mitchell Jr. and Leon W. Spears of the 301st Fighter Squadron and 2d Lieutenants Ronald Reeves and Robert C. Robinson of the 100th Fighter Squadron. McDaniel, commander of the 301st Fighter Squadron, was shot down by enemy aircraft, and Spears might have been, as well, south of Berlin, at about 1215 hours. Reeves and Robinson ran out of fuel over the Udine area of northern Italy at about 1400 hours, and Mitchell probably experienced mechanical failure south of Chemnitz, Germany, at 1315 hours. (Missing Air Crew Reports 13266, 13267, 13268, 13269, and 13270) Enemy fighters also shot down 3 of the escorted bombers. (Missing Air Crew Reports 13274, 13278, and 13375, and mission reports of the 2d, 463d, and 483d Bombardment Groups for 24 March 1945) A combination of enemy antiaircraft artillery (flak) and enemy aircraft shot down two additional escorted bombers. (Missing Air Crew Reports 13374 and 13271) For their heroic actions on this day, 1st Lt. Earl R. Lane and 2nd Lt. Charles V. Brantley, both of the 100th Fighter Squadron, each earned a Distinguished Flying Cross (Roscoe Brown, the other pilot with an aerial victory credit over a jet this day, had already earned a Distinguished Flying Cross for an earlier mission). (Fifteenth Air Force General Order 2834 dated 28 Apr 1945)

24 March: The *Chicago Defender* newspaper published an article stating that the 332d Fighter Group had flown its 200th mission without losing any bombers, despite the fact that 24 group-escorted bombers had been shot down by enemy airplanes the previous summer. A bomber under the escort of the 332d Fighter Group had not been shot down by enemy aircraft since at least September 1944, a period of more than six months. On this same date, three more bombers under Tuskegee Airmen escort were shot down by enemy aircraft, making a total of 27 bombers under Tuskegee Airmen escort shot down by enemy airplanes.

25 March: Despite the very long mission of the previous day, the 332d Fighter Group flew two missions, one to escort a P-38 on a photographic reconnaissance mission over Linz, Austria, and one to escort B-24 Liberator bombers of the 49th Bombardment Wing to, over, and from the Prague/ Nbely Airdrome in Czechoslovakia. One witness saw what appeared to be a Russian aircraft attacking the P-51s. (332d Fighter Group mission report numbers 247 and 248)

c. 25 March: Capt. Walter M. Downs assumed command of the 301st Fighter Squadron, succeeding Capt. Armour G. McDaniel. (301st Fighter Squadron lineage and honors history)

26 March: The 332d Fighter Group again flew two missions, one to escort a Mosquito type aircraft on a photographic reconnaissance mission over Munich, Germany, and one to escort B-17 Flying Fortress bombers to, over, and from the Wiener Neustadt marshalling yards. (332d Fighter Group mission report numbers 249 and 250)

28 March: A P-38 racing with another P-38 dropped its two wing tanks for greater speed. One of the tanks crashed into a tent at Ramitelli Air Field and burst into flames, killing 1st Lt. Roland W. Moody of the 332nd Fighter Group. (332nd Fighter Group history, March 1945). A witness from the 52nd Fighter Group, which was stationed near Ramitelli, reported the incident. Both the 52nd and the 332nd Fighter Groups flew P-51s. The P-38s were from another Fifteenth Air Force fighter group. (Richard K. Curtis, *Dumb but Lucky: Confessions of a P-51 Fighter Pilot in World War II* [New York: Ballantine Books, 2005], 281–282)

29 March: 2nd Lt. Roland M. Moody of the 301st Fighter Squadron died while serving overseas. (American Battle Monuments Commission)

30 March: The 332d Fighter Group sent P-51s to escort a P-38 on a photographic reconnaissance mission over Munich, Germany. (332d Fighter Group mission report number 251)

30 March: Captain Elwood P. Driver, a black pilot with overseas combat experience with the 99th Fighter Squadron, became the new director of the ground school at Tuskegee Army Air Field, back in Alabama. (History of Tuskegee Army Air Field, 2143rd AAFBU, Mar–Apr 1945, vol. 1, AFHRA call number 289.28–9)

31 March: The 332d Fighter Group conducted a fighter sweep and strafing mission against railroad and other targets in the Munich area of southern Germany. (332d Fighter Group mission report number 252) During the mission, twelve members of the group shot down a total of 13 enemy airplanes, including FW-190s and Me-109s. The victors included 1st Lt. Robert W. Williams, who shot down 2 FW-190s, and Maj William A. Campbell, 1st Lts Roscoe C. Brown, Earl R. Lane, and Daniel L. Rich, 2d Lts Rual

W. Bell, Thomas P. Brasswell, John W. Davis, James L. Hall, Hugh J. White, and Bertram W. Wilson, Jr, and Flight Officer John H. Lyle, who each shot down one enemy aircraft. (Fifteenth Air Force General Orders 2292 and 2293 from 1945) Three 332d Fighter Group P-51D pilots were reported missing that day, including 2d Lt. Arnett W. Starks, Jr and 1st Lt. Clarence N. Driver of the 100th Fighter Squadron, and 2d Lt. Frank N. Wright of the 99th Fighter Squadron. Driver went missing at 1315 hours over northern Italy probably because of low fuel. Wright went into a spin while in pursuit of the enemy at 1420 hours over Landshut, Germany. Starks was hit by enemy antiaircraft artillery at 1430 hours over Voklammerkt, Germany. (332d Fighter Group mission report number 252 and Missing Air Crew Report numbers 13211, 13212, and 13216) 1st Lts. Robert W. Willliams and Bertram W. Wilson Jr., both of the 100th Fighter Squadron, each earned a Distinguished Flying Cross for heroic actions on this day. (Fifteenth Air Force General Order 3484 dated 29 May 1945)

March: During that month, members of the 332d Fighter Group and its squadrons shot down a total of 17 enemy airplanes.

March: Eighteen replacement pilots arrived at Ramitelli Air Field in Italy for the 332nd Fighter Group. Among them were 2nd Lieutenants William H. Holloman III and George E. Hardy, who were assigned to the 99th Fighter Squadron, and Leo R. Gray, who was assigned to the 100th Fighter Squadron. (332nd Fighter Group history, March 1945)

Late March: TB-25 airplanes, training versions of the B-25s, arrived at Tuskegee Army Air Field. Before that, twin-engine pilots had used AT-10s. The B-25s would later fly training missions between Tuskegee and Troy, Alabama. (Thole, 17)

April: By this month, the basic flying training department at Tuskegee Army Air Field included 34 instructors, 14 of whom were black. (History of Tuskegee Army Air Field, 2143rd AAFBU, Mar–Apr 1945, vol. 1, AFHRA call number 289.28–9)

1 April: Seven members of the 332d Fighter Group's 301st Fighter Squadron shot down a total of 12 enemy airplanes during a mission to escort B-24s of the 47th Bombardment Wing to raid the St. Polten marshalling yard and conduct a fighter sweep of Linz, Austria. The victors included 1st Lt. Harry T. Stewart, who shot down 3 FW-190s, 1st Lt. Charles L. White, who shot down 2 Me-109s, 2d Lt. Carl E. Carey, who shot down 2 FW-190s, 2d Lt. John E. Edwards, who shot down 2 Me-109s, 2d Lts Walter P. Manning and Harold M. Morris, who each shot down one FW-190, and Flight Officer

James H. Fisher, who shot down another FW-190. Two of the 332d Fighter Group P-51 pilots were reported missing: 2d Lt. Walter P. Manning and Flight Officer William P. Armstrong, both of the 301st Fighter Squadron, at 1400 over Wels, Austria, after encountering enemy aircraft. (332d Fighter Group mission report number 253 and Fifteenth Air Force General Order 2294 of 1945; Missing Air Crew Report numbers 13376 and 13377). Flight Officer James H. Fisher shot down the German pilot who had shot down his wingman, Flight Officer William Armstrong. (Tuskegee Airman Leo Gray supplied this information). For their heroic actions on this date, 1st Lt. Charles L. White, 1st Lt. John E. Edwards, 1st Lt. Harry T. Stewart Jr., and 2nd Lt. Carl E. Carey, all of the 301st Fighter Squadron, each earned a Distinguished Flying Cross. On the same day, the 332d Fighter Group sent a set of P-51s on a second mission, to escort a single P-38 on a photographic reconnaissance mission over Prague, Czechoslovakia. (332d Fighter Group mission report number 254; Fifteenth Air Force General Order 2834 dated 28 Apr 1945 and Fifteenth Air Force General Order 3484 dated 29 May 1945) Tuskegee Airman Leo Gray reported that on the mission to escort the P-38, the P-51s encountered German Me-262 jet fighters, but the jets departed when the Mustangs dropped their auxiliary fuel tanks.

1 April: Lt. Col. William R. Bradford, commander of Freeman Field, issued an unsigned order specifying which facilities on the base would be for supervisors and which would be for trainees. This affected the members of the 477th Bombardment Group, under Colonel Robert R. Selway, which was composed of both white and black officers, among others. Selway would become commander of the base a few days later, and he continued the policy. (Major John D. Murphy, "The Freeman Field Mutiny: A Study in Leadership," Air Command and Staff College, Air University, Maxwell Air Force Base, Alabama, March 1997)

2 April: The 332d Fighter Group flew three missions. Two escorted P-38s on photographic reconnaissance missions, one to the San Severo area of Italy and one to the Munich area of southern Germany. On the Munich mission, they encountered an Me-262 German jet fighter, which attacked the small formation. On the third mission that day, the 332d Fighter Group escorted B-24 Liberator bombers of the 304th Bombardment Wing over the Krems marshalling yards in Austria (then part of Germany). (332d Fighter Group mission reports 255, 256, and 257)

3 April: The 96th Air Service Group was disbanded at Jesi (Iesi), Italy, along with the 1766th Ordance Supply and Maintenance Company and the 1051st Quartermaster Company, Air Service Group, which were also stationed at Jesi. At the same time, the 366th Air Service Squadron, the 1765th Ordance Supply and Maintenance Company, and the 1000th Signal Company, Service Group (Aviation), all at Ramitelli, Italy, were disbanded. On the same day, the 367th Air Service Squadron at Falconara, Italy, and the 43rd Medical Supply Platoon (Aviation) at Seracapriola, Italy, were also disbanded. (XV Air Force Service Command General Order 23 dated 28 Mar 1945, copy furnished by Craig Huntly)

3 April: Black officers at Freeman Field met to plan a non-violent method for desegregating the white officers' club, a few officers at a time. (Major John D. Murphy, "The Freeman Field Mutiny: A Study in Leadership," Air Command and Staff College, Air University, Maxwell Air Force Base, Alabama, March 1997)

4 April: The 523rd Air Service Group was activated at Ramitelli, and the 524th Air Service Group was activated on the same date at Jesi (Iesi), Italy, where the 96th Air Service Group had been stationed. Organizations assigned to the groups and activated at the same time were the 949th and 950th Air Engineering Squadrons and the 773rd and 774th Air Materiel Squadrons. These organizations, stationed at Jesi, Ramitelli, and Faconara, assumed the functions of the organizations that had been disbanded the previous day. (Organizational record cards of the 523rd and 524th Air Service Groups at the Air Force Historical Research Agency and XV Air Force Service Command General Order 23 dated 28 Mar 1945, copy furnished by Craig Huntly)

4 April: Major Robert Long, who had been serving for years as head of the advanced single engine flying school at Tuskegee Army Air Field, departed the base for a new assignment. Captain John H. Foregger took his place. (History of Tuskegee Army Air Field, 2143rd AAFBU, Mar–Apr 1945, vol. 1, AFHRA call number 289.28–9)

5 April: 332d Fighter Group P-51 fighters escorted a P-38 on a photographic reconnaissance mission over Linz, Austria, while other group fighters, on another mission, escorted B-17s Flying Fortress bombers of the 5th Bombardment Wing on a raid against a major enemy airfield at Udine, Italy. (332d Fighter Group mission report numbers 258 and 259)

5 April: Colonel Robert R. Selway, commander of the 477th Bombardment Group that had been stationed at Freeman Field, Indiana, since 5 March, became commander of Freeman Field, in place of Lt. Col. William R. Bradford. Selway maintained the policy of two separate officers clubs on the base. Officers Club 1 was to be for black officers of the 477th Bombardment Group, "E" Squadron (Trainee), and the 118th Army Air Force Base Unit, while Officers Club 2 was to be for base and supervisory personnel who were white. When the 477th Bombardment Group, under Selway, was at Godman Field, the white base and supervisory personnel had gone to the white officers club at neighboring Fort Knox, leaving the officers club at Godman for the black officers. There was no such neighboring white base near Freeman Field. (History of Freeman Field, Indiana, 1 Mar-15 Jun 1945, AFHRA call number 283.28–6). Selway apparently intended to maintain separate black and white officers' clubs. Black officers of the 477th Bombardment Group had tried to enter Officers' Club 2 before, on 7, 8, and 9 March. On 5 April, 1945, 36 officers of E Squadron, 118th Army Air Forces Base Unit (AAFBU), which consisted of replacements for the 477th Bombardment Group, attempted to enter Officers Club 2. The Assistant Base Provost Marshall told them to leave. Three of the black officers allegedly pushed him aside as they entered. They were Lieutenants Roger C. "Bill" Terry, Marsden A. Thomson, and Shirley R. Clinton. (History of Freeman Field, Indiana, 1 March-15 June 1945, AFHRA call numbers 283.28–6J and 283.48–7, 31–32; J. Todd Moye, *Freedom Flyers* [Oxford University Press, 2010], 133 and 138)

6 April: 25 additional black officers attempted to enter Officers' Club 2 at Freeman Field, that had been reserved for white "base and supervisory" personnel. They and the 36 black officers who had attempted to enter the club the day before, at total of 61, were arrested in quarters and charged with disobeying an order of a superior officer, some with violence. (History of Freeman Field, Indiana, 1 March-15 June 1945, AFHRA call numbers 283.28–6 and 283.48–7, 32). At the same time, Freeman Field was made a Control Base, and base functions changed. The 387th Air Service Group was made responsible only for the supply and maintenance of the 477th Bombardment Group, and its squadrons were moved to another part of the base, which lowered group morale. (387th Air Service Group history for the period February-April 1945)

6 April: The 332d Fighter Group flew two missions, one to escort B-24 Liberators of the 304th and 47th Bombardment Wings to, over, and from the Verona ordnance depot and marshalling yards in northern Italy, and the other to escort a P-38 on a photographic reconnaissance mission over Prague, Czechoslovakia. (332d Fighter Group mission report numbers 260 and 261)

7 April: The 332d Fighter Group again flew two missions. One escorted six groups of 5th Bombardment Wing B-17s raiding the Vipiteno, Camp Di

Trens, and Bressanone railroad bridges in northern Italy. One of the group P-51 fighter pilots was initially reported missing, but he later returned. On the second mission that day, 332d Fighter Group P-51s escorted a P-38 on a photographic reconnaissance mission over Munich, Germany. (332d Fighter Group mission report numbers 262 and 263) 2 Lt. Ferrier H. White of the 100th Fighter Squadron died while serving overseas. (American Battle Monuments Commission)

7 April: Back at Freeman Field, Indiana, Colonel Robert Selway, commander of both the 477th Bombardment Group and the field, ordered Officers' Club 2, which had been reserved for white officers, closed, except for the mess hall. (History of Freeman Field, Indiana, 1 Mar-15 Apr 1945, AFHRA call number 283.48–7, 32)

8 April: The 332d Fighter Group flew three missions. One escorted a Mosquito-type aircraft on a photographic reconnaissance mission over the Linz and Munich areas of Austria and southern Germany. Another escorted a P-38 on a similar photographic reconnaissance mission over Prague, Yugoslavia. The third mission escorted B-17 Flying Fortresses of three groups of the 5th Bombardment Wing on a raid against the Campdazzo railroad bridge in northern Italy. On that mission, one of the B-17s was seen to crash into the Adriatic Sea. The mission report noted that "Bombers were strung out making them difficult to cover." (332d Fighter Group mission report numbers 264, 265, and 266) 1st Lt. Robert L. Martin of the 100th Fighter Squadron, who was reported Missing in Action on 3 March 1945, returned after having evaded enemy forces in Yugoslavia for more than a month. (Escape, Evasion, and Repatriation Reports, 332d Fighter Group)

9 April: The 332d Fighter Group again flew three missions in one day. The first escorted a P-38 airplane on a photographic reconnaissance mission over the Linz and Nurnberg areas of Austria and Germany. On that mission an enemy Me-262 was seen. On the second mission, group P-51 fighters escorted another P-38 on a photographic reconnaissance mission over the Linz and Prague areas of Austria and Czechoslovakia. On the third 332d Fighter Group mission of the day, Tuskegee-trained pilots escorted B-17s of the 5th Bombardment Wing and B-24s of the 304th Bombardment Wing to and from the vicinity of Bologna in northern Italy. On that mission, a B-17 was seen spinning down, with three crewmen parachuting out of it. (332d Fighter Group mission report numbers 267, 268, and 269)

9 April: All but 3 of the 61 black officers who had been arrested in quarters at Freeman Field for attempting to enter an officers' club closed to them were released. The three not released had been accused of disobeying the orders of a superior officer and offering violence to him. They included Lieutenants Roger C. "Bill" Terry, Marsen A. Thomson, and Shirley R. Clinton. At the same time, Colonel Robert Selway, commander of the base and of the 477th Bombardment Group there, issued Base Regulation 85–2, noting which personnel were to use each of the two sets of buildings on base. The regulation specified not only two separate officers clubs, but also two separate recreational buildings, two separate mess buildings, two different sets of base officers' quarters, and two separate sets of latrines. One set was reserved for personnel undergoing training, by which Selway meant black officers, and the other set was reserved for base, supervisory, instructor, and command personnel, by which Selway meant white officers. Of the 422 black officers at Freeman Field, 101 refused to sign the new regulation, which contradicted War Department policy, and were taken into custody. They included members of the 619th Bombardment Squadron, 477th Bombardment Group, and "E" Squadron of the 118th Army Air Forces Base Unit (AAFBU), which consisted of replacements for the 477th Bombardment Group. 318 of the other black officers (not counting the 3 still under arrest from the first round) signed the regulation, some of them adding notes that they disagreed with the segregated facilities policy. Among them were 16 of the officers initially arrested. If one counts all of the black officers arrested at Freeman Field during April 1945, the number is 120 (19 arrested first time but not second, 42 arrested first and second times, and 59 arrested second time only). (History of Freeman Field, Indiana, 1 March-15 June 1945, AFHRA call numbers 283.28–6 and 283.48–7, 32; J. Todd Moye, *Freedom Flyers* [Oxford University Press, 2010], 133, 135, 138; James Warren, *The Tuskegee Airmen Mutiny at Freeman Field* [Vacaville, CA: Conyers Publishing, 2001), 195–197)

9 April: Captain John H. Foregger took the place of Major Robert M. Long as director of advanced single engine flying training at Tuskegee Army Air Field. Major Long had been the leader of that training since the first class of pilots graduated in March 1942. (Tuskegee Army Air Field history, Mar–Apr 1945, vol. 1, call number 289.28–9 at the Air Force Historical Research Agency)

10 April: The 332d Fighter Group flew two missions. One of them escorted B-17s of the 5th Bombardment Wing and B-24s of the 304th Bombardment Wing on a raid to Bologna, Italy. The other escorted a P-38 on a photographic reconnaissance mission over the Munich area of southern Germany. (332d Fighter Group mission report numbers 270 and 271)

10 April: The 115th Army Air Forces Base Unit was discontinued, but the

387th Air Service Group remained to take up its functions, supporting the 477th Bombardment Group. (115 AAF Base Unit organization record card)

10–11 April: 101 African-American officers of the 477th Bombardment Group who had twice refused to sign Base Regulation 85–2, Colonel Selway's directive specifying separate sets of facilities at Freeman Field, were confined. That was about one-fourth of the black officers assigned to Freeman Field. (Benjamin O. Davis Jr., *Benjamin O. Davis, Jr., American* [Washington: Smithsonian Institution Press, 1991], 142–143; Alan L. Gropman, *The Air Force Integrates* [Washington: Office of Air Force History, 1985], 22–25; Zellie Rainey Orr)

11 April: The 332d Fighter Group flew two missions again. One escorted B-24 Liberators of the 304th Bombardment Group to the Ponte Gardena railroad bridge in northern Italy. The mission report noted that the bombers were strung out, making them difficult to cover. The second mission of the day escorted a P-38 on a photographic reconnaissance mission over Munich, Germany. (332d Fighter Group mission report numbers 272 and 273)

12 April: The 332d Fighter Group flew four missions in one day. Two of them escorted photographic reconnaissance aircraft, one over Linz, Austria (then part of Germany) and one over Munich, Germany. The other two missions escorted B-24 Liberator bombers, one for the 47th Bombardment Wing on a raid against the Casarsa Diversion railroad bridge of northern Italy, and one for the 49th Bombardment Wing against the St. Veit railroad bridge. On the last mission, two of the escorting P-51s collided. One pilot was reported lost, and the other one was reported as missing. (332d Fighter Group mission report numbers 274, 275, 276, and 277) 2d Lt. Samuel G. Leftenant of the 99th Fighter Squadron was reported missing with his P-51C at 1508 hours north of Klagenfurth after the mid-air collision. (Missing Air Crew Report number 13984)

13 April: The 101 black officers who had been confined at Freeman Field for refusing to sign a regulation requiring two separate officers' clubs were flown in six C-47 airplanes to Godman Field, Kentucky. Once there, the officers were placed under arrest in quarters. (History of Freeman Field, Indiana, 1 March-15 June 1945, AFHRA call numbers 283.28–6 and 283.48–7, 32; LeRoy F. Gillead, "The Tuskegee Experiment and Tuskegee Airmen, 1939–1949," call number 289.28–18 at the Air Force Historical Research Agency)

14 April: The 332d Fighter Group flew two missions. One escorted a photographic reconnaissance aircraft over Munich in southern Germany. The other escorted four British Halifax bombers of the 148th Squadron (Royal

Air Force) to, over, and from Voschia. The British bombers dropped supplies to friendly personnel on the ground. (332d Fighter Group mission report numbers 278 and 279)

15 April: The 332d Fighter Group flew three missions. The first escorted a single P-38 on a photographic reconnaissance mission over Bolzano and Prague, Czechoslovakia. The second escorted B-24 bombers of the 304th Bombardment Wing ("Blue Force" section) to, over, and from an ammunition factory and storage facility at Ghedi. The third mission strafed railroad targets in the areas of Munich, Salzburg, Linz, Pilzen, and Regensburg in Germany and Austria (then part of Germany). On this last mission, Lt. Jimmy Lanham of the 301st Fighter Squadron shot down an Me-109 in the Munich area. One of the 332d Fighter Group pilots was reported lost, one was reported missing, and two were reported to have landed at friendly fields. There are missing air crew reports on Flight Officers Morris E. Gant and Thurston L. Gaines, both of the 99th Fighter Squadron, who flew P-51Cs. Gaines went missing at 1430 hours about 40 miles from Muhldorf, Germany after being hit by enemy antiaircraft artillery fire, and Gant was reported missing at 1600 hours about 12 miles east of Pescara, Italy after running low on fuel. For his leadership of this outstanding railroad strafing mission, in which the 332d Fighter Group destroyed or damaged 35 locomotives, 8 oil cars, 44 other units of rolling stock, 4 barges, 4 motor transports on a flat car, and one aircraft in the air, Colonel Benjamin O. Davis earned the only Silver Star awarded to any member of the 332d Fighter Group. (Fifteenth Air Force General Order 3496 dated 31 May 1945; 332d Fighter Group mission report numbers 280, 281, and 282; Missing Air Crew Report numbers 13798 and 13813; and Fifteenth Air Force General Order 3484 issued in 1945) For their heroic actions on this day, Capt. Gordon M. Rapier and 1st Lt. Jimmy Lanham of the 301st Fighter Squadron and Capt. William A. Campbell and 1st Lt. Gentry E. Barnes of the 99th Fighter Squadron each earned the Distinguished Flying Cross. (Fifteenth Air Force General Order 3324 dated 21 May 1945 and Fifteenth Air Force General Order 3484 dated 29 May 1945)

15 April: Thirty new black military pilots graduated from advanced pilot training at Tuskegee Army Air Field. Twenty-three of them belonged to class SE-45-B for single engine pilots, and seven belonged to class TE-45-B for twin engine pilots.

15 April: Captain Wendell O. Pruitt, who after distinguished combat service overseas had returned to Tuskegee Army Air Field to be a flight instructor for advanced single-engine training, was killed in an aircraft crash. (Tuskegee Army Air Field and 2143rd Army Air Force Base Unit history, Mar–Apr 1945, vol. 1, call number 289.28–9 at Air Force Historical Research Research Agency)

16 April: The 332d Fighter Group flew five missions in one day. The first escorted three C-47 transports that went to northern Yugoslavia. Three of the missions escorted P-38s on photographic reconnaissance missions to the Munich and Linz areas of southern Germany and Austria. The other mission escorted B-24 Liberators of the 49th and 55th Bombardment Wings to the Bologna area of northern Italy. The latter mission report noted that the bombers were "strung out and difficult to cover." (332d Fighter Group mission report numbers 283, 284, 285, 286, and 287)

16 April: Andrew J. McCoy Jr., a black cadet at the United States Military Academy at West Point, New York, entered primary flight training at Moton Field. (History of 2164 AAFBU at Moton Field, AFHRA call number 234.81, Mar–Apr 1945)

16 April: The world premiere of *Wings for This Man*, a short motion picture about black flying training at Tuskegee, and what the black pilots did in combat, was held at Tuskegee Army Air Field. Much of the movie had been filmed during the field's third anniversary celebration. Actor Ronald Reagan narrated the film. (History of Tuskegee Army Air Field, 2143rd AAFBU, Mar–Apr 1945, vol. 1, AFHRA call number 289.28–9)

17 April: Class 45-F graduated from primary flight training at Moton Field. Of the 81 students who entered the class on 6 February, 60 completed it and became eligible to move on to basic and advanced flight training at Tuskegee Army Air Field. (History of 2164 AAFBU at Moton Field, AFHRA call number 234.81, Mar–Apr 1945)

17 April: The 332d Fighter Group flew two missions, one to escort a P-38 on a photographic reconnaissance mission over the Linz area of Austria and the Munich area of southern Germany. The other escorted B-17s of the 5th Bombardment Wing and B-24s of the 304th Bombardment Wing over and from Bologna, Italy. The report noted that the B-24s were split up by enemy antiaircraft artillery fire (flak) in the target area, and fighter coverage was quite difficult. (332d Fighter Group mission report numbers 288 and 289)

18 April: The 332d Fighter Group again flew two missions. One escorted a P-38 on a photographic reconnaissance mission over the Brno area. The other escorted B-24s of the 304th Bombardment Wing (although originally assigned to escort B-17s of the 5th Bombardment Wing) over and from Bologna, Italy. (332d Fighter Group mission report numbers 290 and 291)

19 April: The 332d Fighter Group flew two missions, one to escort B-24 Liberator bombers to, over, and from the Pucheim railroad yards and Wels, and one to escort a P-38 on a photographic reconnaissance mission over the Munich area of southern Germany. (332d Fighter Group mission report numbers 292 and 293)

20 April: The 332d Fighter Group again flew two missions, one to escort B-24s of the 49th and 55th Bombardment Wings raiding railroad bridges in northern Italy, and one to escort a P-38 on a photographic reconnaissance mission over the Praha and Brno areas of Czechoslovakia. On the first mission, one of the P-51 pilots was at first reported missing, but he eventually returned. (332d Fighter Group mission report numbers 294 and 295)

20 April: The War Department directed the release of the 101 black officers who had been confined at Godman Field one week earlier for insubordination at Freeman Field. Three days later, the officers were released. They were transferred to the 126th Army Air Forces Base Unit at Walterboro Field in South Carolina. (LeRoy F. Gillead, "The Tuskegee Experiment and Tuskegee Airmen, 1939–1949," call number 289.28–18 at the Air Force Historical Research Agency). In 1995, the Air Force announced the removal of the reprimand from the personnel files of those who requested such removal.

21 April: The 332d Fighter Group flew three missions in one day. It flew a fighter sweep south of a line running from Augsburg to Munich to Regensburg. Another mission escorted B-24 Liberators of the 49th Bombardment Wing to, over, and from the Attang and Pucheim marshalling yards. The third mission escorted two British bombers, one Halifax and one Lancaster, on a supply-dropping mission over Yugoslavia. (332d Fighter Group mission report numbers 296, 297, and 298) Flight Officer Leland H. Pennington of the 301st Fighter Squadron was reported missing with his P-51B at 1050 hours 15 miles west of Zara off the coast of Yugoslavia. (Missing Air Crew Report number 14022). 1st Lt. Hugh J. White of the 99th Fighter Squadron was also reported missing on 21 April. He returned eight days later, having evaded enemy forces in Italy. (Escape, Evasion, and Repatriation Reports, 332d Fighter Group)

22 April: The 332d Fighter Group was assigned to escort a photographic reconnaissance aircraft over Brno, Czechoslovakia. (332d Fighter Group mission report number 299) On the same day, the group conducted an armed reconnaissance mission over northern Italy. This was the 300th mission the 332d Fighter Group flew for the Fifteenth Air Force. (332d Fighter Group mission report number 300)

23 April: The 332d Fighter Group flew three missions, one to escort a P-38 on a reconnaissance mission over the Prague area of Czechoslovakia, one to escort another P-38 on another reconnaissance mission over the Linz and Brno areas, and one to escort B-24 Liberators of the 55th and 304th Bombardment Wings to and over the Padua and Cavarzere areas of Italy. On the latter mission one of the 332d Fighter Group P-51 fighters was hit by enemy antiaircraft artillery, but the pilot bailed out safely. He was 1st Lt. Hugh J. White of the 99th Fighter Squadron, who was reported missing at 1150 hours over Stanghella, Italy. (332d Fighter Group mission report numbers 301, 302, and 303; Missing Air Crew Report number 14035)

23 April: The 101 black officers who had been arrested at Freeman Field and later transported to Godman Field, for refusing to sign a base regulation calling for segregated base facilities, were released by order of Major General Frank O'D Hunter, commander of the First Air Force. At the same time, Colonel Robert Selway gave each of the officers a written administrative reprimand to become a part of their records. (History of Freeman Field, Indiana, 1 March-15 June 1945, AFHRA call numbers 283.28–6 and 283.48–7, 33) The three officers who had been arrested at Freeman Field on April 5, and were still being held for that incident, remained under arrest, awaiting court martial.

24 April: The 332d Fighter Group escorted B-24 bombers of the 47th and 49th Bombardment Wings to, over, and from enemy targets in northern Italy. (332d Fighter Group mission report number 304)

25 April: The 332d Fighter Group flew four missions, including one armed reconnaissance mission over the Verona area of northern Italy. Two other missions escorted Mosquito-type aircraft on reconnaissance missions, one over the Munich area of southern Germany and one over the Linz area of Austria (then part of Germany). The fourth mission escorted a P-38 on a reconnaissance mission over the Salzburg area of Austria. (332d Fighter Group mission report numbers 305, 306, 307, and 308)

26 April: The 332nd Fighter Group scored the last four aerial victory credits in the Mediterranean Theater of Operations (MTO) (USAF Historical Study no. 85, 334–335). The 332d Fighter Group flew two missions. One escorted a P-38 on a reconnaissance mission over Linz, Prague, and Amstettin in central Europe. On that mission, the group encountered German Me-109 fighters. 2d Lieutenant Thomas W. Jefferson shot down two of the enemy airplanes, and 1st Lieutenant Jimmy Lanham and 2d Lieutenant Richard A. Simons each shot down one. (332d Fighter Group mission report number 309 and Fifteenth Air Force General Orders 2990 and 3362 from 1945) These were the last aerial victories of the Tuskegee Airmen during the war. The 332d Fighter Group had shot down a total of 94 enemy aircraft during World War II. The 99th Fighter Squadron had shot down a total of 18 enemy airplanes before joining the 332d Fighter Group. Together, African-American pilots shot down a total of 112 enemy airplanes during World War II. The other mission that day was the 332d Fighter Group's final bomber escort for the Fifteenth Air Force, protecting B-24s of the 47th and 55th Bombardment Wings on raids over the Casarsa and Malcontenta ammunition storage dumps. (332d Fighter Group mission report number 310) 1st Lt. Thomas W. Jefferson of the 301st Fighter Squadron earned a Distinguished Flying Cross for his heroic actions on this day. (Fifteenth Air Force General Order 3343 dated 22 May 1945)

26–27 April: In the United States, the 477th Bombardment Group and its four squadrons (616th, 617th, 618th, and 619th) moved from Freeman Field, Indiana, where there had been a racial incident, back to Godman Field, Kentucky, where the group had been based before 5 March. (477th Bombardment Group history for the period 16 April-15 July 1945). The move delayed the group's training, not only because of the time it took, but also because Godman Field lacked the abundant space of Freeman Field.

28 April: The 387th Air Service Group moved back from Freeman Field, Indiana, to Godman Field, Kentucky, where it had been stationed before 7 March. (387th Air Service Group history for the period February-April 1945)

28 April: Back in Alabama, a severe storm damaged the roofs of approximately 76 buildings at Tuskegee Army Air Field. The source does not indicate if the storm was a tornado. The same severe thunderstorm damaged 24 primary flight training aircraft at Moton Field. Eleven of them were PT-13s and six were PT-17s. Two other primary flight schools in Florida lent PT13s to Moton Field so that the training could continue there. (History of Tuskegee Army Air Field, 2143rd AAFBU, Mar–Apr 1945, vol. 1, AFHRA call number 289.28–9; History of 2164th AAFBU at Moton Field, Mar–Apr 1945, call no. 234.821)

29 April: 1st Lt. Hugh J. White of the 99th Fighter Squadron, who had been reported Missing in Action on 21 April, returned, after evading enemy forces in Italy for eight days. (Escape, Evasion, and Repatriation Reports, 332d Fighter Group)

30 April: The 332d Fighter Group flew its 312th mission for the Fifteenth Air Force, when the 99th Fighter Squadron provided escort for a reconnaissance aircraft to Bolzano, Italy. (332d Fighter Group mission report number 311; one of the earlier reports covered two different missions) Since the 332d Fighter Group was assigned to the Fifteenth Air Force, which managed U.S. strategic bombing in the Mediterranean Theater of Operations, the group had flown 179 bomber escort missions, 172 of them to protect heavy bombers such as B-17s or B-24s. This is the last 332d Fighter Group combat mission for the Fifteenth Air Force for which a mission report was found.

April: During that month members of the 332d Fighter Group and its squadrons shot down a total of 17 enemy airplanes.

May: For the first time, the number of black Army Air Forces personnel overseas exceeded the number of black Army Air Forces personnel back in the United States. The number of white Army Air forces personnel overseas began to exceed the number of white Army Air Forces personnel back in the United States by January 1945. (Wesley Frank Craven and James Lea Cate, editors, *The Army Air Forces in World War II*, volume VI, *Men and Planes* [Washington: Office of Air Force History, 1983], 524)

1 May: The 332d Fighter Group was scheduled to launch 48 P-51s to escort bombers to Klagenfurt, Austria, and also to escort a reconnaissance mission over San Severo, Italy, but no narrative mission reports for these missions were found. The 332d Fighter Group might have flown more than 312 missions for the Fifteenth Air Force, but no reports on other missions were found. (XV Fighter Command Field Orders 323a and 325a, both dated 30 Apr 1945, and a message in the Fifteenth Air Force mission folder for 1 May 1945)

c. 4 May: The 332d Fighter Group moved from Ramitelli Airfield, Italy, to Cattolica, Italy. (Maurer, *Air Force Combat Units of World War II*; 332d Fighter Group lineage and honors history; the May 1945 history of the 332nd Fighter Group notes that the group moved from Ramitelli to Cattolica during the first week of May 1945)

4 May: Troy Municipal Airport in Alabama, which had served as an auxiliary field for Maxwell Field for B-24 training, became an auxiliary field for Tuskegee Army Air Field for B-25 training for black pilots in the twin-engine advanced flying training phase. (History of Tuskegee Army Air Field and 2143rd AAF Base Unit, May-Jun 1945, call number 289.28–10 at the Air Force Historical Research Agency)

c. 5 May: The 99th Fighter Squadron moved to Cattolica, Italy. (Maurer, *Combat Squadrons of the Air Force, World War II*)

6 May: 1st Lt. Hugh J. White of the 99th Fighter Squadron returned to his unit after repatriation from northern Italy. On the same day, an armada of "Red Tails" took part in a Fifteenth Air Force Review over Caserta and Bari, Italy. (332d Fighter Group history, May 1945) A note in the Fifteenth Air Force mission folder for 6 May 1945 notes that "48 P-51s of the 332nd Fighter Group taking off at 0800 will intercept 304th Wing at 0912 and provide close escort on PTW" (penetration, target cover, and withdrawal), but this was all part of the simulation, which involved all the bomb and fighter groups of the Fifteenth Air Force. The pass in review was conducted as a tribute to the Fifteenth Air Force accomplishments. (Fifteenth Air Force Mission Folder for 6 May 1945)

7 May: 1st Lt. Herbert V. Clark, who had been missing in action since 16 Aug 1944, returned to the 99th Fighter Squadron, after having evaded capture for more than 8 months. During that time, he had led a band of partisans in northern Italy that conducted raids against German forces there. (332d Fighter Group history for May 1945)

8 May: The 332d Fighter Group held a ceremony to celebrate VE (victory in Europe) Day. During this ceremony, Colonel Yantis H. Taylor, commander of the 306th Fighter Wing, and Colonel Benjamin O. Davis Jr. awarded honors to 332d Fighter Group personnel. (332d Fighter Group history, May 1945) The ceremony probably took place at Cattolica Airdrome, Italy, to which the 332nd Fighter Group moved during the first week of May.

10 May: Flight Officers James T. Mitchell and Leon W. Spears of the 301st Fighter Squadron returned to their unit after repatriation from Poland. (332d Fighter Group history, May 1945)

11 May: 2d Lt. James L. Hall Jr. of the 99th Fighter Squadron returned to his unit after repatriation from Romania. That same day, the 332d Fighter Group assembled for a ceremony in which Major General Nathan F. Twining, commander of the Fifteenth Air Force, presented various honors, including the Distinguished Flying Cross, the Air Medal, and the Bronze Star, to various members of the 332d Fighter Group. (332d Fighter Group history, May 1945)

18 May: The War Department's McCloy Committee published a report on the April 1945 Freeman Field incident, noting that Colonel Robert Selway's 9 April 1945 order for separate officers' clubs for 477th Bombardment Group and other base personnel conflicted with U.S. Army regulations such as 210–10.

23 May: Twenty-one new black military pilots graduated from advanced pilot training at Tuskegee Army Air Field. Nineteen of them belonged to class

SE-45-C for single engine pilots, and two belonged to class TE-45-C for twin engine pilots.

29 May: Maj. William A. Campbell was awarded the first oak leaf cluster to his Distinguished Flying Cross (DFC), becoming the first black pilot to earn two DFCs. (332d Fighter Group History, Oct 1942–1947)

30 May: The 332d Fighter Group held a Memorial Day ceremony to honor members of the organization who died during the war. The program included a reading of the Gettysburg Address. (332d Fighter Group history, May 1945) The ceremony took place at Cattolica Airdrome, Italy.

June: Capt. Roscoe Brown assumed command of the 100th Fighter Squadron, succeeding Major Andrew D. Turner. (100th Fighter Squadron lineage and honors history)

1 June: The 67th AAF Base Unit (Tuskegee Weather Detachment) was discontinued. (organization record card)

8 June: In an impressive ceremony, Colonel Yantis H. Taylor, commander of the 306th Fighter Wing, presented Colonel Benjamin O. Davis Jr., commander of the 332d Fighter Group, the Silver Star for gallantry in action. He also awarded five Distinguished Flying Crosses, five Air Medals, and one Bronze Star to others. The troops passed in review to bid farewell to Colonel Davis as commander, who departed that day for the United States. Colonel Davis had been chosen to command the 477th Composite Group at Godman Field, Kentucky. In his farewell speech, Colonel Davis noted that the 332d Fighter Group had been a credit to itself and the Army Air Forces. (332d Fighter Group history, Jun 1945) On the same date, other key personnel of the 332nd Fighter Group and the 523rd Air Service Group were reassigned from the Fifteenth Air Force so that they could assume key staff positions with the 477th Composite Group. (Craig Huntly)

9 June: Maj. George S. Roberts resumed command of the 332d Fighter Group, succeeding Col. Benjamin O. Davis. (Maurer, *Air Force Combat Units of World War II*) At the same time, Capt. Wendell M. Lucas succeeded Maj. William A. Campbell as commander of the 99th Fighter Squadron. Both Davis and Campbell were moving back to the United States, Davis to eventually assume command of the 477th Bombardment Group, and Campbell to eventually resume command of the 99th Fighter Squadron after its own move to the United States later that summer. (332nd Fighter Group history for June 1945)

12 June: The 332d Fighter Group was relieved of its assignment to the XV Fighter Command (Provisional) and was assigned to the 305th Bombardment Wing, despite the fact that the group flew fighters. (332d Fighter Group history, June 1945)

21 June: Colonel Benjamin O. Davis Jr. flew from Washington, D.C. to Godman Field with General Eaker, then deputy commander, Army Air Forces, Truman Gibson, and Brig. Gen. Benjamin O. Davis Sr. The younger Davis that day assumed command of the 477th Bombardment Group, replacing Colonel Robert R. Selway Jr. At the same time, Colonel Davis also became temporary commander of the 387th Air Service Group, which supported the 477th Bombardment Group at Godman Field. Davis succeeded Lt. Col. David H. Thomas, a white officer who had been in command of the 387th Air Service Group since July 1944. (387th Air Service Group history for period April-July 1945; 387th Air Service Group Special Order 51 dated 23 June 1945). All of the white personnel who had been members of the 477th Bombardment Group and its bombardment squadrons, in leadership positions, transferred to other organizations, and the 477th Bombardment Group became an all-black organization. (477th Bombardment Group/477th Composite Group history, 16 Apr-15 Jul 1945)

22 June: Effective this date, a War Department AG letter issued on 27 July 1945 inactivated the 616th and 619th Bombardment Squadrons of the 477th Bombardment Group, which was redesignated the same date as the 477th Composite Group. That left the group with two of its bombardment squadrons, the 617th and 618th, at Godman Field. The Combat Crew Training School for the 477th Composite Group was moved from Godman Field, Kentucky, to Walterboro Army Air Field, South Carolina, because of limited space at Godman Field. Effective this date, the same War Department AG letter dated 27 July 1945 reassigned the 99th Fighter Squadron from the 332nd Fighter Group in Italy to the 477th Composite Group at Godman Field, Kentucky, moving the unit without personnel or equipment. However, members assigned to the 99th Fighter Squadron remained in Italy that summer, flying P-51s under the 332nd Fighter Group alongside members of the 100th and 301st Fighter Squadrons. Documents indicate that during the summer of 1945, members of the 99th Fighter Squadron were stationed in Italy flying P-51s with the 332nd Fighter Group even as other members of the 99th Fighter Squadron were stationed at Godman Field, Kentucky, flying P-47s while assigned to the 477th Composite Group. (War Department AG letter 322 dated 27 July 1945; 332nd Fighter Group histories, June and July 1945; 477th Bombardment Group/477th Composite Group history, 16 April-15 July 1945)

26 June: Major Elmer D. Jones Jr. assumed command of the 387th Air Service

Group, relieving Lt. Col. Benjamin O. Davis Jr., who remained commander of the 477th Bombardment Group. (387th Air Service Group history for the period April 1945-July 1945; 387th Air Service Group General Order 11 dated 26 June 1945)

27 June: Class SE-45-D graduated from advanced pilot training at Tuskegee Army Air Field. There were 29 in the class. They had trained in single engine aircraft to be future fighter pilots.

29 June: The emblem of the 301st Fighter Squadron was approved. It consisted of a disk depicting a cat on a flying machine gun. (Unit emblem folder)

30 June: During the January-June 1945 period, 422 black personnel entered primary flight training at Moton Field, but only 270 of them graduated from there to move on to basic and advanced flight training at Tuskegee Army Air Field. In other words, sixty-four percent of those who began primary flight training at Moton Field completed that phase, and thirty-six percent, or more than a third, "washed out" during that six-month period. (History of 2164th AAFBU at Moton Field, AFHRA call number 234.821, May-Jun 1945)

July: 74,272 black Army Air Forces personnel were overseas, more than the number of black Army Air Forces personnel that were still in the United States. 347 of them were commissioned officers (although not all of them were Tuskegee Airmen). (Wesley Frank Craven and James Lea Cate, editors, *The Army Air Forces in World War II*, volume VI, *Men and Planes* [Washington: Office of Air Force History, 1983], 524)

1 July: Colonel Benjamin O. Davis Jr. assumed command of Godman Field, Kentucky, becoming the first black officer to command a major Army Air Forces base. He had already become commander of the 477th Bombardment Group there, since 21 June. (History of Godman Field, Kentucky, 1 Mar-15 Oct 1945, AFHRA call number 283.48–8, which includes Godman Army Air Base General Order 16 dated 1 July 1945)

2 July: A court martial trial began for two of the three black officers who had been arrested initially at Freeman Field on April 5 for forcibly entering an officers' club reserved for whites. The defendants were Lieutenants Marsden A. Thomson, and Shirley R Clinton. The court found Thomson and Clinton not guilty. (Lt. Col. James C. Warren, *The Tuskegee Airmen Mutiny at Freeman Field* [Vacaville, CA: Conyers Publishing Company, 1995), 170–180; J. Todd Moye, *Freedom Flyers* [Oxford University Press, 2010], 133, 138, 141–142)

3 July: A court martial trial began for Lieutenant Roger C. "Bill" Terry, one of three officers who had been arrested at Freeman Field on April 5 for forcibly entering an officers' club reserved for whites. Terry was the only one of the "Freeman Field Mutiny" arrestees who was convicted. He was fined $150 and confined to base for three months because of "jostling." (Lt. Col. James C. Warren, *The Tuskegee Airmen Mutiny at Freeman Field* [Vacaville, CA: Conyers Publishing Company, 1995), 181–186.

3 July: Maj. William A. Campbell assumed command of the 99th Fighter Squadron, which he had commanded in the autumn of 1944. (Lineage and honors history of the 99th Fighter Squadron; 477th Bombardment Group/477th Composite Group history, 16 Apr-15 Jul 1945)

13 July: P-47 airplanes for the 99th Fighter Squadron began arriving at Godman Field. Around the same time, fighter pilots for the 99th Fighter Squadron were arriving from Walterboro Army Air Field, South Carolina. (477th Bombardment Group/477th Composite Group history, 16 Apr-15 Jul 1945.)

c. 18 July: The 332d Fighter Group and its squadrons moved from Cattolica, Italy, to Lucera, Italy. (Maurer, *Air Force Combat Units of World War II*; 332d Fighter Group lineage and honors history)

26 July: Pilot training continued at Tuskegee Army Air Field, Alabama, despite the fact the war in Europe had ended. A Tuskegee cadet Perry A. Dillman, crashed in his AT-6C training aircraft near Tallassee, Alabama. (Aircraft record card for aircraft serial number 42–48885, provided by Archangelo Difante)

27 July: The War Department issued an AG (Adjutant General) letter that redesignated the 477th Bombardment Group, Medium, as the 477th Composite Group and assigned the 99th Fighter Squadron from the 332nd Fighter Group in Italy to the 477th Composite Group, but effective 22 June 1945. By the same authority, the squadron was moved without personnel or equipment, from Italy to Godman Field, Kentucky, the base of the 477th Composite Group. By the terms of the same letter, the 616th and 619th Bombardment Squadrons of the 477th Composite Group were inactivated, effective 22 June 1945. However, members of the 99th Fighter Squadron continued to fly P-51 aircraft in Italy under the 332nd Fighter Group that summer.

4 August: Thirty-seven new black military pilots graduated from advanced pilot training at Tuskegee Army Air Field. Nineteen of them belonged to class SE-45-E for single engine pilots, and eighteen belonged to class TE-45-E for twin engine pilots.

6 August: Colonel Benjamin O. Davis Jr., then commander of the 477th Composite Group at Godman Field, visited Tuskegee Army Air Field, after having been invited to speak at the fourth anniversary celebration of the field's opening as a flying school site. It was the first time Davis had been back since 2 April 1943, when the 99th Fighter Squadron deployed from Tuskegee under Davis for overseas combat duty. (B. O. Davis Jr. autobiography)

7 August: Pilots assigned to the 99th Fighter Squadron flew their final mission in Italy. (Craig Huntly)

8 August: Twenty-five pilots assigned to the 99th Fighter Squadron were reassigned to the 7th Replacement Depot for transportation back to the United States. (Craig Huntly)

22 August: The 332nd Fighter Group issued orders that reassigned 99th Fighter Squadron personnel in Italy to other organizations. Capt. Wendell Lucas, who had been commander of the squadron, was reassigned and appointed deputy commander of the 332nd Fighter Group. Other personnel were reassigned to the 100th or 301st Fighter Squadrons. (Craig Huntly)

August: Only two primary flight schools remained operational: Tuskegee Institute's Moton Field, which trained black pilots; and a school at Orangeburg, South Carolina, which trained French pilots. (Wesley Frank Craven and James Lea Cate, editors, *The Army Air Forces in World War II*, volume VI, *Men and Planes* [Washington: Office of Air Force History, 1983], 457)

August: Of 2,253,182 Army Air Forces personnel at the time, 139,559 were black. That was 6.2 percent of the total (blacks at the time constituted about 10 percent of the USA population). 1,533 of the black Army Air Forces personnel were commissioned officers. Most but not all of these were Tuskegee Airmen. (Wesley Frank Craven and James Lea Cate, editors, *The Army Air Forces in World War II*, volume VI, *Men and Planes* [Washington: Office of Air Force History, 1983], 523)

September: The 332d Fighter Group and its squadrons departed Lucera, Italy, for movement to the United States of America. (Maurer, *Air Force Combat Units of World War II*; 332d Fighter Group lineage and honors history)

8 September: Thirty-nine new black military pilots graduated from advanced pilot training at Tuskegee Army Air Field. Twenty of them belonged to class SE-45-F for single engine pilots, and nineteen of them belonged to class TE-45-F for twin engine pilots. Class 45F was the largest class of pilots to graduate at Tuskegee Army Air Field.

11 September: Forty-one students graduated from primary flight training at

Moton Field, in class 46-A. Eighty-three had begun the class on 28 June. (History of 2164th AAFBU at Moton Field, AFHRA call number 234.821, Sep-Nov 1945)

4 October: The War Department directed that a 3-man board of officers prepare a policy for the use of Negro manpower in the post-war period, "including the complete development of the means required to derive the maximum efficiency from the full authorized manpower of the nation . . ." (Preface of the Gillem Report, AFHRA call number 170.2111–1, Nov 1945)

20 September: Joe Louis, the heavyweight boxing champion of the world, visited Godman Field, home of the 477th Composite Group, and the only "all Negro Army Air Base in the history of the Army Air Forces." Around the same time, Walter White and Roy Wilkins of the National Association for the Advancement of Colored People also visited the group at the base. (Godman Field History, 15 Oct 1945–15 Jan 1946, call number 283.48–9 at the Air Force Historical Research Agency.)

1 October: The 332nd Fighter Group departed Montecorvino, Italy, and soon thereafter boarded a liberty ship to cross the Atlantic Ocean to return to the United States. The ship was the USS *Levi Woodbury.* (332nd Fighter Group organizational record card; telephone conversation of Daniel Haulman with Lt. Col. Leo Gray, a member of the group's 100th Fighter Squadron.)

8 October: The 618th Bombardment Squadron was inactivated, leaving the 477th Composite Group with only two squadrons, the 99th Fighter Squadron and the 617th Bombardment Squadron. (Maurer, *Combat Squadrons of the Air Force, World War II*)

9 October: Primary Flight Training for black military pilots, which had been conducted at Moton Field, moved to Tuskegee Army Air Field as Captain Robert A. Ports became Director of Primary Flight Training there. During the same month, twelve TP-13 primary training aircraft were transferred from Moton Field to Tuskegee Army Air Field. (2143d Army Air Forces Base Unit, Tuskegee Army Air Field, Sep-Oct 1945, AFHRA call number 289.28–11A)

16 October: Twenty-one new black military pilots graduated from advanced pilot training at Tuskegee Army Air Field. Eight of them belonged to class SE-45-G for single engine pilots, and thirteen of them belonged to class TE-45-G for twin engine pilots. This was the first day that more twin engine pilots graduated at Tuskegee Army Air Field than single engine pilots.

17 October: The remaining members of the 332d Fighter Group arrived at the

New York Port of Embarkation aboard the ship *Levi Woodbury*, and there was a welcome ceremony as the ship docked. Members of the 332nd Fighter Group and its squadrons moved on to Camp Kilmer, New Jersey. (Organization record card for 332nd Fighter Group; telephone conversation of Daniel Haulman with Lt. Col. Leo Gray, who was aboard the ship; Maurer, *Air Force Combat Units of World War II*)

18 October: Thirty-five students graduated from primary flight training at Moton Field, in class 46-B. Eighty-three had begun the training on 8 August. (History of 2164th AAFBU at Moton Field, AFHRA call number 234.821, Sep-Nov 1945)

19 October: The 332d Fighter Group was inactivated, along with the 100th Fighter Squadron and the 301st Fighter Squadron. (Maurer, *Air Force Combat Units of World War II;* Maurer, *Combat Squadrons of the Air Force, World War II*) The 302d Fighter Squadron had already been inactivated in March. That left only the 99th Fighter Squadron active, and it had already been assigned to the 477th Composite Group, stationed at Godman Field, Kentucky.

17 November: A War Department board of general officers headed by Lieutenant General Alvan C. Gillem Jr. submitted a report, "Policy for Utilization of Negro Manpower in the Post-War Army" to U.S. Army Chief of Staff, General George C. Marshall. Besides General Gillem, Maj. Gen. Lewis A. Pick and Brig. Gen. Winslow C. Morse served on the board. Although the so-called "Gillem Report" called for more Negro officers, more Negro combat units, more opportunities for professional and leadership development for Negroes, equal treatment of all officers, and continued "experimental groupings of Negro units with white units in composite organizations," it did not call for immediate or complete desegregation of the Army. The report compared the 332d Fighter Group with the other three P-51 fighter escort groups in the Fifteenth Air Force during World War II, but was somewhat contradictory. On the one hand, it praised the bomber escort performance of the 332d Fighter Group and its leader, Col. Benjamin O. Davis Jr., and on the other hand the report negatively criticized the group for staying with the bombers (which was the policy of Colonel Davis) instead of racking up higher numbers of aerial victory credits by leaving the bombers in search of enemy airplanes to shoot down. It claimed that the other three P-51 groups each destroyed more than two enemy aircraft for each one it lost in combat, but that the 332d Fighter Group lost more aircraft in combat than it destroyed. (This statement was not true, since the 332nd Fighter Group shot down 94 enemy aircraft between the start of June

1944 and the end of April 1945, and lost far fewer airplanes in air-to-air combat). The Gillem Report also criticized the 332d Fighter Group for not taking part in any major air battles, despite the fact that did indeed take part in some major air battles, during which it both shot down large numbers of enemy aircraft and sometimes also lost some of its escorted bombers to enemy aircraft. For example, on the June 9, 1944 mission, the 332d Fighter Group encountered very many enemy fighters, and while it shot down five of them, two of the escorted bombers were shot down. On July 18, 1944, on the Memmingen mission, the 332d Fighter Group encountered more than a hundred enemy fighters, and while it shot down 12 German airplanes that day, fifteen of the bombers it was assigned to escort were also shot down. The report implies that the group had a choice between protecting bombers and shooting down enemy fighters, and that it chose to protect bombers instead, resulting in lower aerial victory credit totals. However, the mission reports indicate that, regardless of group, when more enemy airplanes showed up, there were both more aerial victory credits and more bombers lost. Certainly, on a mission in which no enemy aircraft were encountered, which was a majority of the missions for all the groups, there could have been no bombers shot down by enemy aircraft, and no aerial victory credits, either. In other words, a group did not really have much control over whether a mission would produce more opportunity for aerial victory credits, and at the same time, more bomber losses. (Gillem Report, AFHRA call number 170.2111–1; IRIS number 00128007; War Department Circular 124)

20 November. Twenty-five new black military pilots graduated from advanced pilot training at Tuskegee Army Air Field. Five of them belonged to class SE-45-H for single engine pilots, and twenty of them belonged to class TE-45-H for twin engine pilots.

23 November. Twenty-two students graduated from primary flight training at Moton Field, in class 46-C. Ninety-Five had begun the training on 11 September. (History of 2164 AAFBU, AFHRA call number 234.821, Mar–Apr 1945)

28 November. In a memorandum to Secretary of War Robert B. Patterson, Truman K. Gibson Jr., Civilian Aide to the Secretary of War, criticized the Gillem Report for failing to clearly address the issue of segregation and called for the War Department to issue a clear policy statement on the issue. ("Supplemental Report of War Department Special Board on Negro Manpower," AFHRA call number 170.2111–1A, 26 Jan 1946)

1 December. The 2164th AAF Base Unit (Contract Pilot School Primary), which operated the primary flight training school at Tuskegee, was discontinued. The basic and advanced flight training at Tuskegee Army Air Field, about six miles to the northwest of Moton Field, continued until the end of June 1946.

10 December: Lieutenants Spurgeon N. Ellington and Richard W. Hall were killed in an airplane accident while stationed at Tuskegee Army Air Field. Both had graduated from advanced pilot training there in 1943, had served in combat overseas, and had returned to Tuskegee Army Air Field to train other black pilots. (History of Tuskegee Army Air Field, Nov–Dec 1945)

18 December: Major Harold C. Magoon became Personnel Staff Officer with the 2143rd Army Air Force Base Unit at Tuskegee Army Air Field, after having served with administration of the primary flight training at Moton Field. (History of Tuskegee Army Air Field, Nov–Dec 1945)

31 December: Of 16 "key personnel" leaders listed at Tuskegee Army Air Field, 13 were white. The great majority of personnel at the base, however, were black. Of the 435 officers, 380 were black, and 55 were white. Of the 1661 enlisted personnel, 1640 were black, and 21 were white. (Histories of Tuskegee Army Air Field at the Air Force Historical Research Agency)

1946

29 January: Nine new black military pilots graduated from advanced pilot training at Tuskegee Army Air Field. Four of them belonged to class SE-45-I for single engine pilots, and five belonged to class TE-45-I for twin engine pilots.

31 January: The 126th Army Air Forces Base Unit at Walterboro Army Air Field, South Carolina, was inactivated.

28 February: The United States Navy announced that it was lifting racial restrictions in personnel assignments, and that black personnel would be eligible to serve in any position on any ship. Implementation of the new policy followed gradually. At the end of World War II, the U.S. Navy had 52 black officers, and no black pilots, while the Army Air Forces had 1,191 black officers, with many black pilots. (Benjamin O. Davis Jr., *Benjamin O. Davis, Jr., American* [Washington: Smithsonian Institution Press, 1991], 154)

13–15 March: The 477th Composite Group moved to Lockbourne Army Air Base, Ohio. (B. O. Davis Jr. autobiography; Maurer, *Combat Squadrons of the Air Force, World War II*; Maurer, *Air Force Combat Units of World War II*)

23 March: Twelve new black military pilots graduated from advanced pilot training at Tuskegee Army Air Field. Eight of them belonged to class SE-

46-A for single engine pilots, and four of them belonged to class TE-46-A for twin engine pilots.

14 April: The 2143rd AAF Base Unit and the Army Air Forces Pilot School [Basic-Advanced), Tuskegee Army Air Field, Tuskegee, Alabama, was discontinued. The field did not close immediately, and the last class, (46-C) continued training there. (organization record cards for both organizations; folder on Tuskegee Army Air Field at Air Force Historical Research Agency). By then, the base had 367 black and 46 white officers, and 1129 black and 7 white enlisted personnel, for a total of 413 officers and 1136 enlisted personnel. In addition, approximately 500 civilians still worked on the base. The total numbers, however, had declined significantly since the end of 1945. (Histories of Tuskegee Army Air Field at the Air Force Historical Research Agency)

15 April: The 385th AAF Base Unit was organized at Tuskegee Army Air Field, Alabama, replacing the 2143d AAF Base Unit that had served there. (385 AAF Base Unit organization record card). At the same time, the Army Air Forces transferred the field from Flying Training Command to Tactical Air Command. Col. Noel F. Parrish remained commander of the base, but the base was scheduled to end its flying training mission. At the time, the base had 45 AT-6D airplanes that had been used for basic and advanced single engine flying training, and 12 TB-25J airplanes that had been used for twin engine advanced flying training. By this date, 1682 black cadets had entered flying training at Tuskegee Army Air Field, but only 992 had completed that training. Approximately 59 percent completed the training, and 41 percent did not. (Histories of Tuskegee Army Air Field at Air Force Historical Research Agency)

14 May: Seven new black military pilots graduated advanced flying training at Tuskegee Army Air Field in class 46-B. Three were single-engine pilots, and four were twin-engine pilots.

29 June: The last class of pilots (46-C) graduated at Tuskegee Army Air Field. There were only 9 pilots in the class. Seven were single engine pilots and two were twin engine pilots. A total of 930 pilots graduated from advanced pilot training there since March 1942. In addition to those, there were also 51 liaison pilots and 11 service pilots who trained at fields in the Tuskegee area during World War II, for a total of 992. (385th AAF Base Unit history, Jun–Oct 1946, vol. I; Thole, 19; Tuskegee Army Air Field roster of pilot graduates, with dates of graduation; Craig Huntly). A member of class 46-C-TE, 2nd Lt. Claude A. Rowe of Detroit, Michigan, had already completed pilot training in 1944 with the Royal Canadian Air Force. (Gerald A. White, "A

Tuskegee Airman with a Difference," *Air Force Print News*)

Summer: Black pilots at Tuskegee Army Air Field who did not choose to separate from the service transferred to Lockbourne Army Air Field in Ohio, where the only black flying group left in the Army Air Forces at the time, the 477th Composite Group, was stationed. It was under the command of Col. Benjamin O. Davis Jr. (Histories of Tuskegee Army Air Field at the Air Force Historical Research Agency)

30 June: Tuskegee Army Air Field was placed on temporarily inactive status, with permanent inactivation to come, because personnel were still assigned to the base. (385th AAF Base Unit history, Jun–Oct 1946, vol I). New African American pilots who received their flight training between the middle of 1946 and the middle of 1949 received that flight training beyond Tuskegee at other flight schools that were predominantly white.

20 August: Col. Noel F. Parrish was reassigned from Tuskegee Army Air Field, which he had commanded, to Air University at Maxwell Field, Alabama. He became a student at the Air Command and Staff School, home of the 42nd Army Air Forces Base Unit. He eventually wrote a thesis there advocating racial integration in the Air Force. (385th AAF Base Unit history, Jun–Oct 1946, vol. I; Histories of Tuskegee Army Air Field at Air Force Historical Research Agency)

22 Aug 1947: Colonel Benjamin O. Davis Jr. assumed command of the 332nd Fighter Wing, which had been organized over the 332nd Fighter Group a week earlier at Lockbourne Army Air Base (later, Lockbourne Air Force Base). He remained commander of the wing and the base until inactivation of the wing there in 1949.

28 August: Major Gabe C. Hawkins, a white officer, ended his service as Director of Training and Operations at Tuskegee Army Air Field. He had held that position since March 1945. (Histories of Tuskegee Army Air Field at Air Force Historical Research Agency)

31 August: Lt. Col. Donald G. McPherson, who had served as deputy commander under Col. Noel F. Parrish, assumed command of the 385th AAF Base Unit, the only unit remaining at Tuskegee Army Air Field. (385th AAF Base Unit history, Jun–Oct 1946, vol. I)

1 September: The training department at Tuskegee Army Air Field inactivated. It had remained active after pilot training at Tuskegee ended (29 June) in order to help the remaining pilots at the base to maintain their flying proficiency. (385th AAF Base Unit history, Jun–Oct 1946, vol. I)

5 October: The Army Air Forces Weather Station at Tuskegee Army Air Field closed. (Histories of Tuskegee Army Air Field at Air Force Historical Research Agency)

22 October: Army Air Forces officials at Tuskegee Army Air Field met with representatives of the U.S. Army Corps of Engineers to hammer out details of transfer of the base by the end of the year.

5 December: President Harry S. Truman issued Executive Order 9808, establishing a President's Committee on Civil Rights. Among the members he appointed to the committee were Charles E. Wilson, president of General Electric, and Franklin D. Roosevelt Jr., son of the late president. The findings of the commission encouraged Truman to announce a civil rights campaign early in 1948. (Chauncey Spencer; David McCullough, *Truman* [New York: Simon and Schuster, 1992], 587; Lawrence P. Scott and William W. Womack Sr., *Double V* [East Lansing: Michigan State University Press, 1994], 274–275)

1947

May: Col. Noel F. Parrish's thesis for Air Command and Staff School at Maxwell Field, entitled "Segregation of Negroes in the Army Air Forces," was published. He condemned the continuing racial segregation in the Army Air Forces and called for integration instead. His thesis noted that most black persons in America were part white, and many white persons in America were part black, and that persons should be judged as individuals, not as part of some amorphous racial group.

4 June: Col. Noel F. Parrish graduated from Air Command and Staff School of Air University at Maxwell Field.

12 June: Tuskegee Army Air Field closed permanently when the 385th AAF Base Unit, the last unit there, was discontinued. (385th AAF Base Unit organization record card)

1 July: The 477th Composite Group and the 617th Bombardment Squadron, which had been assigned to it, were inactivated at Lockbourne, Ohio. At the same time, the 99th Fighter Squadron, which had also been assigned to the 477th Composite Group, was reassigned to the newly reactivated 332d Fighter Group at Lockbourne. Capt. Melvin T. Jackson was commander of the 99th Fighter Squadron at the time. At the same time, the inactivated 100th and 301st Fighter Squadrons were activated again, and assigned, like the 99th Fighter Squadron, to the 332d Fighter Group. Maj. Andrew D. Turner became commander of the 100th Fighter Squadron. The group and its squadrons were equipped with P-47 aircraft. (Maurer, *Combat Squadrons of the Air Force, World War II;* Maurer, *Air Force Combat Units of World War II;* Lineage and honors history of the 99th Fighter Squadron; 100th Fighter Squadron lineage and honors history) The bombardment pilots and crews who had been assigned to the 477th Composite Group and its bombardment squadrons had to undergo transition training with AT-6s and P-47s to become fighter pilots. The 99th Fighter Squadron, however, did not need such transition flying training.

28 July: The 332d Fighter Wing was established.

15 August: The 332d Fighter Wing was activated under the command of Major Edward C. Gleed at Lockbourne Army Air Base. The 332d Fighter Group was assigned to the wing. At about the same time, Capt. Elwood T. Driver assumed command of the 100th Fighter Squadron, succeeding Maj. Andrew D. Turner. (100th Fighter Squadron lineage and honors history)

28 August: By this date, Maj. William A. Campbell had assumed command of the 332nd Fighter Group. (332nd Fighter Group lineage and honors history)

September: After W. Stuart Symington was sworn in as first Secretary of the Air Force on 18 September, Secretary of Defense James W. Forrestal ordered air personnel, bases, and materiel transferred from the Army to the new Department of the Air Force on 26 September. All African American personnel in the air units of the United States Army transferred to the United States Air Force at the same time, but they were still in segregated organizations such as the 332nd Fighter Wing and 332nd Fighter Group and its squadrons at Lockbourne Army Air Base, which became Lockbourne Air Force Base. There was a smooth transition. Symington, who, like Truman, was from Missouri, supported the idea that the new United States Air Force should be racially integrated, and later helped the President draft Executive Order 9981 which mandated the racial integration of all the military services. Symington had to wait for the executive order before he could implement the policy. (Alan Gropman, *The Air Force Integrates* [Washington: Office of Air Force History, 1985], 89–90)

October: By this month, Capt. Charles I. Williams had assumed command of the 301st Fighter Squadron. (301st Fighter Squadron lineage and honors history)

October-November: The 99th Fighter Squadron of the 332d Fighter Group (332nd Fighter Wing) took part in Operation Combine and performed so well that it was awarded a certificate of appreciation signed by Maj. Gen.

William D. Old, commander of the Ninth Air Force. The certificate noted that the squadron's personnel worked under difficulties and handicaps not normally expected, but in spite of them, performed with exceptionally high efficiency. Operation Combine was a training exercise involving a simulated invasion of the United States, and involved the dropping of airborne forces and tactical air support for them. (Certificate of Appreciation, Ninth Air Force, to 99th Fighter Squadron, 332d Fighter Group, 1947, sent by Zellie Orr; Ninth Air Force History, Jul–Dec 1947, part 2)

1948

7 January: Several individuals at Lockbourne Air Force Base, including Albert R. Pickering, Alex A. Boudreaux, Franklin G. Eisele, and Captain Charles E. McGee, reported having witnessed an unidentified flying object in the night sky a few miles west and southwest of the base. Their accounts are very similar, and describe an object unlike any existing aircraft. (Guy E. Franklin, *The Tuskegee Airmen UFO Connection* (e-book, 2014)

April: Capt. Marion R. Rodgers replaced Capt. Melvin T. Jackson as commander of the 99th Fighter Squadron. (Lineage and honors history of the 99th Fighter Squadron). Capt. Herbert V. Clark replaced Capt. Elwood T. Driver as commander of the 100th Fighter Squadron. (100th Fighter Squadron lineage and honors history)

5 April: In a letter to Lemuel E. Graves of the *Pittsburgh Courier*, General Carl A. Spaatz, the first Chief of Staff of the United States Air Force, stated "the ultimate Air Force objective must be to eliminate segregation . . .," although he did not give a date when that would be accomplished. (Alan L. Gropman, *The Air Force Integrates, 1945–1964* [Washington: Office of Air Force History, 1985] p.88.)

9 April: Capt. Alva N. Temple and 1st Lt. Halbert L. Alexander, two Tuskegee Airmen pilots, completed a fighter gunnery class at Williams Air Force Base, Arizona, in class 48B-G. They had started the class on 16 February. Both would later serve on the 332nd Fighter Group team that won the non-jet aircraft category at the Las Vegas Gunnery Meet the following year. (History of Williams AFB, AZ and the 3010 Air Force Base Unit, AFHRA call number 289.80–25 Apr–Jun 1948)

April: In testimony to the National Defense Conference on Negro Affairs, Assistant Secretary of the Air Force Eugene Zuckert confirmed that the Air Force supported racial integration, because the "Air Force accepts no doctrine of racial superiority or inferiority." Lt. Gen. Idwal H. Edwards, Air Force Deputy Chief of Staff for Personnel, agreed that the Air Force needed to integrate, because he thought that racial segregation was a waste of manpower. (Alan L. Gropman, *The Air Force Integrates, 1945–1964* [Washington: Office of Air Force History, 1985] pp. 87–89)

26 April: General Carl A. Spaatz, first Chief of Staff of the United States Air Force, announced his policy for the racial integration of the Air Force. The announcement confirmed what he had earlier communicated in his letter to Lemuel Graves of the *Pittsburgh Courier*. (John T. Correll, "The Air Force 1907–2007," *Air Force Magazine,* September 2007; information provided by Tuskegee Airman George Hardy, chairman of the Harry A. Sheppard Historical Research Committee of the Tuskegee Airmen Incorporated)

May: Capt. Joseph D. Elsberry assumed command of the 100th Fighter Squadron, succeeding Capt. Elwood T. Driver. (100th Fighter Squadron lineage and honors history)

19 May: 1st Lt. Daniel "Chappie" James was involved in an aircraft accident at Eglin Air Force Base, Florida. After a runaway P-47 engine, he overshot the runway and the aircraft flipped over on its back. He was not seriously injured, and was extricated from the aircraft. His unit was stationed at Lockbourne Air Force Base, Ohio, but he was on temporary duty at Eglin. (332nd Fighter Wing history, Apr–Jun 1948)

June: 1st Lt. Samuel W. Watts Jr. succeeded Capt. Joseph D. Elsberry as commander of the 100th Fighter Squadron. (100th Fighter Squadron lineage and honors history)

4 June: Having graduated from Air University's Air Command and Staff School at Maxwell Field (Maxwell Air Force Base), Alabama, the previous June, Col. Noel F. Parrish graduated from the Air War College there, a year later.

25 June: 2d Lt. Claude R. Platte graduated from advanced flight training at Williams Air Force Base, Arizona. He was the first black pilot to complete fight training at Williams. (History of Williams AFB, Arizona, and 3010 Air Force Base Unit, 1948, call number 289.80 at Air Force Historical Research Agency)

14 July: Capt. Joseph D. Elsberry resumed command of the 100th Fighter Squadron, a position he had held in May. (100th Fighter Squadron lineage and honors history)

26 July: President Harry S. Truman signed two executive orders, 9980 and 9981. The first set up a Fair Employment Board for federal civil service. The second, Executive Order 9981, mandated the racial integration of all the military services. The order stated "It is hereby declared to be the policy of the President that there shall be equality of treatment and opportunity for all persons in the Armed Services without regard to race . . ." The same order called for the creation within the national Military Establishment of "an advisory committee to be known as the President's Committee on Equality of Treatment and Opportunity in the Armed Services . . ." which he authorized to examine the "rules, procedures, and practices of the Armed Services . . .to determine in what respect such rules, procedures, and practices may be altered or improved with a view to carrying out the policy of this order." While the order did not specifically mention the words "integration" or "desegregation," that is what eventually resulted. Stuart Symington, the Secretary of the Air Force who had already announced his support of the racial integration of the Air Force, had helped President Truman draft Executive Order 9981. USAF Chief of Staff General Carl A. Spaatz had already announced in April that the Air Force would integrate, and that was accomplished in 1949. (Alan L. Gropman, *The Air Force Integrates, 1945–1964* [Washington: Office of Air Force History, 1985], 89 and 109) Black pilots were already training at integrated bases such as Williams Field in Arizona.

26 July: A. Philip Randolph ended his call for massive black civil disobedience against the draft, which he had planned to start on 18 August to pressure the Truman administration to integrate the armed forces.

2 August: Staff Sergeant Malvin C. Whitfield, a member of the 100th Fighter Squadron of the 332nd Fighter Group stationed at Lockbourne AFB, Ohio, won a gold medal for first place in the 800 meters track and field event at Wembley Stadium in England in the 1948 Summer Olympic Games, bringing honor to himself, the Tuskegee Airmen, and the United States. He set a new Olympic record in the event, breaking the old record by six tenths of a second. Later at the same Olympics, Whitfield earned a bronze medal for third place in the 400 meters. (332d Fighter Group history for Jul-Sep 1948)

August: Col. Joseph F. Goetz, chief of the entertainment section of the United States Air Force, visited Lockbourne AFB, Ohio, and saw a talent show there. He agreed to arrange USAF funding for a traveling version of the show, which became "Operation Happiness," and which began performing in November. (332nd Fighter Wing history, Dec 1948-Jan 1949)

25 August: Capt. Richard C. Pullam assumed command of the 301st Fighter Squadron, succeeding Capt. Charles I. Williams. (301st Fighter Squadron lineage and honors history)

13–16 September: The 332nd Fighter Group and its 99th, 100th, and 301st Fighter Squadrons took part in Operation Combine III with other United States Air Force units at Elgin Air Force Base, Florida. They flew P-47s in simulated combat missions. (332d Fighter Group history, Jul-Sep 1948)

30 September: Capt. Elwood T. Driver succeeded Capt. Joseph D. Elsberry as commander of the 100th Fighter Squadron. He remained commander until the squadron was inactivated and ceased to be a segregated unit on 1 July 1949. (100th Fighter Squadron lineage and honors history)

8 October: The 387th Air Service Group was inactivated and disbanded at Godman Field, Kentucky. (387th Air Service Group organization record card.)

12 October: Five Tuskegee Airmen pilots completed their advanced flight training at Williams AFB, Arizona. They included 2d Lieutenants Lawrence E. Campbell, Milford S. Craig, and Harold K. Hoskins and 1st Lieutenants Edgar L. Kellam and George H. O. Martin. (History of Williams AFB, AZ and 3010 Air Force Base Unit, 1948, call number 289.80 at Air Force Historical Research Agency)

November: Operation Happiness, a traveling entertainment group composed of African American performers from Lockbourne Air Force Base, began performing. It included the 766th USAF Band and 1st Lt. Daniel "Chappie" James, a pilot, as a singer. He led an 85-member cast which soon began performing at other USAF bases. (332d Fighter Wing history, Dec 1948-Jan 1949)

1949

20 January: Members of the 332d Fighter Group took part, as ordered by 332d Fighter Wing Special Order 15 dated 19 January 1949, in the inaugural parade for President Harry S. Truman, who had in the previous year issued Executive Order 9981 calling for equality of treatment and opportunity in the Armed Forces. (332d Fighter Wing Special Order 15 dated 19 January 1949, copy of which was provided by Zellie Orr)

23 February: 2d Lieutenants Ernest Craigwell, Thomas D. Sims, and Thelbert B. Wormack graduated from advanced flying training at Williams Air Force Base, Arizona, and were assigned to the 301st Fighter Squadron of the 332nd Fighter Group of the 332nd Fighter Wing at Lockbourne AFB, Ohio. They were the last Tuskegee Airmen pilots trained before the integration of the Air Force and the inactivation of the 332nd Fighter Wing and its group and squadrons, the last all-black flying units, in July.

2–11 May: At the 1949 USAF Gunnery Meet in Las Vegas, Nevada, the 332d Fighter Group, flying F-47N airplanes, won top honors in the conventional (propeller-driven) aircraft division. Team members were: Capt. Alva N. Temple, 1st Lt. James H. Harvey Jr., 1st Lt. Harry T. Stewart Jr. (whose names appear on the trophy), and 1st Lt. Halbert L. Alexander (who served as alternate pilot). At the same meet, the 4th Fighter Group won the jet aircraft division, which had a different number of events. (332d Fighter Group history, May 1949; Zellie Rainey Orr, *Heroes in War—Heroes at Home* [Marietta, GA: Communication Unlimited, 2011], 49)

11 May: The Department of the Air Force issued Air Force Letter no. 35–3, which noted that "all Negroes will not necessarily be assigned to Negro units. Qualified Negro personnel may be assigned to fill any position vacancy in any Air Force organization or overhead installation without regard to race." The same letter noted "All individuals, regardless of race, will be accorded equal opportunity for appointment, advancement, professional improvement, promotion, and retention in all components of the Air Force of the United States." The U.S. Air Force would be the first of the armed services to officially implement its integration plan which it had submitted for approval by the National Military Establishment and its Fay Committee, which was charged with fulfilling President Truman's Executive Order 9981. (Alan L. Gropman, *The Air Force Integrates, 1945–1964* [Washington: Office of Air Force History, 1985], 243, and note from Dr. Gropman to Dr. Haulman, 14 June 2010). As a result of this policy, all-black organizations within the United States Air Force would be inactivated. At the time, the Director of Military Personnel of the United States Air Force was General Dean C. Strother. During World War II, Strother had been commander of the 306th Fighter Wing and the XV Fighter Command, to which the Tuskegee Airmen's 332nd Fighter Group had been assigned. (332nd Fighter Wing history for May 1949, and 306 Fighter Wing histories from 1944 and 1945.) Strother personally opposed rapid integration of the Air Force, but followed the policy of the Secretary of the Air Force Stuart Symington, who was a firm proponent of it. (Alan Gropman, *The Air Force Integrates, 1945–1964* [Washington: Office of Air Force History, 1985], 91–92.)

27 May: General Hoyt S. Vandenberg, Chief of Staff, United States Air Force, announced that the 332nd Fighter Wing and its groups and squadrons at Lockbourne Air Force Base, Ohio, would be inactivated, and their black personnel would be reassigned to formerly all-white USAF organizations. (332nd Fighter Wing history for May 1949)

30 June: The day before the 332nd Fighter Wing and its groups and squadrons were inactivated at Lockbourne Air Force Base, Ohio, it had 215 officers and 1197 airmen assigned, for a total of 1412 black personnel. They would have to be integrated into formerly all-white USAF organizations. Included in that number were black women USAF members of Squadron "W". (332d Fighter Wing history for June 1949)

1 July: The last all-black flying organizations in the Air Force, including the 332nd Fighter Wing, the 332d Fighter Group, and the 99th, 100th, and 301st Fighter Squadrons, were inactivated at Lockbourne AFB, Ohio. Some of the personnel of those organizations were reassigned to formerly all-white USAF organizations, achieving limited racial integration of the Air Force. Other members were reassigned to the 2260th Air Base Squadron, which was activated at Lockbourne on the same date, and which remained active until 5 November 1949. (Organizational record cards of the 332nd Fighter Wing, the 332nd Fighter Group, and the 2260th Air Base Squadron; histories of the 332nd Fighter Wing and the 332nd Fighter Group from June 1949; Maurer, *Combat Squadrons of the Air Force, World War* II; Maurer, *Air Force Combat Units of World War II*)

1 July–5 November: The 2260th Air Base Squadron served at Lockbourne Air Force Base, Ohio. It absorbed personnel of the inactivated 332nd Fighter Wing, 332nd Fighter Group, and their squadrons, until they could be reassigned to formerly all-white Air Force organizations. The unit also transferred the P-47N aircraft that had belonged to the 332nd Fighter Group to Air National Guard squadrons in Georgia, Delaware, and Connecticut. Sources: Craig Huntly; organization record card of the 2260th Air Base Squadron; July 1949 history of the 2260th Air Base Squadron (call number SQ-AB-2260-HI, Jul 1949 at Air Force Historical Research Agency)

END OF THE TUSKEGEE AIRMEN EXPERIENCE

1950–1968

16 June 1950: Col. Benjamin O. Davis Jr. graduated from Air War College of Air University at Maxwell Air Force Base, Alabama. (Source: his autobiography, *Benjamin O. Davis, Jr., American* [Washington: Smithsonian Institution Press, 1991], 174)

17 May 1954: The Supreme Court of the United States issued its famous *Brown v. Board of Education* decision that called for the racial integration of public schools. One of the lawyers who had argued the case for integration before the high court was Robert L. Carter, a Tuskegee Airman. He served on Thurgood Marshall's team of attorneys.

27 October 1954: Benjamin O. Davis Jr. was promoted to brigadier general, the first black general in the US Air Force. His father had been the first black general in the US Army.

1955: Charles Francis published a book, about the first black military pilots in United States history, almost all of whom had trained at Tuskegee, and called it *The Tuskegee Airmen*, coining the term. This was the first book published about the Tuskegee Airmen.

30 June 1959: Benjamin O. Davis Jr. was promoted to major general, the first black major general in the US Air Force.

21–25 March 1965: Dabney N. Montgomery, a Tuskegee Airman, accompanied Rev. Dr. Martin Luther King on his Selma to Montgomery Voting Rights March, which pressured national public opinion to support the Voting Rights Act, which Congress passed later that year.

30 April 1965: Benjamin O. Davis Jr. was promoted to lieutenant general, the first black lieutenant general in the US Air Force.

4 Apr 1968: Rev. Dr. Martin Luther King Jr. was assassinated in Memphis, Tennessee. Although he was not a Tuskegee Airman, many Tuskegee Airmen had taken part energetically in the Civil Rights Movement for which Dr. King had become the leading spokesman.

May 1968: Col. Charles McGee, a Tuskegee Airman who flew fighters in World War II, Korea, and Vietnam, completed his 409th combat mission, one of the highest but not the highest number of combat missions by any USAF fighter pilot in three wars.

1970–1998

1 February 1970: Lt. Gen. Benjamin O. Davis Jr. retired from active duty in the US Air Force.

1 July 1970: Col. Daniel "Chappie" James, a Tuskegee Airman, was promoted to the rank of brigadier general, and he became the second black general in the US Air Force.

25 Jul 1972: Col. Lucius Theus, a Tuskegee Airman, was promoted to the rank of brigadier general, making him the third black general in the history of the USAF. Theus was not a pilot, and he did not serve in combat overseas during World War II. He was the first African American support officer to be appointed as a general in the Air Force. The first three black generals in the history of the United States Air Force, Benjamin O. Davis Jr.; Daniel "Chappie" James; and Lucius Theus, were all Tuskegee Airmen.

11–13 August 1972: Tuskegee Airmen veterans met in Detroit, Michigan, and voted to establish a nation-wide organization. This was the first national reunion of Tuskegee Airmen veterans, and it was held at the Hilton Hotel. (notes from William F. Holton, who served as national historian of the Tuskegee Airmen from 1997 to 2007)

10–12 August 1973: The second national reunion of Tuskegee Airmen veterans met at the Sheraton Park Hotel in Washington, D.C. (notes from William F. Holton, who served as national historian of the Tuskegee Airmen from 1997 to 2007)

1 January 1974: Tuskegee Airman Coleman Young was inaugurated as the first black mayor of Detroit, a position he held for twenty years. He had been elected near the end of 1973.

2–4 August 1974: The third national reunion of Tuskegee Airmen veterans was held at the Hyatt Regency Hotel in Los Angeles, California. (notes from William F. Holton, who served as national historian of the Tuskegee Airmen from 1997 to 2007)

25 February 1975: The Tuskegee Airmen veterans incorporated as the Tuskegee Airmen Incorporated, an educational and charitable organization, and opened its membership to non-veterans.

7 March 1975: President Gerald R. Ford appointed William T. Coleman Jr., a Tuskegee Airman, as the fourth Secretary of Transportation. He was only the second African American to serve in a Presidential Cabinet.

1 May 1975: Brig. Gen. Lucius Theus, the third African American and the third Tuskegee Airman to be appointed to the rank of general in the United States Air Force, also became the third to be promoted to the rank of major general.

1 September 1975: Daniel "Chappie" James was promoted to become the first black four-star general in the Air Force. He was also the first black four-star general in any US military service.

September 1982: The Smithsonian Institution opened a new exhibit, "Black Wings: the American Black in Aviation," in Washington, DC. The exhibit focused attention on the Tuskegee Airmen and other black aviation pioneers, and set the stage for other exhibits and research.

3 February 1990: Air Force historian Alan Gropman interviewed Lt. Gen. Benjamin O. Davis Jr. and asked him about the accuracy of the "never lost a bomber" claim regarding the escort record of the 332nd Fighter Group. Davis told Gropman he questioned the claim, possibly because his own Distinguished Flying Cross citation from World War II noted he had so skillfully led a bomber escort mission that "only a few bombers were lost."

1991: Benjamin O. Davis Jr.'s autobiography, *Benjamin O. Davis, Jr., American* was published by the Smithsonian Institution Press. Davis was the most important of all the Tuskegee Airmen, because of his leadership of the 99th Fighter Squadron, then the 332nd Fighter Group, then the 477th Composite Group, and then the 332nd Fighter Wing.

General Daniel "Chappie" James, the first four-star African American general, had been a Tuskegee Airman in the 477th Bombardment Group, which flew B-25s but did not deploy overseas during World War II. James flew fighters in Korea and Vietnam.

1992: Robert "Jeff" Jakeman's book about black military flight training at Tuskegee, called *The Divided Skies*, was published by the University of Alabama Press.

12 August 1995: Rodney A. Coleman, assistant secretary of the Air Force for manpower, reserve affairs, installations, and environment, announced vindication of black officers who had been arrested at Freeman Field in April 1945 for resisting segregated officers' clubs. Letters of reprimand were removed from the permanent military records of fifteen who requested such action. At the same time, Roger C. Terry, the only one of the officers convicted in court martial, was exonerated. The Air Force restored all the rights, privileges, and property Terry had lost because of his conviction. (Lt. Col. James C. Warren, *The Tuskegee Airmen Mutiny at Freeman Field* [Vacaville, CA: Conyers Publishing Company, 1995], 209)

26 August 1995: The Home Box Office (HBO) motion picture *The Tuskegee Airmen*, the first full-length movie ever made about the first black pilots in American military history, was broadcast on television. While it made the Tuskegee Airmen nationally famous, and honored their achievements, it also spread the myth that the Tuskegee Airmen had "never lost a bomber."

February 1997: John B. Holway's book about the Tuskegee Airmen, called *Red Tails, Black Wings*, was published by Yucca Tree Press of Las Cruces, New Mexico.

1997: A book by Lt. Col. Charles W. Dryden called *A-Train: Memoirs of a Tusekgee Airman* was published by University of Alabama Press. Dryden was one of the most famous members of the 99th Fighter Squadron, having graduated in the second class of Tuskegee Airmen pilots and having flown P-40 combat missions in the Mediterranean Theater of Operations.

9 May 1997: Mr. William F. Holton assumed the position of national historian of the Tuskegee Airmen Incorporated, after having been elected. He held that position for ten years. (notes from William F. Holton, who served as national historian of the Tuskegee Airmen from 1997 to 2007). Holton was a black World War II veteran, but he had served in the U.S. Navy, and was not a Tuskegee Airman. He had served as a professor at Howard University.

6 November 1998: President Bill Clinton signed Public Law 105–355, which Congress passed to establish the Tuskegee Airmen National Historic Site at Moton Field in Tuskegee, Alabama.

9 December 1998: President Bill Clinton promoted retired Lt. Gen. Benjamin O. Davis Jr. to four-star general, to honor him for his historic career.

2004–

2–8 August 2004: At the Tuskegee Airmen Incorporated national convention in Omaha, Nebraska, William F. Holton, who was then serving as national historian of the Tuskegee Airmen Incorporated, spoke about and distributed 450 copies of a booklet he had written and published called "332nd Fighter Group in World War II: 60th Anniversary Commemoration." In his booklet, Holton described his visit to Italy and the old Ramitelli Airfield where the 332nd Fighter Group had been based. He also declared that it was time to "dispel the myth" that the Tuskegee Airmen, on their escort missions, had never lost a bomber to enemy aircraft fire. The booklet revealed evidence that bombers under Tuskegee Airmen escort had been shot down by enemy aircraft, although such cases were rare.

13–19 August 2005: At its national convention in Orlando, Florida, the Tuskegee Airmen Incorporated leadership asked the Harry A. Sheppard Research Team (HASRT), headed by Tuskegee Airman William H. "Bill" Holloman III, and composed of other Tuskegee Airmen, to investigate Bill Holton's claim that the "never lost a bomber" claim was false. Members of that committee, like Holton, himself, sought originally to find evidence to support the claim, but eventually found evidence that the claim was false.

2006: The book *Black Knights: The Story of the Tuskegee Airmen*, by Lynn M. Homan and Louis R. Purnell, was published by Pelican Publishing Company of Gretna, Louisiana.

11 April 2006: To recognize the achievements of the Tuskegee Airmen, Congress passed Public Law 109–213 which authorized a Congressional Gold Medal to be struck. The medal was awarded collectively to the Tuskegee Airmen, and not to each one as an individual.

Spring 2006: Daniel Haulman, a historian at the Air Force Historical Research Agency, wrote a paper about the aerial victory credits of the Tuskegee Airmen ("112 Victories"). In the course of his research, he examined daily mission reports of the 332nd Fighter Group that convinced him that sometimes bombers under Tuskegee Airmen escort were shot down by enemy aircraft. He included mention of that discovery when he read a paper at the Society for Military History meeting at Kansas State University in Manhattan, Kansas, in May. He did not know that William Holton of the Tuskegee Airmen Incorporated had already come to that conclusion, while looking at some of the same 332nd Fighter Group mission reports. When Haulman returned from the meeting, Joseph Caver, who had attended the 2004 Tuskegee Airmen national convention in Omaha, told him. Now there were two historians questioning the "never lost a bomber" claim.

3 November 2006: The Tuskegee Airmen were inducted into the Alabama Military Hall of Honor at Marion Military Institute. At the ceremony, Tuskegee Airmen Incorporated national president Lt. Gen. Russell Davis gave a speech during which he repeated the "never lost a bomber" claim, and received much applause and cheers, although the claim had already been called into question by Mr. William F. Holton, the national historian of the Tuskegee Airmen Incorporated. Attending the ceremony was a reporter for *The Montgomery Advertiser* newspaper, Alvin Benn, who reported the speech.

November or December 2006: Hugh Ahmann, a retired historian at the Air Force Historical Research Agency, who had become aware of Daniel Haulman's research, contacted Alvin Benn and questioned the accuracy of the "never lost a bomber" statement.

December 2006: *The Montgomery Advertiser* reporter Alvin Benn contacted Daniel Haulman about his research showing that the Tuskegee Airmen sometimes escorted bombers that were shot down by enemy aircraft. Haulman told Benn not only about his own research, but also about that of William Holton. After interviewing both Haulman and Holton, Benn published a new article about the questioning of the Tuskegee Airmen "never lost a bomber" claim. The article received national circulation, and many other reporters subsequently interviewed Haulman and Holton about their discovery.

Early 2007: Representatives of the Harry A. Sheppard historical research team of the Tuskegee Airmen Incorporated, William Holloman, Alexander Jefferson, and William Ellis, all original Tuskegee Airmen, visited the Air Force Historical Research Agency and met with Daniel Haulman. Together they researched the "never lost a bomber" issue, looking at monthly histories of the 332nd Fighter Group, daily mission reports of the group, mission reports of the bombardment groups the 332nd Fighter Group escorted on particular dates, and reports on missing air crews. They determined conclusively that on 12 July 1944, at least three bombers under 332nd Fighter Group escort were shot down by enemy aircraft, and that the "never lost a bomber" statement was false.

15 February 2007: The Tuskegee Airmen Incorporated national board of directors voted to deny funding to its national historian, William F. Holton, possibly because of the unpopularity of his challenge to the "never lost a bomber" claim.

29 March 2007: President George W. Bush presided at the Congressional Gold Medal Ceremony for the Tuskegee Airmen at the U.S. Capitol building in Washington, DC. The ceremony was broadcast on national television, and the gold medal honoring the Tuskegee Airmen collectively was unveiled, although Congress had already voted the previous year to award it. While the President did not mention the "never lost a bomber" claim during the ceremony, it was mentioned by Congresswoman Nancy Pelosi, who was not aware that it had been called into question. (Ron Brewington, Public Relations Director, Tuskegee Airmen Incorporated at the time)

11–13 August 2007: The Tuskegee Airmen Incorporated held its national convention in Grapevine, Texas. At that convention, Tuskegee Airman William Holloman, head of the Harry A. Sheppard Research Team, reported that after research among original Tuskegee Airmen documents at the Air Force Historical Research Agency at Maxwell Air Force Base, Alabama, the team had discovered that sometimes bombers under the escort of the Tuskegee Airmen had been shot down by enemy aircraft. The convention received the report, but did not pass any resolution regarding the "never lost a bomber" claim, since research was continuing.

17–20 July 2008: At the Tuskegee Airmen National Convention in Philadelphia, Pennsylvania, William Holloman of the Harry A. Sheppard Research Team reported that his team's research determined that on 12 July 1944, at least three bombers escorted by the Tuskegee Airmen were lost to enemy aircraft. The team recommended that Tuskegee Airmen Incorporated members "refrain from saying that 'the 332nd Fighter Group never lost a bomber to enemy aircraft.'" The organization passed no resolution regarding that conclusion.

10 October 2008: Tuskegee Airmen National Historic Site opened at Moton Field in Tuskegee, Alabama, with a grand ceremony that first allowed the public to view displays in hangar 1. A second hangar was being rebuilt for additional displays in the future.

2010: J. Todd Moye's book about the Tuskegee Airmen of World War II, called *Freedom Flyers*, was published by Oxford University Press. This was the first book about the Tuskegee Airmen that recognized the "never lost a bomber" statement was probably false.

28–31 July 2010: The Tuskegee Airmen Incorporated national convention met at San Antonio, Texas. During the convention, the members passed a resolution recognizing that sometimes bombers under the escort of the Tuskegee Airmen had been shot down by enemy aircraft, and urged that its members not repeat the "never lost a bomber" claim, and challenge the statement when it was made. The resolution supported the research results of William Holton, Daniel Haulman, and the Harry A. Sheppard Research Team, led by William Holloman (who had died within weeks of the convention)

January 2011: Daniel Haulman's article, "The Tuskegee Airmen and the Never Lost a Bomber Myth" was published in *The Alabama Review*, the scholarly publication of the Alabama Historical Association. It documented 27 bombers under Tuskegee Airmen escort that were shot down by enemy aircraft, on 7 of the 179 bomber escort missions the 332nd Fighter Group flew for the Fifteenth Air Force.

May 2011: New South Books of Montgomery, Alabama published the book

The Tuskegee Airmen: An Illustrated History, 1939–1949, by Joseph Caver, Jerome Ennels, and Daniel Haulman. Although the book did not focus on the inaccuracy of the "never lost a bomber" claim, it did include a detailed chronology that noted the seven days on which Tuskegee Airmen-escorted bombers were shot down by enemy aircraft. It also noted the 112 aerial victories of the Tuskegee Airmen, with entries on each day those victories were achieved.

20 January 2012: George Lucas' movie *Red Tails* was released as the first full-length motion picture about the Tuskegee Airmen designed for theatrical release. At about the same time, George Lucas also released a documentary, *Double Victory*, that described the history of the Tuskegee Airmen, with interviews of several of them.

2012: New South Books of Montgomery, Alabama published a book by Daniel Haulman called *Eleven Myths about the Tuskegee Airmen*, which refuted many of the common misconceptions about the record of the Tuskegee Airmen.

15 February 2014: Hangar 2 at the Tuskegee Airmen National Historic Site at Moton Field was opened to the public in Tuskegee, with exhibits about the Tuskegee Airmen in basic and advanced flight training at Tuskegee Army Air Field and their experiences in combat overseas, in the Mediterranean Sea area and Europe. It complemented Hangar 1, which had opened in 2008. Hangar 1 commemorated the primary flight training that had taken place at Moton Field.

16 April 2014: The U.S. Postal Service issued a commemorative stamp in honor of "Chief" Charles Alfred Anderson, one of the most important of the black flight instructors at Tuskegee's Moton Field, where the primary military flight instruction had taken place during World War II. Before moving to Moton Field, Chief Anderson had taught black pilots in the civilian pilot training program at Kennedy Field in Tuskegee. Both Kennedy Field and Moton Field were owned by Tuskegee Institute, although the primary flight school at Moton Field had operated under contract with the Army Air Forces.

2015: New South Books of Montgomery published a book called *Tuskegee Airmen Questions and Answers for Students and Teachers* by Daniel Haulman. It addressed more than 70 of the most common questions asked about the Tuskegee Airmen.

Sources

General Sources for Chronology: 99th Fighter Squadron histories; 332d Fighter Group histories; 332d Fighter Group daily narrative mission reports; Maurer Maurer, *Combat Squadrons of the Air Force, World War II*; Maurer Maurer, *Air Force Combat Units of World War II;* Twelfth Air Force General Orders (for aerial victory credits); Fifteenth Air Force General Orders (for aerial victory credits); Fifteenth Air Force daily mission folders; Missing Air Crew Reports of the Army Air Forces, World War II (for airplane losses)

Some Tuskegee Airmen statistics: 1491 combat missions, including 914 of the 332nd Fighter Group and 577 of the 99th Fighter Squadron before it began flying missions with the 332nd Fighter Group; 1179 combat missions for the Twelfth Air Force.

A total of 930 pilots, in 44 classes, graduated from advanced flying training at Tuskegee Army Air Field, either as single engine future fighter pilots (685) or as twin engine future bomber pilots (245). In addition to that, there were 51 liaison and 11 service pilots who trained at Tuskegee, giving a total of 992 Tuskegee Airmen pilots who completed their flight training at Tuskegee during World War II.

At least twelve other African American pilots completed their advanced pilot training beyond Tuskegee, but who could be considered Tuskegee Airmen because they were assigned to Tuskegee Airmen organizations before those units were inactivated in 1949. In fact, between the middle of 1946 and the middle of 1949, all new African American military pilots received their flight training at bases beyond Tuskegee, because Tuskegee Army Air Field ceased pilot training by the end of June 1946, even though they were assigned eventually to the all-black flying units. Among those other flying training bases were Stewart Field, New York; Enid Army Air Base, Oklahoma; and Williams Air Force Base, Arizona. If one considers all twelve of these pilots as Tuskegee Airmen, there were at total of at least 1004 Tuskegee Airmen pilots.

The number of black military pilots before the integration of the United States Air Force in 1949 varies depending on what is being considered. There were 992 Tuskegee Airmen pilots who graduated from flight training at Tuskegee, including 5 Haitians. Besides that, there were 4 black liaison pilots and 11 other black pilots who received their pilot training beyond Tuskegee Army Air Field, which gives a total of 1007 black pilots who trained with the Army Air Forces or the United States Air Force before the integration of the Air Force in 1949. If you subtract the 5 Haitians, who did not serve with the Army Air Forces after their pilot training, you get 1002 black Americans who completed military pilot training in the United States before the integration of the United States Air Force in the middle of 1949.

179 bomber escort missions of the 332d Fighter Group for the Fifteenth Air Force; 172 heavy bomber escort missions of the 332d Fighter Group for the Fifteenth Air Force; 112 aerial victories of the 99th Fighter Squadron and the 332d Fighter Group combined during World War II; 96 Distinguished Flying Crosses awarded to members of the 332d Fighter Group or its squadrons; 94 aerial victories of the 332d Fighter Group for the Fifteenth Air Force between June 1944 and the end of April 1945; 61 missions under the Fifteenth Air Force for which the 332d Fighter Group reported one or more of its own aircraft lost or missing; 46 the average number of bombers shot down by enemy aircraft for each of the other six fighter groups of the Fifteenth Air Force; 35 missions in which the 332d Fighter Group reported enemy aircraft encounters; 27 bombers shot down by enemy aircraft when those bombers were in groups the 332d Fighter Group was assigned to escort; 25 is the number of 332d Fighter Group missions for the Fifteenth Air Force on which its members reported seeing bombers go down (some of these were bombers not assigned to the 332d Fighter Group to escort); 21 additional missions in which the 332d Fighter Group reported seeing enemy aircraft but reported no encounters with them; 21 is the number of 332d Fighter Group missions for the Fifteenth Air Force in which Tuskegee Airmen shot down enemy aircraft; 18 aerial victories earned by the 99th Fighter Squadron before it joined the 332d Fighter Group; 9 black liaison

pilots who did not graduate from pilot training at Tuskegee Army Air Field but at Fort Sill instead; 7 bomber escort missions of the 332d Fighter Group for the Fifteenth Air Force on which bombers under escort were lost to enemy aircraft; 4 is the highest number of aerial victory credits scored by a Tuskegee Airman, but three Tuskegee Airmen earned that number of aerial victories (Lee Archer, Joseph Elsberry, and Edward Toppins); 4 is the number of types of aircraft the Tuskegee Airmen flew in combat (P-40s, P-39s, P-47s, and P-51s); 4 is the number of Tuskegee Airmen who each earned 3 aerial victory credits in one day (Joseph Elsberry, Clarence Lester, Lee Archer, and Harry Stewart); 3 German jets shot down by the Tuskegee Airmen; 3 Distinguished Unit Citations earned by Tuskegee Airmen organizations (99th Fighter Squadron earned two before it was assigned to the 332d Fighter Group, and the 332d Fighter Group earned one after the 99th Fighter Squadron was assigned to it)

The outstanding performance of the 332nd Fighter Group, in comparison with other fighter escort groups, is possibly partly a result of the following factors:

The Tuskegee Airmen were not allowed to enter combat overseas for so long, their period of flying training was longer than the members of most fighter groups or squadrons; After June 1944 and before early March 1945, the 332nd Fighter Group had four squadrons instead of the three that other fighter groups had, giving them more pilots and more planes than the average fighter group; There were only two black flying groups and eight black flying squadrons in the Army Air Forces (they could draw the best African American human resources from all over the country).

Also from NewSouth Books

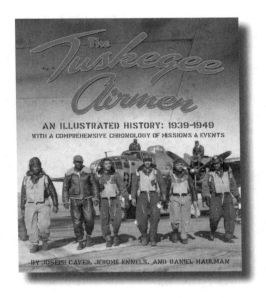

Experience the visual history of the Tuskegee Airmen . . .

Many documentaries, articles, museum exhibits, books, and movies have treated the subject of the Tuskegee Airmen, the only black American military pilots in World War II, but most of these works have focused on their training and their subsequent accomplishments during combat.

The Tuskegee Airmen: An Illustrated History goes further, using captioned photographs to trace the Airmen through the various stages of training, deployment, and combat in North Africa, Italy, and over occupied Europe. Included for the first time are depictions of the critical support roles of nonflyers: doctors, mechanics, and others, all of whom contributed to the Airmen's success. This volume by historians Joseph Caver, Jerome Ennels, and Daniel Haulman makes vivid the story of the Tuskegee Airmen and the environments in which they lived, worked, played, fought, and sometimes died.

ISBN 978-1-58838-244-3 • Hardcover • 232 pages • $27.95
Learn more at www.newsouthbooks.com/tuskegeeairmen

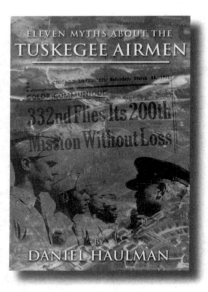

Learn more about the Tuskegee Airmen . . .

The members of the 332d Fighter Group and the 99th, 100th, 301st, and 302d Fighter Squadrons during World War II are remembered in part because they were the only African American pilots who served in combat with the Army Air Forces during the war. They are more often called the Tuskegee Airmen since they trained at Tuskegee Army Air Field. In the more than sixty years since World War II, several stories have grown up about the Tuskegee Airmen, some of them true and some of them false.

This book focuses on eleven myths about the Tuskegee Airmen, throughly researched and debunked by Air Force historian Daniel Haulman, with copious historical documentation and sources to prove Haulman's research.

ISBN 978-1-60306-147-6 • Paperback/ebook • 74 pgs • $7.95
Learn more at www.newsouthbooks.com/elevenmyths

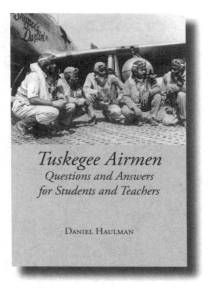

A resource for classrooms or general interest . . .

Almost everyone you meet has heard about the Tuskegee Airmen, but surprisingly few can answer with accuracy questions relating to their most important leaders, aircraft, missions, stations, phases of flight training, and unique accomplishments. Some of the Tuskegee Airmen stories in circulation are downright false. This book, designed primarily for students and teachers but also useful for general readers, answers 76 of the most common questions that people ask about the Tuskegee Airmen, enabling readers to separate the facts from the fictions.

This short and accurate summary of Tuskegee Airmen history honors the first African American pilots in U.S. military service—pioneers in the continuing struggle for racial equality.

ISBN 978-1-60306-381-4 • Paperback/ebook • 40 pgs • $7.95
Learn more at www.newsouthbooks.com/airmenqa

In the aftermath of Pearl Harbor . . .

One of the most heroic World War II air raids by US forces was the one that killed Admiral Isoroku Yamamoto, the commander of the Combined Japanese Fleet and the man who planned the Pearl Harbor and Midway attacks in 1941 and 1942. The raid occurred on April 18, 1943, exactly one year after the famous Doolittle raid on Japan, but it accomplished more by eliminating Japan's most important admiral and leading strategist.

This account stresses the crucial teamwork and planning, by code-breakers, strategic leaders, and pilots of the US Marine Corps, the US Navy, and the Army Air Corps, which achieved an almost miraculous interception. Those issues outweigh in significance the great controversy that emerged over the question of which of the pilots actually shot down the Yamamoto aircraft.

ISBN 978-1-60306-387-6 • Paperback/ebook • 34 pgs • $7.95

Learn more at www.newsouthbooks.com/yamamoto

Investigating the "Never Lost a Bomber" myth . . .

During the first sixty years following World War II, a powerful myth grew up claiming that the Tuskegee Airmen, the only black American military pilots in the war, had been the only fighter escort group never to have lost a bomber to enemy aircraft fire. The myth was enshrined in articles, books, museum exhibits, television programs, and films.

This ebook explores how the "never lost a bomber" myth originated and grew, and then refutes it conclusively with careful reference to primary source documents located at the Air Force Historical Research Agency. By piecing together these historical documents, Daniel Haulman not only proves that sometimes bombers under the escort of the Tuskegee Airmen were shot down by enemy aircraft, but when and where those losses occurred, and to which groups they belonged.

ISBN 978-1-60306-105-6 • Available as an ebook
Learn more at www.newsouthbooks.com/bombermyth

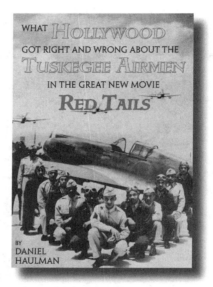

The movie is only the beginning . . .

The new George Lucas movie called *Red Tails* focuses attention on the Tuskegee Airmen of World War II and their combat operations overseas. Loaded with special effects and a great cast, the movie is thrilling and inspiring, but how accurate is it historically? Military historian Daniel Haulman takes an appreciative look at *Red Tails*, comparing it to the actual missions of the Tuskegee Airmen and offering places where interested viewers could study the events further.

"This list of differences between the *Red Tails* depiction of the Tuskegee Airmen and the real Tuskegee Airmen story is not intended to denigrate the movie," Haulman writes in his introduction, "but merely to caution those who might mistakenly take the fictional account as history."

ISBN 978-1-60306-160-5 • Available as an ebook
Learn more at www.newsouthbooks.com/redtails